The Dream-Hunters of Corsica

DOROTHY CARRINGTON

PHŒNIX

A PHOENIX PAPERBACK

First published in Great Britain by Weidenfeld & Nicolson in 1995
This paperback edition published in 1996 by Phoenix,
a division of Orion Books Ltd,
Orion House, 5 Upper St Martin's Lane, London WC2H 9EA

A CIP catalogue record for this book is available
from the British Library.

ISBN: 1 85799 424 8

Typeset by Deltatype Ltd., Ellesmere Port, Cheshire

Printed and bound in Great Britain by
The Guernsey Press Co. Ltd.,
Guernsey, C.I.

FOR KATHLEEN RAINE
*who for so long has encouraged
me to write this book*

CONTENTS

ILLUSTRATIONS

The baroque campanile of la Porta d'Ampugnani
(Editions A. Tomasi)
San Michele de Murato (Jonathan Robertson)
Statue-menhir at Filitosa (Jonathan Robertson)
Statue-menhir at Tavera (Joseph Cesari)
Shepherds of the Niolo (Jonathan Robertson)
A goatherd at milking time, Niolo (Jonathan Robertson)
The bard Jean-André Culioli and the *oriu* of Chera
(author's collection)
An *oriu* in southern Corsica (author's collection)
Barbara de Benedetti, *voceratrice* (author's collection)
La Mora, the hunting shepherdess c. 1900 (private collection)
Dispelling the *occhiu*, or Evil Eye (Jonathan Robertson)
Catenacciu, Sartene (Jonathan Robertson)
The Devil's sculpture near Piana (Stephen R. Bateson)
Rockscape in southern Corsica (David Williams)
The 'Bridal Veil' near Bocognano (F. Desjobert)
Bonifacio (Jonathan Robertson)

ACKNOWLEDGEMENTS

My first thanks go to Jean Cesari who has given me the matter of this book. By encouraging me to come to Corsica, with my husband, in 1948, and arranging our stay there, he offered me an intimate vision of the island at a period when the line of its tradition, reaching back to remote periods, was still unbroken. I owe a further introduction to the Corsican heritage to M. Alexandre Mondoloni, mayor of Sollacaro, and to M. Charles-André Culioli, Chera, to whom I offer my sincere thanks.

I am also greatly indebted to Mme Rotily-Forcioli, who generously communicated to me the text of her book concerning her acquaintance with a *mazzeru*, shortly to appear; to M. Pierre Lamotte, who, as Directeur des Services d'Archives de la Corse, allowed me to collaborate in his researches on Corsican occultism; to the historian of the village communities, Mme Lucette Poncin, and to Mme Claude Robertson-Forcioli and Mme Noëlle Vincensini, who have shared with me their close knowledge of Corsican rural life.

I wish to express my gratitude to the people who have given me the benefit of their special knowledge on various subjects, lent me rare publications and otherwise facilitated the preparation of this book: M. l'Abbé Gauge, curate of the parish of St Roch, Ajaccio; M. Charles Adreani, Nice; M. Bertrand Bardot, sculptor, Porticcio; Professor Stanley Barrett, professor of social anthropology, Guelph University, Ontario; Maître de Conférences Jean Cancellieri, historian, Université de Corse; M. Joseph Cesari, Conservateur Régional d'Archéologie, Direction Régionale des Affaires Culturelles de la Corse; Mme Annette Olsen-Fazi, docteur des lettres, Université de Corse; Mme Rosalind Fiamma, Zicavo; M. Louis-Mathieu Genty, Guagno; Maîtres de Conférences Suzanne and Gérard Girolami, Université de Corse; Professors Jean and Laurence Jehasse, Université de Saint-Etienne; M. Olivier Jehasse, classical scholar; Mrs Terri Madison, social anthropologist, University of Edinburgh; Professor J. M. P. McErlean, historian, York University, Toronto; M. François Mercury, Paviglia; M. Alain Piazzola, libraire-éditeur, Ajaccio; M. and Mme Jean-Claude Sillamy, Ajaccio; Mr Bill Sands, Ajaccio, member of the RAF forces that landed in Corsica in 1944.

I offer my thanks for the help I have received from the staff of INSEE (Institut National de la Statistique et des Etudes Economiques), Direction Régionale de Corse; from M. Michel Leenhardt, Directeur du Parc Naturel Régional de Corse, M. Simonpoli and members of the personnel of the Parc; from M. Noël Pinzuti, Conservateur Général du Patrimoine et Directeur des Archives départementales de la Corse-du-Sud and from the personnel of the Archives; from Mme Noël Pinzuti, Conservateur de la Bibliothèque municipale d'Ajaccio and the personnel of the Bibliothèque; and from the personnel of the London Library, who have answered my queries by telephone and sent me books with exemplary promptitude.

I acknowledge my profound debt of gratitude to those organizations that have supplied me with material aid to carry out this task: the Royal Literary Fund and La Société des Gens de Lettres de France. I am sincerely grateful to Mrs Fiona Clark and M. Pierre Rossi for their kind encouragement. I offer my thanks to my friend and translator M. Roland Muraccioli who has supplied me with many pertinent suggestions.

I acknowledge my thanks to M. René Durando, professor of Italian and to Mme Angelina Pirrolo for their translation of Italian texts, and to Mme Anghjulamaria Carbuccia for help in transcribing from the Corsican language. Translations from French are my own.

I also thank Bureau-Service, and M. and Mme Hognat, 'Aux Beaux Livres', Ajaccio, for aid in the technical presentation of my manuscript.

Genoa

ITALY

Adriatic Sea

CORSICA

Tyrrhenian Sea

SARDINIA

SICILY

Mediterranean Sea

Rogliano

Monte Minervio
Minerbio

Cagnano

Cap
Sisco
Corse
Brando • Lavasina

Saint-
Florent • **BASTIA**

Furiani

Nebbio

Santo-Pietro-
di-Tenda
Murato
Mariana

Balagne
Calvi **HAUTE - CORSE**

• Calenzana
Golo
Ponte Novo
Venzolasca

Casinca

Asco

En-Deçà-des-Monts
Castagniccia

*Cinque
Frati* △ **Niolo**
Rusio • Cambia
Alesani

*Capo
Tafonato* △
Casamaccioli

Santa-Lucia-
di-Mercurio • Cervione

Corte

Porto
Spelunca
Evisa

Golo

Piana
Porto

Marignana

*Les
Calanques*

Col de Manganello

Tavignano

• Guagno

• Etang de Diane

Sagone

Liamone

Salice

Forêt de Vizzavona
Col de Vizzavona

Bocognano
Ghisoni
△ *Christe Eleison*
△ *Kyrie Eleison*

Aleria

Tavera

Gravona

CORSE-

Palneca

AJACCIO

Ciamanacce

• Zicavo

DU - SUD

Au-Delà-des-Monts

Serra-di-Scopamene

Filitosa

Alta Rocca
Fozzano
Levie
• Carbini

*Forêt de
l'Ospedale*

Propriano

Golfe de Valinco

Rizzanese

Sainte-Lucie-
de-Tallano

Sartene
*Montagne
de Cagna*

Sartenais
—L'Omo di Cagna

Chera

Figari

Golfe de Santa Manza

Bonifacio

CORSICA

CHAPTER I

Bread of Wood, Wine of Stone

Villages – cemeteries – prehistory – history –
Pisans – Genoese – Pasquale – Paoli – French
occupation – vendetta – bandits

The baroque campaniles proclaim the villages from afar. Columns of local stone, granite or schist, often undisguised by stucco, they soar above the plain classical façades of the churches and the lines of tile-roofed houses strung along mountain flanks and spurs. Crowned with little spires or cupolas, they are pierced by two or three superimposed round-arched openings that may shelter venerable clocks and bells, or else, empty, frame views of wooded escarpments or vacant sky.

By the campaniles one can spot distant villages, however deeply encased in the exuberant Corsican vegetation: clusters of dark mountain oak, feathery olive groves, grandiloquent chestnut trees and pines. There, one knows, a group of human beings live, toil, rest and die. In the church, usually uncompromisingly plain in architectural style, but legatee of a noble tradition, they are baptized and married amid crowds of joyful relatives and friends. Later, watched by mourners, they lie in coffins draped in black while a priest intones the Mass for the dead. The coffin is then borne on strong shoulders to the cemetery, usually situated on a slope just outside the village, to be laid in the family tomb, one of the little buildings aligned as in the streets of a miniature town. The coffins are stacked in superimposed recesses in the lateral walls.

These chapel-tombs are designed with more imagination than the homes of the living, which are usually quadrilateral stone-built blocks almost devoid of decoration. The tomb architecture of Corsica ranges through the centuries and across the world: Gothic spires of northern

Europe and Italianate baroque façades, often more elaborate than that of the village church, are juxtaposed. Other tombs are unashamedly Islamic; the so-called 'marabout tomb' is circular, topped with a high, round dome. Only the little crosses standing on the roofs of the buildings remind one that this is a Christian burial ground.

In fact the cemeteries, in spite of their evocation of past ages, date only from the last century, when it was decreed, for reasons of hygiene, that bodies could no longer be interred in the *arca*, a vault beneath the church floor. This had been a common practice since the sixteenth century; earlier burials were in graveyards near the churches without monuments. Pride in a family as opposed to a collective sepulchre developed strongly in the nineteenth century; while many families acquired building space in the newly created cemeteries, others erected highly decorated tombs on their own land, as close as possible to their homes.[1] The Islamic influence in the tomb architecture is explained by the Corsicans' frequentation, at this period, of the French North African colonies, and not by any memory of a Saracen occupation of the island.

The traditional Corsican village, with which this book is concerned, stands seldom less than twenty or so kilometres (twelve miles) from the sea, and at any altitude between one and eight hundred metres (328–2783 feet) in the tumultuous Corsican landscape. Corsica offers a constant vision of mountains, range piled on range receding into blue distances, rising to jagged silhouettes of peaks snow-streaked half the year. No less than two hundred of them reach about 2000 metres (6500 feet). They spring from the granitic range that divides the island, running from northwest to southeast, with long spurs dropping to the coasts. The northeast of the island, less rugged, presents a formation of schist mountains never exceeding 1760 metres (5772 feet). For the curious I should add that the island measures at its extreme length 185 kilometres (116 miles), and at its widest 83 kilometres (51 miles), and that it covers 8,681 square kilometres (3,351 square miles).

These two areas, separated by the granite mountains, have been known through history as the *Di qua dai Monti* or *En-Decà-des-Monts* (the northern and north-eastern area), and the *Dila dai Monti* or *Au-Dela-des-Monts* (the southern and south-western). They differ like two distinct countries, perhaps in their ethnic composition, most certainly in their customs, traditions and their social and economic development. The *En-Deçà*, the country of easily negotiated mountains and fertile coastal plains, enjoyed a relative prosperity stimulated by commercial and cultural contacts with neighbouring Italy; Bastia, on the northeast coast, is only 117 kilometres (73 miles) from Leghorn. Cap Corse, the northernmost peninsula, produced and exported wine; the Balagne, on the north-west coast, produced olive oil from Greco-Roman times which was sold abroad and all over the island transported by caravans of mules. The Castagniccia, an area of chestnut forest in northeastern Corsica, was densely inhabited by a population of skilled craftsmen who exported their wares to the rest of the island, as well as chestnut flour, much valued as an alternative to cereals which in some regions could be cultivated only on terraces, by hand.

The *Au-Delà*, beyond the mountains, was poorer, less populated, more archaic in its methods of production, an altogether harder and rougher world. Its economy was predominantly pastoral. Corsican shepherds, in accordance with a primeval tradition, are semi-nomadic, transhumant; that is to say, they take their flocks in summer to the high plateaux, to camp in huts above the topmost villages at 4500 feet and more. In autumn they bring their livestock down to lower altitudes, where they sometimes become sedentary and attach themselves to village communities. Much of the material for this book has been collected in the *Au-Delà*, where tradition has survived longest. The people of the two areas feel themselves to be very different, so that one sometimes hears them speaking of '*les deux Corses*': 'the two Corsicas'.

Hundreds of villages are perched on the mountain slopes: Corsica counts 360 *communes*; the populations of those in the interior vary from a few hundreds (or thousands in one or two country towns such as Corte and Sartene) to a few dozen, always dwindling now that the rural people here, as in other countries, are moving into the towns. Ajaccio, on the west coast, since 1811 the French administrative capital, with over 59,000 inhabitants, and Bastia, the old Genoese capital on the northeast coast with over 38,000, have sucked in more than a third of the total Corsican population: 249,000 in 1990.[2]

Yet in spite of these modernized, rapidly expanding urban centres, the coastal areas of Corsica have an oddly desolate air. Mile on mile of the seaboard is a waste of wild shrubs, the richly scented maquis made up of lentisk, cistus, arbutus, myrtle, rosemary and thyme, with masses of dark holm oak. Here and there it is interrupted by jerry-built hamlets hastily run up by eager capitalists, often foreigners or at least non-Corsicans, to the indignation of many local inhabitants who view this development as yet another invasion. 'We've clung to our rocks through the centuries,' a wayside acquaintance said to me, 'we're not going to be dislodged now.' He evidently sympathized with the Corsican nationalist movement which erupted in the 1970s and has become a force to be reckoned with, as will be told.

Rocks were indeed the Corsicans' defence and refuge. Retreating into their barely accessible mountains, they were able to preserve their specific customs and beliefs in the face of repeated foreign incursion, invasion, occupation, colonization. Beliefs deriving from prehistory were maintained and respected: the cult of the dead, the phenomenon of the dream-hunting *mazzeri*. Hunters and food-gatherers settled the island from perhaps as early as 7000 BC; a skeleton recently brought to light is dated by radiocarbon to 6570 BC. Pottery, stockbreeding and agriculture appeared with the development of Neolithic culture between 5000 and 4000 BC; sheep and goats and cattle were raised, while agriculture remained for a long time minimal. The discovery of elaborate individual burials in rock shelters, where the corpses were sometimes daubed with a reddish clay to ensure their conservation, points to an early veneration of the dead. So indeed does the proximity of the dead with the living; some were interred under the soil of inhabited shelters and so shared their kinsmen's home. Subsequently incineration became the rule, with the remains of the half-burned bodies being placed in funeral urns.[3]

By the third millennium BC the Megalithic faith had reached Corsica, a compelling religion of the dead, apparently originating in the Near or Middle East, and carried round western Europe by missionary seafarers from Malta to the Orkneys. In Corsica they found a people predisposed to accept their message. It was exterior-ized in a dramatic display of stone monuments. None is very large; but all are spectacular: the dolmens, burial chambers erected above ground in conspicuous sites; the menhirs, a thousand or so in all, aligned in the maquis like the ranks of armies. Smaller than the giants of Avebury and Carnac, they stand little more than man-high, from eight feet to ten; carefully shaped and dressed, and tapering towards their summits, they in fact suggest human beings, as though the bodies were struggling to emerge from the granite. The evolution to anthropomorphic form took place, it seems, between 2000 and 1000 BC, creating a powerful and original insular art.[4]

Menhirs with roughly carved human heads appear in the alignments, or grouped together, as at Filitosa, that centre of megalithic art in southwestern Corsica which I had the great good fortune to see in 1948 on my first visit to the island. No less than twenty-four of these so-called statue-menhirs are assembled there; eighty-four have been found in Corsica in all. The figures of Filitosa are locally known as the *paladini* (paladins, knights of Charlemagne); and warriors they certainly represent, though of a more distant epoch. The majority have an intensely ferocious expression; eleven of them carry on their bodies the outline, carved in relief, of daggers and swords. These have been identified as bronze weapons current in the Mediterranean from the middle of the second millennium BC. The Corsicans, evidently, were already at war. Against whom is not known. Triumphant or not, they honoured their fallen heroes with these imposing portraits. The megalithic faith implanted itself in Corsica with a particular vitality, and it endured long after its lifespan elsewhere; in fact relics of its creed can be detected in insular custom and tradition to this day.

From the sixth century BC Corsica was drawn into the commercial circuit of the western Mediterranean. Greeks, Etruscans and Carthaginians settled there, to trade, and also to plunder natural products by imposing tribute in wax and honey, and sometimes to capture slaves. But these intruders brought to Corsica the culture of the olive and the vine. In 565 BC Greeks from Asia Minor, flying the menace of Persian invasion, founded a port on the east coast, Alalia; as Aleria, it was to become the Roman capital. The Romans seized it and laid claim to the whole island in 259 BC. The population of the interior put up a furious resistance, but to no avail. The Romans needed Corsica as a base in their long struggle with Carthage. They won possession of it at the cost of suppressing a sequence of rebellions that lasted till 111 BC, in the course of which Corsica was drained of resources and men. Half the indigenous population, it is estimated, was eliminated in battle, by epidemics, by famine, and by the loss of those who were herded off to slavery on the mainland.[5] Corsica's fate was sealed. Thenceforth the island was to be fought for, fought over, bought and sold by rival maritime powers with little or no regard for its inhabitants.

But first came five centuries of Roman rule, the longest period of peace Corsica has ever known. The Romans introduced many benefits of civilization: new cereal crops, techniques for the irrigation and draining of the fertile coastal plains, where they built a string of ports and made settlements for their own military veterans. They bought literacy, law and the Latin language, which was the origin of the Corsican language, which is still the natural speech of country people. Christianity took root, in defiance of official persecution, from around 200. Though it never obliterated the older cults of the ancestors, it lasted while the Roman achievements were ruined. Vandal invasions from 420 wiped the Roman ports off the map; the irrigation and drainage systems fell out of use, the harbours silted up, the waterlogged plains became infested with malaria as they remained till the Second World War.

The collapse of Rome inaugurated a long period of insecurity and violence, a recurring pattern of invasion, resistance, unhappy subjection, counter-invasion, war. Vandals and Ostrogoths in turn occupied the island before it was incorporated into the Byzantine Empire, which left an even worse memory of tyranny and exploitation. Subsequently annexed to the kingdom of Lombardy, Corsica was overrun by the Saracens during an indeterminate length of time that may have lasted several centuries. They came to pillage rather than colonize. There is no evidence to show that they converted the inhabitants to their faith, and no authentic trace of their art and architecture has been found. The Corsicans, as always when attacked, retreated into the mountainous interior, stronghold of their traditions.

Thanks to the intervention of the Papacy and various Italian crusaders, Corsica was eventually freed from the Saracens, to be taken over, in 1077, by the republic of Pisa. The dark age had ended. The Pisans launched a vast programme of evangelization. Skilled craftsmen, among them Corsicans trained in Pisa where they were employed in the construction of the Duomo, built churches and chapels all over the island. They are distinguished by the elaborate sobriety of their decoration and a perfect mastery of stone. Their architects made good use of what they found on the spot. San Michele de Murato is built of green and whitish serpentine, quarried locally, and arranged in a pattern which might be that of an abstract painting. The cathedral of Nebbio is a Romanesque masterpiece with arcane sculpture in pale local limestone, erected near the little port of Saint-Florent, on the site of an abandoned Roman town.

The Pisans sought to revitalize the centres of Roman occupation. Two of their most impressive monuments, the cathedral of Santa Maria Assunta and the large church of San Parteo, stand on the empty site of the Roman colony of Mariana.[6] But the ancient city never revived. The Pisans' attempt to reverse the inland movement of the population failed; malaria and pirate raids had laid a permanent ban on the coasts. Many Pisan churches can be seen in these deserted areas; one comes upon them stranded in the uninhabited maquis, as are most of the megalithic monuments, manifestations of an earlier faith. Poor in material and economic achievement, the Corsicans excelled in the expression of spiritual values. What is most admirable in their visual art is of religious inspiration; the churches of every period which are invariably the finest edifices in the villages, and the fabulous creations of the megalithic age. In the same way their most memorable verbal art, the lamentations known as *voceri*,[7] of which more will be told, was inspired by the cult of the dead, the primeval insular religion.

Pisan control of Corsica excited the jealousy of the rival republic of Genoa. In the contest between them the Genoese came out victorious in 1284 in the naval battle of Meloria. They lost no time in asserting their possession with a chain of coastal fortresses: Bonifacio, in the extreme south, had already been seized from Pisa in 1187; Calvi was founded in 1268; Bastia, the Genoese capital, developed round a fort built in 1380; Ajaccio was founded just over a century later. Their ruthless colonialism roused the hostility of the Corsican feudal lords. One after another, for a time aided by the kings of Aragon, whom the Pope had invested with the sovereignty of Corsica, they raised revolt after revolt until by the beginning of the sixteenth century they had practically fought themselves to extinction. The struggle for freedom then passed to the leadership of a shepherd's son, Sampiero Corso, supported by France in alliance with the Turks. His campaigns, if successful, could have led only to a change of colonial rule. France in fact administered the island for a couple of years before trading it back to Genoa in 1559 by the treaty of Cateau-Cambrésis.

If Corsica was so much coveted it was not for any riches existing there. The wood, the cork, the minerals – deposits of lead and copper – the semiprecious rocks and stones, all of which could have proved assets to Corsica as an independent state, were not worth fighting for by the foreign powers. The value of Corsica in their eyes was its strategic position: whoever held its ports could dominate the western Mediterranean. In consequence, during more than fifteen hundred years after the fall of Rome the island continued to change hands. Strategic colonialism is colonialism of the worst kind, for while it takes little or no account of the local inhabitants it does little to develop their natural resources. So the Corsicans remained through the centuries poor, angry and dispossessed.

This troubled history left deep scars on the Corsican collective psyche. Attitudes of suspicion, rejection and pessimistic fatalism have prevailed, together with the under and over self-estimation characteristic of people who have been humiliated, or feel themselves to have been so. It might be thought that constant contact with foreigners would have rendered the Corsicans adaptable; quick to adopt new ways. But no. The presence of strangers on their soil served to make them more intensely themselves. Their ideal of freedom was nonetheless contradicted, until very recently, by the rigidity of their own traditional social code. The Corsicans were prepared to conform, but only to what they themselves decreed.

Ancestral custom was upheld in a permanent protest to colonial rule. So the vendetta, the blood feud, continued almost up to the present day. Any and every injury might be punished by the murder of the offender, and this murder had to be avenged by another. The obligation was assumed, like a religious duty, by a close relative of the man who had been slain. The motive was not self-protection, but to appease the victim, otherwise his spirit might return to wreak vengeance on his defaulting kinsman by dragging him down to his own shadowy realm. The vendetta was a spectacular expression of the cult of the dead.

A feud, once declared, might last for generations. It could never be settled by the payment of compensation, in money or in kind, as was the custom in other countries where the blood feud was practised, in the era of antiquity, in the Middle Ages and later. 'Blood is not for sale' is the saying that summed up the Corsicans' view; for them the life of a human being was beyond price. The feud sometimes continued long after its original cause had been forgotten. This might be the seduction of a daughter, or political rivalry, but also a trivial quarrel between neighbours: the last full-scale vendetta in the 1950s was instigated by a donkey straying into a vegetable garden.[8]

A system so brutal suggests ancient origins. The blood feud was in fact current in Europe before the Romans imposed law, as it was or is in any archaic society without a respected organized government. Was Roman law respected in Corsica? Evidence is lacking. Diodorus Siculus paints an idyllic picture of the early Corsicans as a people who treated each other according to the principles of justice. Was this justice guaranteed by the vendetta? Or did the vendetta develop later, on an underlying foundation of the ancester cult, as a reaction against the misgovernment of the Genoese? Their magistrates are remembered as notoriously corrupt, and Genoa's judicial system included such abuses as the right of the governor to condemn to death without trial. The Corsicans, true to their basic disposition, took matters into their own hands. At the beginning of the eighteenth century, towards the end of the Genoese régime, over 900 murders were being committed yearly in a population of not more than 120,000.

After the defeat of Sampiero Corso, who in 1567 died by political assassination, Genoese rule was firmly clamped down and the country reorganized. The population grouped itself in mountain communities away from the dreaded coasts, and the villages as we know them took shape. The seventeenth century was the period of the 'Genoese peace'; so-called, though North African pirates continued to raid the coasts, bypassing Genoese defences, and the majority of the Corsicans were engaged in private war. Their attachment to their customs was unshaken.

The Genoese had the merit of leaving the villages to run their own affairs, according to a system of self-government that was in tune with Corsican temperament and tradition. An elected *podesta* was advised by two elected *padri del comune*, guardians of the not inconsiderable collective property. The Genoese intervened only to send armed agents to collect the bitterly resented taxes. They did on the other hand give some encouragement to agriculture, in particular the planting of the invaluable chestnut tree. Chestnut flour, much easier to produce in mountain territory than cereals, enabled the Corsicans to survive in endurable poverty. '*Pane di legna, vino di petra*' is how the Corsicans describe their traditional fare: 'bread of wood', made from chestnut flour, and 'wine of stone', water from the mountain springs. In fact

Cap Corse from an early date produced and exported wine and vineyards are numerous in the island, but drinking is, or at least was, restrained.

The old proverb is applicable to Corsica as a whole. The luxuriance of the vegetation is misleading: the extreme ruggedness of the terrain, and the resulting difficulties for agriculture and for communications, combined to make life hard and bare, and these conditions were aggravated by recurrent war. Farmers and shepherds subsisted by barter: cheese for olive oil, oil for chestnut flour. Consumption was restricted except on religious feast days and family gatherings such as christenings, weddings, and funerals which were occasions for veritable banquets. The essential austerity of the country is reflected in objects and buildings. Only in the comparatively recent cemeteries was fantasy allowed free play. The homes of the living, the village houses, built of roughly hewn local stone, often left apparent, are so plain that a carved window ledge or doorway, a flight of stone steps running obliquely across a façade to an upper floor, excite comment. The one form of decoration the Corsican country people allow themselves, uncostly but effective, are bands of white paint, about a hand's span wide, laid straight on to the stone, framing windows and doors. Inside one usually finds simple massive furniture, often made from local wood – chestnut, walnut, pine – by local artisans. This represents a fairly recent level of comfort; in the last century furniture in the village houses was often almost nonexistent, and people often slept on makeshift mattresses laid on the floor, as the shepherds still do in their mountain cabins.[9] Today householders sometimes take pains to embroider sheets and repaint walls, but the idea of interior decoration is alien to them. Gardens, other than vegetable plots, were until recently unknown, as water supplies were too meagre to squander on flowers.

Only the churches have any pretensions to fine appearances, though their architecture, in all periods, is resolutely sober. Their interiors, however, often make up for this severity of style. Precious furnishings and objects could be acquired over a period of years: marble polychrome altars imported from Genoa, frescoes and painted wooden statues, the work of Italian or Corsican artists, are arresting; gold and silver candelabra and silver crucifixes were usually donated in the last century. Glowing by candlelight at evening services, they offered the only glimpses of opulence that most of the village people had ever known. Surprisingly, the populations of the smallest villages still contribute to keep the churches in good repair.

If Genoese officials and merchants and their allies, together with some high-ranking Corsican clergy, lived well enough in the Genoese coastal towns, it cannot be said that the mass of the people prospered. Genoese trade monopolies discouraged production and fuelled an increasing sense of injustice. The Corsicans accepted poverty with stoicism, as the natural lot of man. Riches were suspected as ill-gotten, the fruit of collaboration with the enemy overlords, and this was indeed often true. Underlying the traditional Corsican philosophy is the conviction that all men are equal, or at least entitled to be treated as such. Real equality has in fact never existed in Corsican society in historic times, except among the shepherds, but the people have always struggled to bring it about. The feudal lords, who established themselves in the Middle Ages, were as much opposed by the Corsicans as by the Genoese;[10] the rural notables who superseded them held their position at the mercy of the local inhabitants. That colonial rulers should assume superiority was to most Corsicans insupportable.

The age of the Enlightenment inspired rebellion. It broke out in 1729 in the mountainous province of Bozio. The Genoese were taken unawares, and within a short space of time the insurgents gained control of the interior. A German adventurer, Theodor von Neuhoff, equipped with some material means and revolutionary notions, succeeded in making himself king of Corsica in 1736, before leaving the island that same year due to lack of funds. Genoa appealed to France; French forces, surprisingly defeated by the Corsicans at Borgo in 1738, won a temporary victory over the rebels the following year. But the Corsicans got the better of this uneasy alliance, and while French troops reinforced the Genoese coastal garrisons Pasquale Paoli was elected in 1755 general in chief of the Corsican nation.

Now at last the Corsicans could see their ideals of liberty and equality put into practice. Son of a notable of the Castagniccia, Pasquale had been brought up in Naples where his father, a rebel leader, had retired after the previous French victory. There he had studied at the university, absorbed the culture of the period and become a disciple of Montesquieu and Rousseau. Returning to Corsica, he consolidated its independence with a constitution that embodied the most advanced ideas of the age: 'The General Diet of the People of Corsica, legitimately master of itself . . . Having reconquered its Liberty, wishing to give durable and constant form to its government, reducing it (forming it into) a constitution from which the felicity of the nation will derive . . .' So run the opening words of the original constitutional document, dated 16–18 November 1755. The Scottish writer James Boswell, who visited Paoli in 1765 on the advice of his admirer, Jean-Jacques Rousseau, declared it to be 'the best model that hath ever existed in the democratical form'.[11]

Remarkable it certainly was in its time. Parliamentary democracy was embodied in a Diet, a legislative assembly meeting yearly, which included members elected in every village by men of twenty-five years old and over. Paoli lost no time in inciting it to found a university at Corte, the mountain capital of the newborn state. There Boswell was received by the rector, Father Mariani, a Corsican Franciscan, as were the other members of the staff. Charles Bonaparte, father of Napoleon, was among his students and published a dissertation on a course in ethics he had attended, where one can read such statements as 'man is born free', and 'all men are by nature equal'.[12]

But whatever Paoli had done for the island came to nothing when it was invaded by Louis XV. Genoa had ceded her rights over Corsica to France on 15 May 1768 by the Treaty of Versailles, which included clauses financially advantageous to the Genoese. Thus disposed of, unconsulted, the Corsicans went to war, refusing to be treated, in the words of Paoli, like 'a flock of sheep driven to the market'. Outnumbered and outarmed, but adept at guerrilla tactics and recklessly brave, Paoli's little militia held out against the French army for the best part of a year. It was finally defeated and dispersed in a suicidal engagement on the bridge of Ponte Novo on 8 May 1769; according to Voltaire the Corsicans fought behind a barricade built with the bodies of their own dead while the wounded flung themselves on to the pile.[13] Paoli had to flee the island; he took refuge in England.

The rule of the French monarchy was experienced as a cruel deprivation of liberty. In 1774 the people of the Niolo, in the mountainous centre of the island, rose in rebellion. It was crushed with a brutality that became legendary and inspired the young

Napoleon to write a bloodcurdling, fragmentary tale entitled 'Nouvelle Corse' (Corsican Novella).[14]

The French Revolution seemed, however, to promise the Corsicans a better deal. '*Liberté, Egalité, Fraternité*' was a slogan that appealed to them. In November 1789 the French *Assemblée Nationale*, on the plea of the Corsican deputies, voted the permanent integration of Corsica into the French state. Paoli, amnestied, returned to the island in triumph. Disillusionment was in store. After an unsuccessful military expedition to Sardinia, Paoli quarrelled with the Convention and declared Corsica independent for the second time. It was a bold step. Isolated and menaced, he accepted British protection, and in June 1794 the Anglo-Corsican kingdom was proclaimed.

Like the other powers that had occupied the island, the British were primarily interested in its strategic position, so valuable to them in this time of continental war. Though well-intentioned, they had little understanding of Paoli and his fellow countrymen. Offended by the authority of the viceroy, Sir Gilbert Elliot, in 1795 Paoli returned to England. Corsica was abandoned on British government orders in September of the following year, while Napoleon sent in troops from Italy, unopposed.

Contrary to what might have been hoped for by a country that gave him some 10,000 fighting men, including forty-three generals, Napoleon did little for Corsica. The harsh military government imposed with General Morand was as much resented as any colonial régime. Napoleon III made some amends, by extending the road-building programme undertaken by Louis Philippe and offering exalted posts to Corsicans in his entourage. Life improved in Corsica through the nineteenth century, if slowly. Unlike previous conquerors the French were making a genuine attempt to incorporate Corsica into their nation-state. Carriage roads, the first seen in the island, facilitated communications: the *Au-Delà-des-Monts*, granitic Corsica beyond the mountains, was no longer so cut off from the *En-Deçà*. The link was further improved by the building in the 1880s of a daring little single-track railway from Ajaccio to Bastia that burrows its way in a long tunnel through the central hump of the island. A spectacular bridge over a ravine was designed by Gustave Eiffel, architect of the Eiffel Tower. Free education in French schools superseded the teaching of the clergy. Though the new primary schools paid small heed to traditional Corsican culture, and even frowned on the speaking of the Corsican language, they did ensure literacy and so equipped the people with the means to play a part in the outside world.

Little by little living standards rose. The population increased to a maximum of 280,000 in 1891. It was in fact too large to be supported by the archaic agriculture of the time. Emigration was the obvious solution. Thousands of Corsicans entered the French army and civil service; it has been estimated that 80 per cent of the administrators in the French colonies were Corsicans. They retired with pensions to their villages where they came to form a new élite; because, as was explained to me by a woman who had grown up in a mountain community, they were the people who could afford to buy groceries.

A Corsican is bound to his village by ties that he feels to be magical and sacred. The village is a part of himself, an extension of his being. All through life, even when making a career in distant lands – in the time of the French empire in Indo-China, maybe, or central Africa – he will cherish the memory of his birthplace where he intends to retire and to die. Even those who earn their living in the Corsican towns never lose the sense of belonging to their villages. One young couple of my acquaintance – he a doctor – confided to me that whenever they were separated from their village for any appreciable length of time they were haunted by dreams of it being overwhelmed by catastrophe: earthquake, flood or fire.

The population of a Corsican village is soldered together by ties at once sentimental, instinctive and material. Marriage was by tradition endogamous. The custom, encouraged by the difficulty, until recently, of communicating with other villages by the mountain tracks, ensured that no portion of a family's land left the community with the dowry of the bride. In consequence almost everyone came to be related. In a small village like Chera (of which I shall have more to say), nearly everybody carries the name Culioli; in many larger ones only half a dozen surnames are shared. A vendetta within a village had the character of a family war, and caused the participants to suffer the more acutely because they felt it to be something against nature.

The French judicial and police systems, improved living standards and access to the outer world were among the factors that brought about a decrease of the vendetta in the course of the last century. All the same, it was still prevalent and dramatic enough to strike foreigners as an extraordinary insular custom. Prosper Mérimée gave it European celebrity with his masterly novel *Colomba*, based on what he had seen and heard during his tour of Corsica as Inspector of Historic Monuments in 1839.[15] No one actually remembered the incident that had set two family groups at war in the little village of Fozzano, in southwest Corsica, about a century earlier. But murders had recently been committed, and, in spite of an official treaty of peace signed in the church, according to custom, the belligerents still lived barricaded in their fortress-like homes. A formal peace treaty, signed in the church and accompanied by a religious ceremony, was a means by which vendettas might be brought to an end. The Christian faith was relied upon to overcome the primeval religion of the dead. It sometimes failed in its mission, as at Fozzano.

Corsicans were to complain that Mérimée made them known to the world as bloodthirsty barbarians, but in fact *Colomba* is considerably milder than the events by which it was inspired. Moreover Mérimée's story, in life as in fiction, is far surpassed in horror by the very popular book of the Corsican writer J.-B. Marcaggi, first published in 1898, and aptly entitled *Fleuve de Sang*, 'River of Blood'.[16] Report rather than novel, it relates a real vendetta and its consequences, adhering closely to local records.

The vendetta broke out on Christmas Eve of 1840; like many, it was sparked off by a quarrel at a card party. A player accused another of cheating; need I remind the reader that Napoleon was often so accused in his youth? Unforgivable words were exchanged; the accuser promptly killed the accused and disappeared into the night. He had become a bandit, one of the many outlaws who after a murder took to the maquis, where they might survive for years, perhaps to the end of their lives, supported and sheltered by the population as men of honour – ambiguous word – who preferred their own, logical law to that imposed from abroad.

Marcaggi does not hesitate to speak of the 'disturbing fascination of the maquis', as well as terrible impulses lurking in the Corsican psyche: the 'mad desire to kill' and the 'appetite for death'. He tells how the bandits roamed the country, self-appointed 'princes of the maquis', enforcing their will with their guns; how they were joined by relatives and friends so as to form redoubtable armed bands; how a detachment of two hundred armed police was needed, in 1852, to overcome bandits holding out in caves in the Niolo, wounded, dying of thirst and hunger, but still, until receiving the fatal shot, refusing surrender. Was banditry a protest against foreign rule? A frustrated affirmation of Corsican independence? Or was the motivation not perhaps of deeper origin: an urge, welling up from the unconscious, to revert to a primeval way of living? Such an urge, as will be told, impels the *mazzeri*, but it is enacted in the realm of dreams.

Fleuve de Sang describes the last serious episode of banditry in the nineteenth century. The wise, moderate rule of Napoleon III brought about a decline of the vendetta; the number of bandits fell sharply from 168 to 36.[17] But a resurgence of the old wild ways followed the First World War. In the 1920s the bandits were numerous, picturesque and brazen enough to become veritable tourist attractions. Visitors went out of their way to meet them, picnic with them, photograph them, listen to their reminiscences and include them in their own. As a deterrent, the bandit Spada was beheaded by a guillotine brought to Bastia for the purpose in 1935.[18]

My own reminiscences include only one bandit, Bornea, for by the time I reached the island in 1948, thanks to the energetic intervention of the French police and a shift of outlook consequent to the Second World War, the vendetta and banditry had almost come to an end. François Bornea was one of the last bandits alive and at large; having served a prison sentence for the one – only one – murder, he was ending his life in a peaceful domesticity in a southern village. I have a pleasant memory of a Christmas Day party in his home. Fragile-looking and gentle in his speech, he had none of the flamboyance generally associated with the bandits. When I arrived he was quietly but firmly reproving one of his children, a little boy, for having laughed during Christmas Mass. 'But he's so young,' I said, 'perhaps he didn't understand.' 'There are things one must learn when one is very young,' said the retired bandit, 'otherwise one may not come to understand them until it is too late.' Like many bandits, retired or not, Bornea held to the Christian faith. The same is true of the *mazzeri*, though their activities are also alien to Christian precepts.

My afternoon in the ex-bandit's company was reassuring. I have less pleasant memories of being paraded along the main street of a southern village divided by an old vendetta in the company of a

Corsican host. His partisans rushed out of their houses with effusive greetings; those in the enemy camp shut themselves inside, slamming shutters and doors. Most of the men, I noticed, were carrying their shooting guns. So it happened that I witnessed traces of a tradition centuries, perhaps millennia, old. Or so I supposed. 'You were very naïve,' a Corsican friend said to me after I had told him of the experience. 'Don't you realize that all that was theatre? The Corsicans love play-acting.' True enough. Yet I was unable then, as I am now, to believe that the whole show was put on for my benefit. I later learned that this village had been the scene of a bloody vendetta in the early years of the century.

Possibly the villagers exaggerated their attitudes to impress me, the unexpected foreigner, at a period when few tourists visited remote villages of the interior. Play-acting: yes, the Corsicans are very given to it and very dangerous it can be. Little is needed, a trivial irritating circumstance, an unconsidered word or gesture, for the man who habitually carries his gun to fire it on his enemy; someone perhaps who has never harmed him personally but who belongs to a family at odds with his own. The role he has been acting in the tragic drama then becomes real, and he must play it to the end of his days.

So, by accident, I become acquainted with one of the most spectacular aspects of Corsican tradition. Later I came to know others, more enigmatic and arcane: the signs and omens of death, magic healing, a technique of prophecy, the predictions of the dream-hunters, the *mazzeri*, as will be told.

CHAPTER 2

The Dead and the Living

World wars – Liberation – the Corsican flag –
the break with tradition – nationalists – farming –
the *sgio* – shepherds – the Church – the *confréries* –
Good Friday – the day of the dead – *voceri*

Corsica had been through two world wars when I arrived there with my husband in 1948. I found a people sad, poor, proud and fraternal. Poor they had always been, and their modest subsistence economy had taken a hard battering in both wars. The first had entailed an appalling loss of life. Eleven thousand Corsicans had been killed, according to the most conservative estimate; the figures of 20,000 and even 40,000 are also quoted. One reads the tragic lists of their names engraved on the war memorials of every village. Some record only one surname, as though all the able-bodied men of a family had been exterminated. The consequences of this slaughter were for a long time visibly apparent: acres and acres of land went out of cultivation, reverted to maquis; the women put on the mourning black which was so prevalent that foreigners took it to be an inherited local costume. In fact the costume of the past had been colourful enough, and today Corsican women do not shrink from wearing bright clothes.

The Second World War, less costly in human lives, brought the enemy into the heart of the country. On 11 November 1942 Italian troops landed in the island which Mussolini was loudly claiming to be part of his empire. The occupying force eventually amounted to 85,000 men; about one for every two Corsicans, women and children included. They had instructions to treat the Corsicans with a friendliness sufficient to convince them that they naturally belonged to Italy. They failed to do so. They might have gone out of their way to shake hands with peasants, but they ate up most of the available food, including 21,000 tins of sardines, thus depriving the Corsicans not only of food but of means of procuring it, sardines being used as bait for fish.

The Corsicans reacted as they had always done when threatened on their own soil: they took to the maquis and to arms. A redoubtable resistance organization, largely impelled by the Communists, covered the countryside. Thousands, eventually over 11,000, disappeared to camp in rock shelters; like the bandits, and like their first ancestors. The women bravely brought them food. Soon they were drawn into the international theatre of war. Arms and munitions were smuggled in to them by submarine by the Allies, and dropped by parachute; reinforcements from North Africa arrived. The occupants, no longer friendly, were shot down by snipers; patriots were captured, tortured, killed. The name of Fred Scamaroni, who committed suicide to avoid torture, is celebrated in the terrible annals of Corsican history, as is that of Jean Nicoli, who was brutally executed in Bastia only ten days before an armistice was declared.

Mussolini was deposed: Italy signed peace with the Allies. The news was heard in Corsica on British radio on 8 September 1943; regardless of the curfew the population of Ajaccio poured into the streets where the rejoicing continued all night long. The patriots declared their allegiance to the Allies and to de Gaulle. The Italian occupants, abashed, ashamed and quite often relieved, laid down their arms; some joined forces with the Resistants. Thousands of German occupants remained to be dealt with, greatly increased by an armoured division retreating up the east coast from Sardinia, heading for Bastia and the Italian mainland. Tough fighting ensued. By 4 October the last of the enemy had left: Corsica was free, the first *département* of France to be liberated. British and American forces subsequently landed in the island, which became a base for Allied operations. Several Englishmen stayed on after the war, married and made homes there.

The Corsicans were justifiably proud of their performance in the two wars; shared suffering and struggle consolidated their sense of fraternity. They came out of the Second World War with an enhanced international reputation, as well as an important, un-expected gain: American troops stationed on the east coast in 1944 sprayed the marshes with insecticides and so rid the land of the malarial mosquitoes that had made it uninhabitable since the fall of Rome. The victorious days of 8 and 9 September are celebrated every year with pomp and ceremony: French ministers, generals and high-ranking officials are received; processions and military parades are performed amid a flamboyant display of flowers and flags. French flags, nearly all: the Corsican flag, known as the *Tête de Maure*, the 'Moor's head', is only occasionally seen. Startling and enigmatic, like so much else in Corsica, it presents a black silhouette of a Negroid head in profile, wearing a white headband, against a white ground.

Its origin is obscure. Apparently it was brought to Corsica in the later Middle Ages, when the kings of Aragon, backed by the Papacy and supported by certain Corsican nobles, laid claim to the island. Their coat of arms included four such heads to celebrate their victories over the Moors in Spain. A single Moor's head was attributed to Corsica to serve as the island's arms; those of Sardinia, conquered by Aragon in the fifteenth century, included all four. The Corsicans became attached to this emblem. The adventurer Theodor von Neuhoff, who made himself king of Corsica for part of a year during the eighteenth-century rebellion, adopted the Moor's head as the national flag; the Moor was shown with the bandeau over his eyes, to indicate his status as a slave. Pasquale Paoli followed his example, but with the bandeau lifted to the brow of the Moor. Since then this curious image has been regarded as the Corsican flag.[2] Floating alongside the massed blue, white and red flags of France, solitary and incongruous, it welcomes the visiting dignitaries of state while they name streets and unveil monuments in honour of those Corsicans who set all France an example in the struggle for liberty.

War, death, bereavement, enemy occupation and fighting in the maquis had not disrupted the traditional life in the villages, as I soon came to understand. Indeed, foreign invasion, as always, had served to reinforce attachment to ancestral customs and beliefs. The Corsicans, for once at peace, seemed to be drained of vitality, sunk in sleep, dreaming of their own past. To learn about them, I had only to listen to what they said. I had not intended, on my first visit, to stay very long. I had recently published in England a book on British travellers and their journals that had attracted attention. Now I wanted to write a travel book of my own. I went to Corsica to look for material. I found too much; it has held me there ever since. Jean

Cesari, a Corsican I had met in London with my husband at the end of the Second World War, had encouraged us to visit his island. He came to join us there. He led us to Filitosa, and introduced us to the granite heroes of Corsican prehistory.[2] I felt that an island which concealed such astonishing monuments must harbour much else of interest, unknown to the outside world. We returned the following summer. The visits became yearly: not holidays, for they were never restful, but ventures into the unknown that stirred every level of my being. When in 1953 I acquired a flat in Ajaccio to save hotel bills I realized I had found a home.

Most, though not all, of the material presented in the following chapters was gathered in the 1950s, before the modernization of the island that took place in the following decade. Many of my informants were elderly, so their confidences may date from pre-First World War days. Many have since died and with their disappearance some customs and beliefs have faded from the Corsican scene. An abrupt, generalized modernization has cut the line of tradition reaching back into prehistoric times. Certain aspects of it, among the most interesting, have been saved from oblivion by the books of Roccu Multedo, a retired man of law who has become a specialist on Corsican occult phenomena. Other researchers have published evidence of value.[3] Almost all, now, refers to the past. This is why I have undertaken to transmit to an audience outside the island what is remembered, and what has survived.

The break was not so much impelled by any change within Corsica as by the impact of events in the outside world. France was withdrawing from her spheres of influence in North Africa. From 1958 a stream of French refugees reached Corsica, a stream that became a torrent after France abandoned Algeria in 1962. Some 17,000 people poured into the island, about a quarter of them Corsican by origin. They brought with them various skills, and capital partly supplied by the French government in grants and loans. To carry out their plans they imported an Arab labour force that has become a permanent feature of island life.

Corsica was equipped to receive them. In 1957 the French government had taken steps to revitalize two main sectors of the island's economy, agriculture and the tourist trade, by instituting the organizations known as SOMIVAC and SETCO. dams had been built to supply water for irrigation, and roads to open up hitherto derelict areas that were then divided into properties of 20–25 hectares (49–60 acres) and distributed to Corsican applicants.[4]

The refugees from North Africa benefited by these measures, though they owed as much and more to their own funds and to their professional dynamism and experience. Some acquired large properties, comparable in size to those they had left behind them in Africa. Within an amazingly short space of time Corsica was transformed. Physically. The bulldozer, an innovation, drove tracks into untamed maquis and revealed new perspectives. Wide expanses were mechanically cultivated. The east coast plain, formerly known as the 'green desert', now no longer unhealthy, was covered with vineyards, which have been recently superseded by plantations of citrus fruit. Villages sprang up on sites uninhabited since Roman times. The repatriates, known as the *pieds noirs*, settled also in the towns, where they found scope for their competence. Some built hotels for tourists. Money drew money. Foreign investors – many from northern Europe – ran up hotels, motels and holiday villages around the coasts; the yearly intake of tourists rose and has continued to do so, to reach 280,000 in 1970 and about 1,400,000 in 1993.[5]

Simultaneously, customs changed. Television came into country people's homes. Staring at the screen, they learned many things about the outside world, and forgot many others pertaining to their own tradition. The French cultural upheaval of May 1968 was echoed mildly but perceptibly in the island: manners became more relaxed, especially between the sexes, clothes less formal; women as well as men took to wearing jeans. Women's emancipation forged ahead from this time.[6] Only half willingly, the Corsicans were jolted into the modern world. Some welcomed the change as a release from ancient servitudes. But for many people the new developments were seen as yet another invasion, to be repelled. Corsica, they argued, was being cheated, denatured and abused. Foreigners were degrading the landscape with their gimcrack accommodation for tourists who swarmed in every summer to degrade it still further. Strangers with no respect for the Corsican way of life had occupied the east coast where formerly shepherds had pastured their sheep in winter on common land for minimal fees. Now the land was alienated and the shepherds deprived.

The nationalist movement was already latent: a number of Corsicans felt that the Corsicans should have more voice in running Corsican affairs. When indignation broke into action in 1975 it was, significantly, directed against one of the newcomers. Twenty or so armed militants led by Edmond Simeoni, who has since become a reputed political leader, occupied the wine cellar of a *pied noir* who owned no less than 2000 hectares (2900 acres) of land on the east coast that could well have been distributed to young Corsican farmers. He was moreover held guilty of practising scandalous illegalities in the fabrication and marketing of wine, which the French government had left unpunished. Luckily for him he was absent on the day when the angry Corsicans took possession of his premises. The authorities lost no time in sending a large detachment of armed police against them, it has been said more than a thousand strong. The nationalists resisted; one was badly wounded and two policemen were killed. A few days later a violent incident in Bastia led to the death of another member of the French police. War had been declared.

Since then the nationalist movement has spread, gained in power and in numbers, made itself felt in almost every sphere of island life. This was inevitable. Too many grievances had accumulated, and these had been brought to a head by the abandonment of the French colonies which for so long had provided work, incomes, pensions, and an outlet for Corsican energies. At the same time work had become more difficult to find in mainland France, flooded with ex-colonials in search of jobs and homes. Corsicans now had to look to their island for their living, their fulfilment. For many of the younger generation this necessity corresponded with natural emotional drives. Corsica was beautiful, it was unique, it was heroic; it was where they felt they belonged. Many became aware that it had been neglected for decades, that its agriculture was archaic, its economy in a lamentable state of stagnation. Meanwhile, they reflected, its cultural heritage was being slighted by the French educational system to the point of being threatened with extinction.

The nationalists went into action with a vast programme for the renovation of their island. A surprisingly large part of it has been achieved, if at the cost of recurrent violence. Activists have blown up many buildings, while however giving their occupants time to evacuate without danger. Principal targets have been holiday villas belonging to people from mainland France, condemned as intruders. The motivation was more political than chauvinistic: the homes of the scattering of foreign residents from various European countries have been left unharmed. Less unjustified destruction has been directed against holiday villages, often erected on or near beaches by foreign speculators with a total disregard of official planning regulations.

It can be said of the nationalists that they endeavour less to innovate than to conserve. The protection of the environment, the restoration of ancient monuments, the revival of traditional Corsican music and of the Corsican language are among their major aims. Thanks to their campaigning, the Corsican language is now taught in schools; the gospels, part of the Roman Catholic liturgy and certain religious chants are now translated into Corsican. The language is also a subject of study at the university that opened in Corte in 1981, named for Pasquale Paoli, who in 1765 founded the original university in that town. The creation of Université de Corse, sponsored by the French Minister of Education, represents the triumph of the nationalists and their allies, although the nationalists are not specifically entrusted with the running of it. Whereas previously, in flagrant contradiction to Corsican principles of equality, university education was a privilege reserved for those whose parents could afford to send them to study on the mainland, it is now available to all who reach the required grade in secondary school. Numbers at the university have risen to 3000; premises are being planned to accommodate as many more.

Corte, since the French conquest a bleak garrison town, has recovered its former dignity as a seat of learning. The huge stark old Palazzo Nazionale, where Paoli presided over the government of independent Corsica, now houses the Centre d'Etudes Corses, an institution for the study of the Corsican heritage with all that it implies. In the campus built on the edge of the town various branches of learning are dispensed, with a marked orientation towards pure and applied science. The little Corsican university has always been up to date in the context of its age: while Paoli sought to teach the avant-garde ideology of the Enlightenment, the university now seeks to inculcate the latest developments in contemporary research.

The nationalist movement has split into several groups. Some, classed as terrorist, have been outlawed by the French authorities but continue to operate in secret. Extremists – a minority – call for total independence from France. Moderates demand only greater autonomy in the management of Corsican internal affairs. This was in some degree satisfied when in 1972 Corsica was given the status of a *région* of France; three years later it was divided into two *départements*, *Haute-Corse* and *Corse-du-Sud*, with boundaries more or less corresponding with the ancient limits of the *En-Deçà* and the *Au-Delà-des-Monts*. In 1982 the *région* was endowed with an elective assembly with executive though not legislative powers. In response to the requests of certain Corsicans a *Parc naturel régional* was instituted in 1972 with the mission of preserving wildlife and nature which extends over 330,000 hectares (more than 815,000 acres) of the interior and along some forty miles of spectacular coastline; in 1976 the DRAC (*Direction régionale des affaires culturelles*) was charged with the encouragement and promotion of insular culture.

Are the Corsicans the happier for what has been done for them, for what they have done for themselves? There is no easy answer to this question. Never have they been so divided. Conservatives and moderates, that is to say the adherents of the reigning political parties, proud to be French, and aware of many advantages in the relationship, accuse the nationalists of betraying France. The nationalists accuse their opponents of betraying Corsica. To those who contend that tourism is the best means of bringing wealth to the island, the nationalists retort that the Corsicans should do without wealth if it means the ruin of their landscape. Meanwhile the Communists, who represent only a small proportion of the electorate – around 10 per cent – stand aloof, maintaining that only industrialization will bring Corsica prosperity.

Undoubtedly the general standard of living has risen over the past thirty years. The mass of the people are better, if more casually dressed, and certainly better housed. To say better fed would invite a comparison between home-grown and supermarket food. Whatever may be said against the latter, elderly people visibly put on weight, while younger people are noticeably taller than their elders. Are the Corsicans, as a whole, more contented with their lot? It would hardly seem so. The satisfaction of one need engenders another. Families that grew up with a single donkey as their means of transport now clamour for a car or at least a motorbike a head. In fact there are more cars per inhabitant in Corsica than in mainland France. In a country carved up by mountain ranges this is of course an asset rather than a luxury.

More money is in circulation than ever before; but never have the Corsicans had so much craving for it. The aristocratic disdain for money, even among unrich peasants and shepherds, that so much struck me when I first went to the island has become a thing of the past. In the course of my first journey with my husband I left on a beach a bag containing the money, in notes, for the rest of our tour; banks then existed only in Ajaccio and Bastia. It was returned to me intact by a little boy from a neighbouring peasant family. Neither he nor his parents would accept any reward. The anecdote now rings like a fairy tale.

Commercial rivalry, in a country where commerce had always been minimal, now provokes violence and threats of violence. Armed robbery, with kidnapping, of banks and shops and post offices is an almost daily occurrence. When I first went to Corsica, when the vendetta still operated, the murder rate was about twenty a year. In 1992 twice as many murders were committed. They could not possibly be explained by motives of so-called honour, or duty to the dead. Many, perhaps most, were incidents in gang warfare: Corsica has not escaped the barbarities of the international drug trade. But while in the past this was in the hands of a few sinister professionals, many more people are now involved. The drugs, which formerly touched Corsica only in transit, usually for Marseilles, now find a market in the island among a people formerly rigidly abstemious. The nationalists, true to their self-imposed role of vigilantes, stigmatize traffickers and addicts in a strenuous propaganda campaign.

This dramatic sequence of events, constructive and destructive, was unimaginable when I first arrived in the island that seemed so little changed by the centuries and unlikely to change ever. Though the vendetta dragged on in at least one of the villages, as I have described, the majority bathed in an aura of blessed serenity. The houses, built in local stone, seemed to be growing out of the soil. In the church square, in the shade of an ancient elm, men strolled in groups discussing local affairs. On a stone bench running the width of the church's façade the village elders sat smoking their pipes, and hailed the younger men returning at dusk from their flocks and fields. Here everything spoke of durability, of the suspension of time; misleadingly, for the church squares are now most often car parks and there are ever fewer young men to till the land. Subsistence agriculture no longer satisfies tastes and needs; commercial agriculture is handicapped by the limitations of the local market and the difficulty of securing markets abroad.

Corsicans may dream of their villages, but they avoid living in them until they retire. When I first saw them their populations were already predominantly old. People returned from all over the world dwelt side by side with those who had never left their birthplace nor wanted to do so. Meanwhile, young men were leaving almost every family to take up salaried posts in the French civil service, or in the colonies. Their parents spoke of their departure with mingled sorrow and pride. A time may well come when mass unemployment in the towns will drive Corsicans back to win a living from their soil. When I first went there I was impressed by the way in which those who remained managed to supply their essential needs. The country people I stayed with were pleased with my gifts of sugar and coffee brought from England, luxuries they could neither produce nor easily obtain during the years of war. But they were much better fed than the wartime urban British crowds. Home-grown fruit and vegetables were plentiful, home-made sheep and goats' cheese was bartered with neighbours for local olive oil; home-cured hams and sausages hung from the rafters. Bread, made from locally cultivated wheat and baked in the domed village bread ovens that suggested prehistoric monuments, tasted like an unfamiliar delicacy. In fact all the food produced in Corsica has strong, characteristic flavours: the cheeses that burn one's tongue, the olive oil with an intriguing, slightly musty taste, the honey, at once sweet and bitter.

This well-balanced subsistence farming was carried out on small properties of 10–20 hectares (24–49 acres). Large estates were exceptional, and rarely, I observed, so well tended. The feudal lords were crushed and dispossessed early on in Corsican history, by the Genoese and by the Corsicans themselves.[7] The survivors who contrived to draw benefit from their land mostly left their villages to spend their money out of the sight of envious neighbours. A few – very few – have kept up their ancestral homes, filled with costly furniture imported in the last century from the mainland. Others, less fortunate, regarding manual work as derogatory and unqualified to do anything else, have sunk into pitiable poverty. They can still be met with, dragging out wretched existences under the leaking roofs of their huge houses. A friend of mine, a foreigner to Corsica, who lodged with one such family as a paying guest, told me that she was given a vast bedroom containing only a Napoleonic bed; the rest of the furniture had been sold. The drawing room and dining room were empty; the family made do with a kitchen table and some stools.

The residences of such people, known as the *sgio*, the *signori*, are invariably in the village streets, in line with the other houses and differing from them only by their size. There are no equivalents to the English country mansion or the French *château*. Conditions in the Corsican countryside have always been too precarious to encourage that style of living. Only the transhumant shepherds, at the opposite end of the social scale, will face living away from the communities. Taking their flocks to the high plateaux between May and September, they inhabit one-roomed stone cabins that mark the limit of Corsican austerity. A cabin is furnished only with a wooden, or more often stone, platform. The occupants sleep on it in a row on mattresses made from sacks and stuffed with straw or dry leaves. A space between the end of the platform and the outer wall is just large enough for a fire, which is always kept burning; the smoke creeps out through the door that is seldom closed. I must add that I slept soundly enough on my mattress stuffed with dry leaves gathered from the roots of the beech trees that in Corsica grow among the pines and even higher up the mountains. The shepherds' cabins stand always on bare ground, away from the woods and maquis. Nothing is planted near them except a small dead tree, on the branches of which are hung the pails used in cheese-making.

The villages, in conformity with the French constitution, are democratic in their usages and social structure. Authority is vested in the municipal council, elected every sixth year, which elects from its members the mayor, chief magistrate of the community, an organization not unlike that existing under the Genoese régime and before. The village schoolmaster or schoolmistress is another person of importance, often solicited by the population for help in drafting official letters or filling in forms. The reassuring presence of a schoolteacher is, however, becoming increasingly rare, for the French government pursues the regrettable policy of closing the schools of the smaller communities and sending the children by bus to study in larger villages. At the same time many villages have suffered the loss of a parish priest, a figure always held in high esteem.

When I first went to Corsica there was a priest in every village; but in consequence of the falling off of vocations since the Second World War, each of the sixty-one priests now has to minister to several of the 410 parishes. Christianity, established in the island since Roman times, has struck deep roots into the Corsican collective psyche. It is adhered to with fervour and respect, in exaltation and in grief, as a counter-force to all the harm inherent in the universe. Slow to accept technical innovations from abroad, the Corsicans were responsive to spiritual influences: the megalithic faith in pre- and proto-historic times, then Christianity from the second century. They co-existed, not without conflict. Environed by pagan forces, Christianity, militant, proclaimed itself with its churches and chapels all over the island. The massive wooden crosses standing by the roadside in or near every village were placed there to protect the communities from the powers of evil. Some are associated with miracles. A spectacular cross at Guagno, some thirty feet high, was planted on a rocky pedestal in 1837 thanks to the prayers of the saintly Father Albini from the nearby monastery at Vico. He had undertaken a preaching mission to this village where the population was notoriously given to vengeance and sexual sins. Moved by his words the people made peace, repented and performed the arduous task of raising the cross. Or, according to some accounts, it raised itself, at the mere touch of Father Albini's hand.[8]

The Corsican year is punctuated by religious festivals that give colour and meaning to the routine of living. On Palm Sunday palm leaves, twisted into intricate shapes (a local craft), are blessed in the church square. Good Friday night is the occasion, in various villages and small towns, of penitential processions in which the whole population takes part. The pagan celebration of the solstices is incorporated into the practice of the Catholic Church. Huge bonfires are lit in the church square on the eve of the midsummer festival of Saint John the Baptist, and on Christmas Eve.[9]

On the eve of the feast of Saint John the fire is made from aromatic plants – arbutus, lentisk, rosemary, the incense-scented *immortelle* – collected by the boys of the village in the maquis during the day. That night is the occasion of the *cumparaggiu*, a traditional non-religious rite much prized by the inhabitants. Young girls and young men – up to the age of about twenty – engage in bonds of lifelong friendship which are sealed when they jump twice over the bonfire holding hands. The link may be made between two girls, two young men, or a girl and a man, and may include four persons. They are not relatives nor potential marriage partners. Thereafter they become *commères*, the girls, and *compères*, the young men, and they owe each other affection and loyalty in every circumstance through life.

They may become godparents to each other's children. Charles Bonaparte, Napoleon's father, was *compère* with Lorenzo Giubega, who replaced the count of Marbeuf as godfather to Napoleon, Marbeuf being too busy to attend the ceremony. '*Amattissimo signor compare*,' Charles begins a letter written on 18 March 1776 to Giubega, a reliable supporter in his precarious legal career. A man of wealth and power in the Corsican scene, Giubega consistently befriended the Bonapartes. In June 1793 when they were hounded out of their home by the opposing political faction of Paoli, Giubega came to their rescue and enabled them to get away from Calvi to the mainland.[10]

The *cumparaggiu* is a Corsican institution of altogether exceptional kind. It is unconnected with sexual or blood relationships; it has no connotation of violence or death. And it is based on choice: choice, an advantage which traditional Corsican society offered to few of its members, women or men. It has died out, but quite recently, so that there are still elderly people who cherish an affectionate friendship with the *commères* or *compères* with whom they leapt over the fire fifty or so years ago.

Christmas is the festival of the family: the Holy Family and all others. Young and old gather before and after Midnight Mass round the huge fire built in the church square, symbol of Jesus, light of the world. In Rusio, a mountain village of the southern Castagniccia, where I spent one Christmas in the snow, the Mass was chanted in a wonderful Corsican polyphonic music, and the singers went on singing afterwards around the fire, regardless of the snow, songs sacred and profane, until the small hours of Christmas Day. That night the houses stay open; neighbour visits neighbour, and between eleven o'clock and midnight magic incantations against illness and misfortune, of which I shall later speak, are taught to the young, for it is believed that the forces of evil are inoperative during that one night of the year.

Elaborate cribs are fabricated in the churches for the festival: miniature moss-covered grottoes shelter little carved or moulded figures – the *santons* – representing the scene of the Nativity. In some villages live pageants are staged: a real ox, a real ass, real people personifying Saint Joseph and the Magi, watch over a young mother and her baby: the Virgin Mary and the infant Jesus. Crowds pour into the churches, to admire these displays, to attend Midnight Mass. But today, due to the shortage of priests, it cannot always be celebrated. Recently the people of a village who had been at pains to create a live pageant, realizing with dismay as the time passed that no priest would come, stayed in the church to join in the prayers recited by the *confrérie*, the village brotherhood.

The *confréries* are secular associations grouping a number of parishioners who, independently of the clergy, make it their business to carry out certain traditional religious rites and ceremonies. They can be traced in Corsica from the later Middle Ages; numerous and prosperous in the sixteenth and seventeenth centuries, they are still active, though fewer, today. The clergy have always held them in high esteem for their zeal in kindling the faith. Their members, coming from all ranks of society, pay subscriptions into a common fund to provide for their own funerals. The easing of death, the ensuring of a dignified exit from life, is one of their main concerns. It is reflected in the choice of patron saints of the different *confréries*. Saint Anthony the hermit is frequently honoured: he who is well known to have resisted temptation in the desert and less well known to have been helped by a lion to bury a fellow anchorite. He is represented, with a pig beside him, in statues often found in the plain little chapels of the *confréries*, sometimes the vigorous work of local woodcarvers.[11] Saint Roch, who cured the plague, is another figure frequently seen, and Saint Sebastian, who was martyred and clubbed to death in Rome. His corpse, thrown into a sewer, was providentially recovered and buried in a catacomb.

The *confréries* organize the traditional ceremonies of Good Friday night. In certain towns and villages penitential processions enact the Calvary. A repentant sinner, usually masked by a hood through which only his eyes can be seen, carries a heavy wooden cross through the streets; in certain places, as at Corte, the effigy of Christ is carried on an open bier. In the context of Good Friday, Jesus, in the minds of the Corsicans, incarnates the hero who at the cost of his life persisted in opposing the colonial tyranny of Pontius Pilate and Rome. The man who bears the cross may well be an insular patriot; he is also, and essentially, a penitent; according to tradition, a murderer. In times past he might be a bandit come in from the maquis to seek his salvation.

Banditry had died out when I joined in the spectacular Good Friday night procession in Sartene, known as the *Catenacciu*, 'the chained', because the chief penitent drags a chain attached to his right leg through the streets of the town. Fortified by the Genoese in the sixteenth century to police and defend southwest Corsica, the little town has the allure of a medieval stronghold, so bleak and stark are its ramparts and the tall façades of its houses superimposed on the mountainside overlooking the Golfe de Valinco. Surprisingly, it has been administered by Communist municipalities ever since the liberation of the island in 1943. Yet the atheist Marxist creed has in no way impaired its ancient religious traditions, and the *Catenacciu* is celebrated every year with unabated popular enthusiasm.

Candidates for the role of chief penitent are booked by the priest for ten years ahead and more. His identity is known only to the priest and the monks of the little Franciscan monastery on the edge of the town where he must prepare himself during three days before his ordeal by abstinence and prayer. He appears on Good Friday night draped and hooded in red, symbol of Christ's blood, bearing on his shoulder a great black wooden cross, the stem of which is held by a penitent shrouded in white personifying Simon the Cyrene.[12] In spite of the rule of secrecy the identity of the chief penitent had leaked out that Good Friday night when I reached Sartene; he had just terminated a prison sentence, I was told, for killing a faithless wife. He was certainly no tough denizen of the maquis, to judge by his small-wristed, red-gloved hands clutching the enormous cross, and his slender bare feet bending over the cobbles.

The procession, followed by a dense, excited crowd, lasted over three hours. Some people walked in ordered ranks behind the *confrères*, joining in their chant, the hypnotic *'Perdonnu mio Dio, Mio Dio perdonnu'*, chanted to an ancient Corsican air; others pushed, shouted, exclaimed and called to friends massed on the balconies of the houses illuminated by candles in all the windows. According to tradition the penitent must fall three times on his route, as Christ fell on the way to Golgotha; each fall drew a deep cry, almost a howl, from the spectators. Women wailed. Old white faces appeared pressed against the panes of closed windows, watching the spectacle with expressions of intense concentration. They were people, I was told, who never left their homes for years on end. The entire population, it seemed, was united in this collective demonstration of guilt. No one can remain unmoved by the *Catenacciu*. Foreign visitors, aghast and slightly shocked, have described it as a 'half-pagan' ceremony. Mistakenly: the *catenacciu* is essentially Christian, and in a matter-of-fact, historical sense. 'What you will see is not a solemn rite,' the priest warned me, 'but a representation of the Calvary. Disorderly, just as the real event must have been.'

Closer to the pagan heritage is the festival of the dead, All Souls' Day, on 2 November. The Catholic Church has certainly tried to Christianize the occasion. Three different orders of the Mass are prescribed; in the past all three might be celebrated in succession, between five o'clock in the morning and midday. But popular tradition has not lost its vitality. On the eve of 2 November, lighted candles are placed by all the tombs, so that the cemeteries become glowing patches of brightness in the dark maquis. One old lady of my acquaintance used to spend that night every year in the family chapel-tomb; to listen to the dead, so she explained. The dead gave her advice on how to run family affairs during the following year, practical advice on the buying and selling and renting and leasing of property. The dead, if treated with due respect, can be relied upon for guidance. In the Middle Ages and even later village assemblies and tribunals were held in a burial ground, known as the *arringo*, with the participants grouped round a slab of stone, the *petra l'arringo*, laid over a tomb.[13] The dead were trusted to inspire wise decisions.

On the eve of All Souls' Day the dead are thought to return to their homes, a belief that has parallels in Italy, notably in Sardinia. Each family rings the church bell to summon their spirits; in certain villages the bell tolls all night long. The fires in the houses are left burning, and the doors open, to welcome the dead. Food may be laid out for them on the dining table, or on the outer rim of a window ledge. I tasted this food: 'Eat it, it's not been touched,' an old woman said to me when I passed by her home one bitterly cold All Souls' Day morning. Did she imply that I was hungrier than the dead? She offered me an assortment of pasties, with strong unfamiliar flavours. It is in fact the custom to share these refreshments with relatives and neighbours, who by consuming them are thought to give pleasure to the dead. The pasties may be stuffed with onion, or marrow or wild sorrel, and flavoured with salted *brocciu*, a soft cheese made from ewes' or goats' milk.

To partake of the food of the dead; never had I hoped for so great a privilege. In Corsica the dead reign, dictating actions and attitudes. Venerated, they are also feared. If their tombs are uncared-for, and no food or water is prepared for them on the night of their return, if their advice has been disregarded, or worse still, if they suffered a violent death that has been left unavenged, they may wreak their own vengeance on the living by taking them to themselves.

A death in a Corsican household was until very recently the occasion of spectacular traditional ceremonies that owed little to Christianity. The family assembled round the corpse, which was laid out on the dining table. Windows, shutters and doors were closed, the room was lit only by a single candle; sometimes the façade of the house was painted black. Women shrieked and wailed and tore their hair, scratched their faces with their nails, so that some of them remained disfigured for life. This was particularly true of widows, who hoped thereby to appease the spirits of their dead husbands. Meanwhile one of the women, gifted in the art of improvising verses to music, would chant a *voceru*, a song in honour of the deceased. There was even a ritual dance, the *caracolu*, in which the mourners linked hands and gambolled round the corpse. The clergy condemned it as a pagan practice derived from the Saracens. In fact it seems to have been a circular movement of pre-Christian origin designed to restore a natural harmony broken by death, as was the procession known as the *granitola*, of which I shall speak later.[14]

Dancing, singing, shrieking and wailing might accompany the procession of the coffin to the church and to the burial ground. The bishop of Mariana and Accia, presiding over a diocesan synod in 1657, fulminated furiously against this 'abominable spectacle', such 'barbarous and impious customs' and 'superstitious songs', threatening the performers with fines of 'three *scudi*' and 'major excommunication' and to deprive of his office any priest who assisted at such scenes.[15]

Ecclesiastical condemnations of the *voceri* continued till the present day. If one studies their content one can understand why. Passed from mouth to ear and ear to mouth, these songs have been collected and published at intervals since the latter part of the last century.[16] They are usually considered together with the *lamenti*, improvised songs of a milder inspiration which might be composed for any unhappy situation, and not necessarily beside a corpse. The *voceru*, on the other hand, was very often a summons to vengeance, in which any pretence to Christian submission was precluded. The *voceratrice* had no hesitation in naming the murderer and calling for revenge; her words were calculated to stir the bloodthirsty instincts of the men assembled in the background, drumming the floor, I have been told, with the butt ends of their guns. These verses were the more terrible because they often embodied Christian allusions: Christianity was not forgotten so much as rejected. So a *voceratrice* laments the death of her cousin Matteo, a doctor, killed by his client, Natale, who summoned him to his supposed sickbed in order to murder him.

> Oh! Infamous Natale!
> More perfidious than a dog
> He has betrayed his doctor
> As Judas betrayed his Christ!
> . . . If I do not witness vengeance
> I shall want to be de-baptized.

Sometimes, after a death by violence, a bloodstained garment of the victim was exhibited and the women smeared his blood on their faces and hands. A young girl bewailing the death of her father addresses her audience with the words:

> Now bring me the scissors
> Bring them to me quickly
> I want to cut my hair
> To staunch his wounds
> See the blood of my father!
> It covers my hands.

For a woman to shave her head was a fitting sign of grief. Conversely, men engaged in a vendetta would leave their beards unshaven until vengeance had been achieved.

In one celebrated *voceru* for the death of two cousins, it is not the murderer who is execrated but the priest who, being related to the murderer, refused to toll the funeral bell for the slain:

> May I see in a basket
> The entrails of the priest
> May I tear them with my teeth
> And rub them in my hands
> In the house of the priest
> One hears the Devil
> Infamous priest, excommunicated
> Dog-eater of the sacraments
> May you die in anguish
> In spasms and in torments.

Ejected in paroxysms of grief, the *voceri* nearly always tend to extravagance of expression. When the death is by natural causes, the *voceratrice* may pour out a torrent of images comparing the deceased to any and everything she has ever enjoyed or admired. So a woman addresses her dead husband:

> Oh my Petru-Francescu
> Source of my ruin!
> You were my flower,
> My rose without thorns;
> You were my valiant heart,
> Known from the mountains to the sea.

And later:

> Oh my tufted cypress,
> My muscat grape,
> My sugared cake,
> Sweet and good manna . . .
> You were my column
> You were my support,
> You were my grandeur,

You were my brother,
My oriental pearl,
My finest treasure.

The climax of these metaphors is 'You were my brother', for to a Corsican the blood tie is the most sacred bond. Not that incest is approved; on the contrary, it is violently stigmatized by people and clergy alike. Yet marriage between cousins, even first cousins, is frequent and socially approved. Corsican marriage was by tradition endogamous, as I have explained, so that almost everyone in a village became interrelated. Cousin had to marry cousin if he or she was to marry at all. A Corsican family is tight-knit and self-defensive as a regiment. All its members share in its resources, so that destitution, as distinct from poverty, has been extremely rare. Each person has a respected place in the organization, and a function to perform in its economy; the loss of a life was a loss to all. The small groups of the family, the village, which until recently constituted Corsican society, needed their full working force in order to survive. The extreme reactions to death reflected not only sentimental grief but fear: the fear felt by those who had to go on living with one less fellow being beside them. The cult of the dead was also concerned with the living.

Corsica has always been short of men; in work as in war, it has been handicapped by small numbers. The population, estimated at 120,000 during the eighteenth-century rebellions, rose to a maximum of 280,000 in 1895; yet the death rate in the nineteenth century was the highest in France. Medical surveys give a horrifying account of the ravages of endemic malaria, of smallpox due to lack of vaccination, epidemics of cholera as well as typhoid and typhus, known as 'the malady of poverty'.[17] The death of a husband, perhaps the most active member of a family, might mean material as well as emotional tragedy. So a widow improvising a *voceru*, surrounded by her children, reproaches her husband for leaving them penniless:

What, my dear treasure,
Was your intention
When you broke the link
Of so faithful a union?
And left your children

And their mother
In a state of mendicity?
. . . But for charitable people
(It's terrible to say)
My dear sons
We should perish!
Ah! weep for your father.

A *voceratrice* was not necessarily a member of the family affected by the death. Unrelated women of the neighbourhood particularly gifted in this art might be called upon, or spontaneously present themselves at the house of the bereaved. They performed without any thought of material reward, like the village storytellers and bards, and the healers, of whom I shall later tell. Each *voceratrice* chose a particular traditional air which she used, with only slight variations, on every occasion; the words were either composed beforehand or improvised on the spot.

So I learned from a practised *voceratrice*. I met her by chance on a bus journey. She caught a finger in the door. While it was being dressed as well as might be in a wayside café I was struck by her aloofness from blood and pain. This woman, I thought, was an exceptional being. I was not disappointed when I came to know her. Her vocation, she told me, was to visit houses in her neighbourhood where a death had taken place and improvise a *voceru* in honour of the deceased. Recently, she told me, she had improvised a *voceru* for the death of an eighty-four-year-old man.

Nothing in her experience would seem to have prepared her for this role. She had not spent her life in a village, steeped in local tradition, but in Paris where she had worked forty years in the Ministry of Finance. Her husband had been employed in the Préfecture de la Seine. This life-style had been in accordance with her wish. A modern woman of her time, she had married on the understanding that her husband would take her to live in mainland France. How then did it happen that she, who had turned her back on tradition, should have resumed it so willingly? Why had she even wanted to do so? Her answer to my question was brief and conclusive. 'It was death herself who unleashed the gift.' Her husband, then her two sons, had died in the Second World War. When the third, unbearable, death took place of her younger son, she had spontaneously improvised a *voceru*. 'I don't know where it came from,' she told me, 'I heard myself singing for the dead.'

After that she had returned to her Corsican village and pursued her vocation of *voceratrice*. 'The priest disapproves,' she said to me, 'he says it's a pagan custom. But I don't pay much attention; it gives great comfort to the relatives.' I could understand why when she invited me to her home and sang to me a selection of her *voceri*. They impressed me by their serenity. Was it because she was an independent *voceratrice*, not intimately connected with the deceased, or perhaps simply because she was a born poetess, that her *voceri* were untainted by notions of revenge? She made no personal reproaches. For her, death was the sole culprit:

> That miscreant, death
> She roams round the houses
> And enters without knocking
> She blocks her ears
> And leaves us to cry alone.

Her voice was pitched very high; the air was poignant. Corsican traditional music has a searing quality. It is modal and oriental; echoes of the Gregorian chant can be detected mingling with those of an older, harsher music, the primeval music of the Mediterranean from which that of the Arabs also derives; the relationship between Corsican and Arab music is one of cousinship.

So it happened that I was able to hear some of the last *voceri* to be performed in Corsica. Since then the custom has faded out, with many others. Not only the way of living but the way of dying has changed. People now seldom expire in their homes surrounded by their weeping and more or less helpless relatives, but tended by doctors and nurses in clinics and hospitals. It is true that the new environment does not prevent families gathering round the deathbed, and that weeping and wailing often sounds in the corridors. Death is none the less terrible for all the efforts made to prevent it; perhaps it is the more so for being robbed of the poetry by which it was enshrined in tradition.

Corsican tradition is primarily concerned with death. Yet the Corsicans are not a particularly melancholy people. They know how to enjoy themselves with an undisguised zest on appropriate occasions: family weddings and christening parties, local festivals, the carnival which is performed in certain villages. Not to mention the celebration of a successful election, when the partisans of the triumphant candidate let go in outbursts of gunshot, fireworks and song. But the Corsicans have inherited a religion of the veneration of the dead, that of the megalith builders, which was superimposed on an earlier insular cult of the same character; one perhaps natural to a people who attached so great a value to a human life.

The Megalithic faith was a powerful and widespread religion, as compelling as Christianity was later to become. Between about 3500 and 1000 BC it spread over western Europe, leaving enormous, indestructible stone monuments: in these areas some 50,000 have been found. They were created with a conviction comparable to that of the builders of the medieval cathedrals. Their significance was undoubtedly religious, though it is not always easy to interpret today. Archaeology has shown that the dolmens and other types of megalithic sepulchres were designed for collective burial. The meaning of the menhirs, which may stand twenty feet high, is less clear. Does each one commemorate an individual human being? The numbers of the menhirs, arranged in lines and circles, apparently at the same period, weighs against this theory. According to such a supposition the huge menhirs of Brittany, known as 'the hosts of Carnac', 1099 of them placed in eleven parallel lines, would suggest a holocaust of giants. But it seems more likely, at least in northern Europe, that the menhirs were erected to mark processional avenues or delimit sacred grounds. Research has established that at Stonehenge they are building elements in a temple dedicated to the cult of the dead as well as of the sun.

In Corsica the statue-menhirs, at least, are explicit. It can hardly be doubted that they commemorate deceased chieftains, warriors and heroes. Representing a late climax of megalithic art, they are perhaps the earliest portraits of individual human beings in western Europe.[18] A religious movement so highly developed could not easily wither away. In the sixth century Pope Gregory the Great condemned the Corsicans for worshipping stones.[19] In the twelfth century the ancient faith was still alive, to judge by the two statue-menhirs found built into the lower stone courses of the lateral walls of the ruined Pisan cathedral of Sagone. They cannot have been placed there for convenience, for their shape is incongruous in relation to the careful Pisan masonry. They were incorporated, surely, into the Christian edifice to demonstrate the victory of one faith over another.

The victory was never decisive. The Megalithic cult of the dead lingered on in the Corsican collective unconscious, determining beliefs, attitudes and customs. The un-Christian funeral rites, the *voceru*, the *caracolu*, the practice of collective burial in the *arca*, the more recent elaborate family tombs, the attentions paid to the dead on All Souls' Day, the vendetta itself, which decreed that murder should avenge murder to appease the spirit of the murdered man; all these customs, as well as various popular beliefs which I shall describe, must surely hark back to the Megalithic faith. Like a dark, rank plant of the maquis, it survived through the centuries alongside Christianity, sometimes intertwining with it, sometimes smothering it, never extirpated to this day.

Yet it is not, I think, the most ancient complex of beliefs enduring in this country where so little has been innovated and so much conserved. The phenomenon of the *mazzeri*, those who hunt and kill by night in dreams, seems to stem from even older origins, as will be told.

CHAPTER 3

Villains, Heroes and Phantoms

Career of a bandit – popular tales – presages of
death – megalithic tradition – the *mazzeri*

My knowledge of the Corsican tradition was gleaned little by little
over a period of years after 1948, when I first arrived in the island with
my husband. Jean Cesari initiated me. People of all kinds and ages
contributed to my understanding of different phenomena, people I
met when moving about the island in the 1950s, on foot, by bus and by
train. These encounters were so rewarding that I never regretted being
unable to afford a car. Again and again I was to be enchanted by the
way the Corsicans, reputedly wary of foreigners, spoke to me so
freely, and to feel grateful for their confidence.

Chance acquaintances invited me into their homes, like the
voceratrice, and the woman who gave me the food of the dead. Poverty
has never made the Corsicans mean. Their traditional hospitality gave
me the key to the rest of their cultural heritage. The best moment for
conversation was the *veillée*, the evening gathering of family, friends
and neighbours, in winter round the hearth, in summer on the little
stone terraces outside the houses, under the stars. The term *veillée* has
been discarded now that television has robbed the custom of its
intrinsic character; in the 1950s it was almost the only available
distraction, the day's work done.

Tales would be told; some relating events that had made recent news,
others belonging to a legendary or semi-legendary past. Favourite
subjects were the exploits of famous bandits, some of whom were
personally known to my hosts. So I learned the life story, at once
pitiable, grotesque and tragic, of the bandit Muzarettu, who died soon
after I came to the island.[1] It was a slap in the face from a nephew at a

card party, no more, that launched him on his terrible career. The insult rankled, incited him to ambush and kill his nephew that same night. Even murder, it seems, was insufficient to wipe out the offence. Perhaps Muzarettu brooded on it until he had projected it into physical form; he died of a cancer of the face.

The tragic sequence of events developed slowly. A few months after the murder Muzarettu gave himself up to the police. He was tried and acquitted; the slap was regarded as sufficient justification for killing. But his life had been fatally dislocated. Menaces from his nephew's family drove him to leave his village, to sell his land. For a time he camped in a cellar in a small seaside resort, and there lived in a ramshackle, bohemian style. Fishermen of Ajaccio told me how they paid him visits and joined him in revels that lasted till dawn. This life of wild pleasure was brought to an end in the Second World War, when Muzarettu was ordered out of the cellar to make way for Italian troops. He retorted by murdering the secretary of the mayor who had evicted him. The family of the secretary bribed a young man to murder Muzarettu; Muzarettu got wind of the deal and killed him too.

This time Muzarettu had no intention of surrendering to the law. But he was captured in an undignified, almost laughable way. Some people he met one day on a lonely beach invited him to share their picnic. No sooner had he sat down than they sprang on him, policemen in disguise, and carried him off to prison. Muzarettu was then over seventy and already suffering from cancer of the face. He was put into the prison hospital, from which he escaped. Regardless of age and illness he took to the maquis, where he spent the rest of his life: more than ten years. He found a hiding place in a rock shelter in a cliff on the then desolate south-west coast. Fishermen I knew in Ajaccio went to visit him, brought him an assortment of useless medicines, so that the whole place smelt, so they told me, like a chemist's laboratory.

He was dying when he made his way to Sartene. Not to the *Catenacciu*; his health was too far gone for him to play the part of the penitent. Moreover Muzarettu was not a religious man, but a notorious blasphemer who scorned God as he scorned the law. He nevertheless accepted the hospitality of the Franciscan monks established in a small monastery near the town, who invited him to end his days in their care. Reviving an ancient tradition according to which the monasteries had the right to give asylum to outlaws and criminals, the Franciscans obtained assurance of his immunity from the police. It is even said that the commandant of the local *gendarmerie* went to visit him on his sickbed. Yet Muzarettu was a far from easy patient. He threatened suicide, yelled for his revolver, tried to poison himself with a tube of strychnine he kept hidden in his wallet. Only at the very end did the fierce old man come to terms with God. Dying, so one of the monks told me, horribly disfigured and beyond speech, he lay quite still, silently and repeatedly making the sign of the cross.

Such Corsican stories are no less violent and dramatic than the half-fictional tales of tradition. Preserved orally through the generations, they have been transcribed and published since the end of the last century.[2] Experts trace their subject matter to international sources: Greco-Roman, Germanic, Celtic, medieval Christian, Indian and Arab. A mingling of these influences can be detected, as though these tales had travelled from hearth to hearth through the generations and across the world. Yet as told in Corsica they have a characteristic tenor. Their dominant theme is the conflict between the bad powerful rich and the good powerless poor. In these conflicts the good poor always come out victorious, though not without trials and tribulations.

Social status is usually associated with evil. Tales of nobles and medieval lords echo ancient grievances of the common people. Orso Alamano lorded it over the shepherds and peasants from his castle in southern Corsica. He dispensed justice, but he also practised the *droit de cuissage*, that is to say he assumed the right to deflower every bride on her wedding night. A young girl consented to marry her fiancé, Piobitto, only on condition that he first killed Orso Alamano. Piobitto, cunning – an asset not unusual among the Corsican good poor – went to Sardinia and there learned the technique of lassoing animals from horseback. On his return he invited Orso Alamano to go for a ride with him, lending him one of his own horses. At a suitable moment he lassoed Alamano, unseated him and dragged him to death over the stony ground. He left his corpse on the spot, unburied. The young couple married. But one day a passing shepherd recognized the skull of Orso Alamano, and cursed it, striking it with his stick. Whereupon a fly emerged from the skull which soon grew to be as big as an ox and killed everyone who approached it with its pestilential breath. The local people, desperate, prepared to abandon their land. But they were delivered by an unknown knight who killed the fly, and who turned out to be Saint George.

The fly no doubt reflects the memory of an epidemic of malaria. Orso Alamano was a real and detested feudal lord: the Corsican chronicler Giovanni della Grossa gives a more detailed and down-to-earth version of the events, emphasizing their importance in a social revolution leading to the establishment of a popular democratic system of local self-government.[3] The knight of Saint George, who appears only in the oral version, proclaims confidence in the Christian faith. The story is a picturesque rendering of a historical episode.

The bad rich, in Corsican tales, are not necessarily noble. Rich people are bad, irrespective of their social origin. The idea probably issues from a long history of colonial exploitation: to be rich was to betray basic Corsican values. Two sisters married two shepherds, the one rich, the other poor. The wife of the bad rich shepherd, who had two children, employed as servant the wife of the good poor shepherd, who had seven. She was so mean as to grudge her good poor sister the flour she took away smeared on her hands after making bread, which could be used for making *fougasse*, a form of soft flat bread, to feed her seven children. The children were starving; yet the bad rich sister obliged her good poor sister to wash her hands after making the bread so as to have nothing to take home. The bad rich well-fed children taunted the good poor hungry children by going to eat on their doorstep.

This was too much for the good poor shepherd. In despair he left home and walked through a forest until, after nightfall, he saw the lights of a house glimmering through the trees. Exhausted, he knocked at the door. He was welcomed by twelve men sitting at table; not the twelve disciples, but the twelve months of the year. February, the smallest and kindest of them, persuaded him to spend the night and fed him with ample helpings of sausage and ham.

The next day he was sent on his way equipped with a little portable mill and instructions to turn it twice when he reached a certain cave. The good poor shepherd followed these directions. February provided his best weather: brilliant sun, that marvellous golden light that heralds the Corsican spring. The good poor shepherd reached the cave and turned the mill twice. Out came a stream of gold coins. Arriving home he bought sheep and pasture: he and his wife had become rich.

The bad rich sister, with a lack of intelligence not uncommon among the bad rich in Corsican tales, sent her husband to the same house in the forest, counting on the same result. The bad rich husband began by insulting February, who offered him only a little thin soup. The following day he was sent home with a portable mill. Reaching the cave, according to instructions, he turned the mill twice. Out came twelve men armed with staves who beat him almost to death. February added his worst weather to the experience: thunder, lightning, hail, frost, wind and snow. The bad rich shepherd arrived home in a state of collapse. He handed the mill to his wife. She turned it ten times. Twelve men came out and she was beaten by each of them. A cautionary tale about the consequences of wealth and pride.

Animals play an important part in the Corsican tales, as might be expected in the context of an archaic rural society. One glimpses reflections of an ancient, widespread belief in a mythical, happy age when men and animals lived on equal terms, understood each other's language, and exchanged identities. Traces of such beliefs exist in the practices of the Corsican *mazzeri*, which will be discussed later. The hero of one bewildering surrealistic tale transforms himself eleven times. A widow had three sons, lazy and disobedient. A tall handsome stranger introduced himself to her as her rich brother from America. The rich relation from America is a not unfamiliar figure in the traditional Corsican scene; from the sixteenth century onwards, adventurous Corsicans made fortunes in the New World.

The widow protested that she did not recognize the stranger as her brother, and with reason: he was not her brother but the Devil in person. The Devil often appears in Corsican tales; he is always outwitted but never destroyed. This brother-Devil offered to help his sister by setting up her sons in advantageous professions, as carpenters or shoemakers. He took away two of them with these expectations; they were never seen again. The third son had meanwhile cunningly learnt some of the Devil's magic. He turned himself successively into a cock, a cow, a horse, a fish, a dove, a falcon and a jewel-studded brooch which the falcon dropped through a window into a princess's bedroom.

The princess was delighted by the brooch, and equally, it seems, by the young man who emerged from the brooch every night. The king, her father, was naturally alarmed by the arrangement, and judging his daughter to be insane sent a doctor to examine her. But the young-man-brooch turned himself into a doctor. The brooch was thrown to the floor and splintered into pomegranate seeds. The young man turned himself into a cock and picked at the seeds, all except one which the princess stamped under her foot. This seed was transformed back into the young man, and with the king's consent he married her.

Surprisingly, kings and queens and their offspring are not classed among the bad in Corsican popular tales. Perhaps because such royal personages, imported with foreign themes, were to the Corsicans alien and unreal. Corsica underwent many changes of régime in its history but it was never controlled by a monarchy for any considerable time. In the fourteenth century the island was theoretically subject to the kings of Aragon, but they never succeeded in implanting themselves on Corsican soil. In the eighteenth century Theodor von Neuhoff was acclaimed king by the anti-Genoese rebels, but his reign lasted less than a year. The subsequent British attempt to rule the island lasted less than three. The intervening twenty-year-long experience of the *ancien régime* never brought the French kings to Corsica in person.

Yet, confusingly, Corsica was referred to in documents as *Il Regno di Corsica*, 'the kingdom of Corsica', from the seventeenth century till the French conquest. This title was insisted on by the doges of republican Genoa because it conferred on them the status of royalty in embassies and in the treating of international affairs. It was preserved by the Corsican leaders of the eighteenth-century rebellion to give dignity to the newly-created state. But none of them, not even Paoli, aspired to kingship.

In the two different versions of the Cinderella story told in Corsica, which, incidentally, are equally brutal in their action, the prince appears as the chivalrous young man of European tradition who restores the missing slipper to Cinderella and makes her his bride. The story as told in the *Au-Delà-des-Monts* begins with a murder: Cinderella, encouraged by her wicked stepmother, kills her own mother by pushing her into a bread chest and slamming down the lid so as to cut her in half. Meanwhile donkeys' ears sprout from the head of the already ugly stepsister so that she has to wear a hat when she goes to the royal ball. Cinderella, magnificently dressed up by her fairy godmother with a golden star on her forehead, wins the heart of the prince. But before he can marry her he has to rescue her from a barrel in which she has been shut up in a cellar by her wicked stepmother. In the other version of the tale, current in the *En-Deçà-des-Monts*, the wicked stepsister is roasted alive in a bread oven.

Fairies of a specifically Corsican type appear in several well-known tales. They are not godmothers, but wild creatures who might be described as water sprites, who inhabit caves near streams. Extremely beautiful, they are dangerous to mortal men.[4] A man in a village of the Sartenais was exceedingly attracted to a fairy living by the Rizzanese, a river that flows to the sea in the Golfe de Valinco. He seized her, protesting, by her hair and forcibly married her. But though she bore him three sons and three daughters she was unable to adapt to village life; she was unhappy and walked about the streets with her head bent, as though in shame. She made her husband promise never to look at her naked left shoulder, which she kept always covered. But the husband, asserting his male prerogatives, disobeyed, and he saw to his horror a hole in her shoulder filled with bones. 'That is the skeleton of our love which you have destroyed,' she cried, and left him for good, taking with her the three daughters. They went to Sardinia and never returned. On departing she told him that his family would never have more than three male heirs, and this prediction came true.

In another tale it was a fairy, again living in a cave near water, who fell in love with a shepherd. When she placed a ring on his finger to symbolize their union he suddenly became very handsome, and attired like a prince. She lent him a chariot drawn by magic horses to take him home to tell his mother the news. On the way he met a queen who was so impressed by his appearance that she proposed to marry him. Tempted by the prospect of power, he agreed. The fairy's chariot and horses vanished on the spot and the shepherd resumed his usual poor, plain appearance. The queen thereupon rejected him; a great storm arose, the earth opened at their feet and swallowed them up. A warning tale against the sins of greed and pride.

Corsican tales, however violent and fantastical, illustrate a clearly defined moral code: avarice and arrogance are punished. Their stock is limited. The same themes turn up in different parts of the country with details changed, added or discarded. Unwritten, they were preserved by storytellers, people gifted in this art who knew how to bring their subjects alive by their intonations of voice, their gestures and asides. Valued guests at the *veillée*, they provided the nearest performance to a theatrical production that most of their audiences had known. Novelty was not necessarily required of them; old tales were greeted like old friends.

Jean Cesari possesses this histrionic gift, as I had occasion to appreciate on my first visits to the island. He has a natural talent for controlling and varying his voice when telling a tale. So I heard him mimic the gruff hoarse voices of old men, the strident accents of argument and menace, female and male, the plaintive tones of distressed women and the high thin voices of the spirits of the dead. For what Jean had to tell me were not only traditional tales, but events that had actually taken place in the experience of people known to him, or in his own. And what has happened in Corsica, or is thought to have happened, is fully as strange as any legend.

So I learned of the signs that give warning of death. The beating, for instance, of an invisible drum. The drum can never be located; when one hears it in the cellar, no sooner has one run downstairs than it sounds in the loft; when one climbs to the loft it sounds from below. In that house someone is doomed to die. Another portent of death, particularly frequent, I was told, in the Castagniccia, is the *mubba*, a procession of phantom pigs passing the house at night. The Castagniccia is in fact overrun with real pigs, half wild, often crossed with boar, which feed on a delicious diet of chestnuts and cyclamen bulbs and so make delicious food for their owners. Equally feared is the appearance outside the window of a large white owl; the so-called 'bird of evil', the *malaceddu*. Or the hooting of an owl in a house where someone is ill. So a young girl sings in a lament for her deceased father:

> When you were ill
> The owl hooted;
> Your soul flew away
> At its sinister cry
> Oh! Why did it leave
> Its dark abode?[5]

If a bird – any bird – taps at a closed window it is thought to be the spirit of a dead person, *u spiritu* or *spirdu*, seeking to communicate with his relatives; to remind them, perhaps, of a duty neglected or an injury unavenged.

The most dreaded of all signs of imminent death is the phantom funeral procession, known as the *Squadra d'Arrozza*. It may be seen in broad daylight, a procession of white-robed penitents, like the members of the local *confrérie* or, according to other accounts, of figures draped in black. From a distance they appear like human beings; but if one looks at them closely one can never distinguish their features, for their faces shimmer and flicker as in a worn-out film. They are in fact the spirits of the dead, the dead of the village towards which they are bound.

Bearing a coffin and lighted tapers they proceed along the road and into the village with the sound, Jean told me, of a tramping army; or they may herald their presence with a drum beating a funeral march. When they reach the house of which one of the occupants is to die they call him by his name, but he is the only person not to hear them. They pronounce his name quite distinctly; but it is impossible to speak with them, for they gabble in high thin whistling voices, Jean told me, like telegraph wires in the wind, and their talk is incomprehensible to human ears. Any contact with them is dangerous, for they will try to capture a human being and drag him down to their spirit world of purgatory. One must never accept the tapers they offer, for these will turn out to be the limbs of dead children. He who accepts them, so I have heard, will become a *mazzere*, enslaved thereafter to sinister practices, of which I shall have more to say. Some believe that even to meet the *Squadra* is to risk death. The best means of self-protection, I was told, is to stand with one's back to a wall as the procession passes by, holding in one's mouth a dagger with its point directed outwards towards the coffin-bearers.

The *Squadra* is often seen in time of war. It was an all too frequent apparition during the two world wars, particularly in the first, which brought a loss of life from which Corsica has never recovered. The word *arrozza* has no meaning in the Corsican language. People of the Sartenais believe it to be a deformation of *Heroda*: Herod, he who massacred the innocents. According to this interpretation the *Squadra* is thought to claim the first-born sons, who may not necessarily be infants. Having summoned its victim the *Squadra* then goes to the village church, where it can be heard chanting the Mass for the Dead, perhaps that rending Corsican Mass sung in polyphony, the *paghiella*, a music said by some scholars to derive from the megalithic age, and which does indeed seem to be torn from the roots of time. If the *Squadra* arrives by night, as often happens, the church will appear lit by candles. The procession can afterwards be seen carrying the coffin to the cemetery.[6]

A somewhat similar premonitory procession is known as the *mumma*. A band of phantom penitents robed in white is seen walking in double file carrying a coffin. It contains the spirit of one who will shortly die. He may be saved if a living person has the courage to stop the procession, break open the coffin, and tear some shreds from the shroud of the phantom corpse. But this must be done before the procession crosses a stream; the river, perhaps, that divides the worlds of the living and the dead. Once the coffin has been carried over the water nothing can help the victim; and within a short space of time his body will die. Roccu Multedo reports that a known seer of Chera, the magic-steeped village of which I shall later tell, saw only and always phantom funerals on 8 September, during the ceremonies in honour of the Nativity of the Virgin.[7]

The accounts of such apparitions, though far from commonplace, seemed not altogether unfamiliar to me. I must already have heard or read about such things, for they are, or until recently were, known in Brittany, in Scotland and in Wales, where the beating of the invisible drum and the sight of phantom funerals are sure signs of impending death. How then could it happen that these beliefs should be, or have been, current in lands geographically so far apart? A possible explanation leaps to mind: were they not inherited from the pre-historic cultural influence shared by those countries, the Megalithic faith? One may readily understand their relevance to a religion based on the cult of the dead, that religion which left so deep and durable a mark on the Corsican psyche. Any idea of a Celtic origin can be dismissed: no evidence of a Celtic penetration has come to light in Corsica; moreover, the Celts were not, anywhere, the artisans of the Megalithic monuments. It must surely have been the itinerant missionaries of the Megalithic faith who, between about 3500 and 1000 BC, spread these beliefs through western Europe, leaving in their wake this disturbing foreknowledge of death.[8]

Yet in some strange way this knowledge reassures the Corsicans. People gifted in foreseeing death are respected, even if they sometimes inspire fear; this is particularly true of the *mazzeri*, as will be told. To know when death will come is considered a privilege. Though it does not empower the seer to prevent or delay dying, it implies that the seer is in communion with the supreme power by which death is ordained. In Corsica death is not looked upon as a natural happening caused by illnesss or age, but as natural because it is inevitable, a happening in the face of which all men are equal. A song current in the Fiumorbo speaks of death in words that can be translated as: 'It is not worth weeping, for death is natural. When death passes by one cannot put back the hour.' The word here used for death is the Corsican *falcina*, meaning she who carries the scythe. Does this personification reflect a distant belief in the primeval Mother Goddess, giver and taker of life, the divinity revered in the megalithic areas of Europe? Perhaps. There is archaeological evidence of her cult in Corsica, though it seems not to have been predominant; the figures of male warriors are much more numerous. Only half a dozen of the eighty-four statue-menhirs are thought to be female, identified as such by indications of breasts, interpretations which have however been contested. One, broken, headless, but with unmistakeable protruding breasts, found in the central south, at Castaldu near Ciamanacce, bears on the shaft of the body the representation, in relief, of a large dagger. A portrait of a divinized female warrior? Of the Mother Goddess? Of the dreaded *falcina*?[9]

The shepherds of the Niolo are sensitive to omens of death apparently peculiar to their region: the *finzione*.[10] In the vast roadless expanses of the upland plateau the sight of a human being is in itself a matter of interest. The shepherds' cabins are often an hour's walk one from another, and two hours or more from the nearest villages at lower altitudes, where their wives and children spend the summer. When an unexpected silhouette appears on the skyline it arouses curiosity, or apprehension. Is it that of friend or foe? In past times the visitor might be a bandit, one of the outlaws who often imposed themselves, gun in hand, on the hospitality of shepherds so that they were drawn, willingly or not, into vendettas.[11] Or it may be someone who has walked up from a village bringing important news; perhaps of a death.

The *finzione* are in fact bearers of this news; but of a death that has not yet occurred. Men and women, they look just like ordinary human beings; the women are most often dressed in white. But it is impossible to converse with them. They enter a cabin without explanation or greeting, while their host, as in a nightmare, finds himself unable to speak. They stand there for a time in silence, then leave, always without a word. Their visit is a presage of death. But the *finzione* are not ghosts of dead people; the shepherds may even recognize them as living people of their acquaintance which makes their appearance the more terrifying.

Curiously enough, there is in Corsica no belief in ghosts similar to that entertained in Britain. Individual spirits are not thought constantly to haunt their earthly homes, but to visit them only during the days immediately after their decease, or on the eve of All Souls' Day, and even then they do not assume the physical images of their living selves. Their presence, felt rather than seen, is none the less alarming, for the dead, if in any way offended by the living, may capture and so destroy them. The best defence, according to tradition, is to keep in the house palm leaves and olive branches blessed on Palm Sunday, and to suspend cutting instruments, preferably made of iron, over the beds and the entrance door, iron being thought to have a magical protective quality. But these precautions, Christian or pagan, are not always observed; on the contrary, on the eve of All Souls' Day elaborate preparations are made to welcome the dead, as has been told.[12] The Corsicans' attitude to the dead is ambivalent, made up of contradictory fears.

Spirits of the dead, *spirdi* or *spiriti*, may be met with by anybody, anywhere, usually unrecognized figures clothed in white. They are often seen near water, Jean told me, or near tombs which are not necessarily their own, or in places where a deed of violence has been committed which need not be associated with the visiting apparition. Whoever sees them risks imminent death. One evening, returning with Jean to his cousins' home in the donkey cart they had lent us, I became aware of a certain nervousness in his manner. Later he confided to me that he had in fact felt uneasy during that stage of our journey. We had passed close by a family tomb – whose, we did not know – isolated in the maquis. Years before, Jean told me, a friend of his grandfather's had met his death there; literally, in the form of a phantom woman. One night the man dreamed he was riding along that track after dark with his dogs following him. Near the tomb he saw a woman in white with seven dogs. 'Are your dogs with you?' she asked him. 'Yes, they are all here,' he replied. 'Then we will make my dogs fight yours,' she said. And there the dream ended. A few days later this man received news of the death of a cousin who lived in that neighbourhood. At once he left for the funeral. He travelled on horseback with his wife riding pillion, by night, to avoid the heat of the day. As they passed the tomb he saw the white woman of his dream with her seven dogs. His horse abruptly stopped and refused to advance another step. His wife saw neither the woman nor her dogs. Then the man realized that the woman was a phantom. 'Have you your seven dogs?' he called to her. 'Yes,' she cried, 'and I will send them to you.' And she thereupon threw something at him that stung his skin like sand. The next day spots appeared on his face and he was stricken by fever – smallpox? – and within a week he died.

It was in the home of his cousins, at the hour of the *veillée*, that Jean told me of such things and taught me of the warnings of impending death. The audience chimed in with eager exclamations and comments, correcting and adding details. A similar scene could hardly be witnessed today. Much of what Jean told me he had learned from his elders, and when they died they took their beliefs with them. Since the wholesale modernization of the island in the 1960s the common lore of the country people has not been so much discredited as laid aside. A vast improvement in communications has shaken traditional perspectives. It was impossible for Corsica to remain a reserve of archaic beliefs and customs when only a little more than half an hour by air from the south of France and less than two from Paris, and when overrun by thousands – now more than a million – of tourists every summer. The phantoms have faded. Dreams no longer foretell. 'We don't dream any more,' I was told. I was questioning an old couple about intimations of death. 'It's because of the modernism,' the woman explained to me, in tones of grief.

The 'modernism': aircraft, bulldozers, motorcars, motorcycles, telephones, television; these convenient innovations, welcomed by the Corsicans, have combined to alienate them from certain areas of their cultural heritage. Not, however, completely. There are still those who dream of death, who predict it, who indeed inflict it, in symbolic form. Death's messengers, as they might be termed, they are a category of people endowed with particular occult gifts exercised in the course of their night-hunting. They are known as the *mazzeri*. The masculine singular form is *mazzeru*, the feminine *mazzera*, plural *mazzere*; but the terms *mazzere* or *mazzeri* are commonly used, in defiance of grammar, to designate the singular of either sex. Regarded with a mingling of awe and dread they cannot be forgotten or ignored; for the *mazzeri* are not phantoms, but real people living in the villages and known to their neighbours while practising their dark calling.

It stems from prehistory, from a period, it would seem, anterior to that of the megalith builders; to consider the phenomenon of the *mazzeri* is to peer down the shaft of time. One can only be astonished by their survival into the twentieth century, surrounded as they are by powerful hostile influences. On the one hand, they are in conflict with the rational positivism of the French educational system, imposed on every child from six years old, at latest, to adolescence. On the other they brave the disapproval of the Catholic Church, which lays its stamp on almost every individual from the candle to the grave. How has it come about that the *mazzeri* have not been crushed by this formidable pincer movement? Nor yet by the 'modernism' that has intruded into almost every home, suppressing dreams and silencing the voices of the dead?

The *mazzeri* have survived, just because of the 'modernism' rather than in spite of it. The movement has stimulated its own counter-reaction, a swing back to the traditional customs and beliefs. Some have been abandoned, but respect for what they once were has revived. It was Jean Cesari who first spoke to me of the *mazzeri*. What he said stirred no echoes in my mind, for the *mazzeri* seemed to belong to a layer of tradition deeper and older than any I had so far apprehended. But my curiosity was aroused; the kind of curiosity that incites investigation. I was not alone in my quest. My friend Pierre Lamotte, director of the departmental archives, was already attracted to the subject, and together we published an article on the *mazzeri* in a Corsican learned journal in 1957. Since then trained ethnologists – Claude Faucheux, Georges Ravis-Giordani, Lucie Désidéri – have all collected valuable material on the *mazzeri*. Roccu Multedo, specialist on Corsican magic, is the author of three works relating to the *mazzeri*, or rather to *mazzerisme*, a word he has coined to designate their activities considered as a whole. Bradley Holway, an American social anthropologist, includes a discussion of the phenomenon in a doctoral thesis on a Corsican village completed in 1978. Others of whom I shall speak have shared with me their first-hand experiences: the late Peppu Flori, a poet of the Niolo, and Charles-André Culioli of Chera. Later I had the privilege of meeting two *mazzeri*, as I shall relate. Recently Madame Rotily-Forcioli has most generously communicated to me the matter of her illuminating little book describing her close acquaintance with a *mazzeru*, shortly to be published.[13]

The sum of these encounters and researches does not constitute a complete picture of *mazzerisme*, still less an explanation of it. *Mazzerisme* is occult, irrational, and various aspects of it have no doubt been discarded and forgotten through the centuries, or the millennia. The wonder is that it has survived at all. True, the numbers of the *mazzeri* are dwindling. When I first arrived in Corsica they were to be found, one or more, in almost every village, at least in the *Au-Delà-des-Monts*. They are much fewer today; but thirty, so I have been told on good authority, are still operating in the extreme south of the island. They have drawn interest from an unexpected quarter, from young people with nationalist tendencies, who feel that their inherited culture has been too long derided and ignored. There are many today to share the view of Roccu Multedo, that the *mazzeru* is 'the incarnation of the Corsican collective unconscious'.[14]

CHAPTER 4

The Dream-Hunters

The *mazzeri* – hunters by night – hunters in dreams –
mazzeri and animals – the 'aware' dream-battles
between *mazzeri*

The *mazzeri* live by night. The *veillée* has ended; neighbours and
friends have taken leave. The ashes have been raked over the live
embers in the hearth; the last of the heavy steps has trudged up the
wooden staircase or ladder leading to the bedrooms on the floor
above. The household sleeps. Apparently. If there is a *mazzere* in its
midst he, or she, will slip out into the dark.

When the *mazzeri* go out at night their purpose is to kill. Not
people, but animals, any animal, wild or domestic. Evidence suggests
that they have a predilection for wild boar. These are very numerous
in Corsica so that even today certain villages count on the weekly boar
hunts for their meat supply throughout the hunting season from
September to mid-January. But the *mazzeri* may also kill pigs, goats,
sheep, oxen, bulls, cows and even dogs, though evidence on this last
point is contradictory. In Corsica domestic animals are hardly ever
shut up at night, but left to wander at will, in the maquis, along the
village streets, or on the roads, to the exasperation of motorists today.
Every one of these animals is potential prey for the *mazzeri*.

According to their own accounts the *mazzeri* go out equipped with
a variety of the weapons known to the Corsicans in their history and
prehistory: guns, spears, axes, daggers, knives, sticks and stones. The
preferred weapon is a heavy staff or cudgel known as a *mazza*, usually
cut from the root and stem of a vine. The word *mazzere* may derive
from *mazza*, or equally well from *ammazza*, meaning 'to kill'. In the
village of Chera, however, in the far southeast of the island, the only
weapons used are knives, if any are used at all. The *mazzeri*, I was told,

who are mostly women, hunt in packs and tear their prey to death with their teeth, like hounds. Their exploits call to mind the belief in the 'wild hunt' and the 'furious horde' once current in certains parts of Europe, of which I shall speak later.[1] In Chera, and in some other parts of southern Corsica, including the Alta Rocca, the *mazzeri* are known as *culpatori* or *culpadori* or *colpadori*, from *culpi*, 'to strike a blow'. They go by other names in different parts of the island, making eighteen in all, which will be listed further on.[2]

Having killed an animal, the *mazzere* rolls it onto its back, stares at it closely, and for a brief moment, 'in a flash' as I have heard say, he recognizes the face of someone known to him, nearly always an inhabitant of his village, who may also be one of his kin. The next day he will tell what he has seen, and the person mentioned invariably dies in the space of time running from three days to a year, and always within an uneven number of days.

Recognition of the victim can come about in other ways. The cry made by the animal as it dies may recall the voice of a particular human being. Or the process may be purely intuitive. How else can one interpret the story, told to me by a reliable informant, of a *mazzere* who caught a trout in a pool with his hand and recognized it as one of his aunts? He promptly released the fish and the next day warned his aunt that she would be very ill, but would recover. And this is in fact what happened.

If an animal is only wounded by the *mazzere*, then the person it represents will meet with an accident or illness, but not death. A *mazzere* of whom I shall later have much to say seized a bull by its leg and stabbed it with his knife. Its human equivalent was seriously injured by a broken leg, but not fatally. I also heard of a young woman, a newly initiated *mazzera*, who flung a stone at a pig which hit the animal on the thigh; three days later a friend of hers broke her hip bone.

As a rule there is a correspondence between the injury inflicted on the animal by the *mazzere* and the accident or illness suffered by the human being it represents. This connection was illustrated by the first story I heard of a *mazzere*, which was related to me by Jean Cesari before I had even set foot on the island. 'It was a cold autumn evening,' he began, in his inimitable storyteller's voice. 'I was sitting with my cousins by the fire roasting chestnuts; we had gone up into the mountains to get chestnut flour from some relative of ours. We heard a tap on the door. It was an old man; we invited him to join us; in Corsica one always welcomes a visitor to one's hearth. The look in his eyes was very strange. The night before, he told us, he had taken part in a boar hunt in the forest of Ospedale. He had shot a boar in the shoulder, the boar got away but he thought he had killed it. About a week later I met the old man again. He was distressed. He had just received news that his nephew in Marseilles had died of a cancer of the lung. Then I knew that the old man was a *mazzere*. I shall never forget the look in his eyes.'

The story left me at once puzzled and intrigued. Intrigued by this esoteric anecdote coming from a country which I had hitherto known only as the birthplace of Napoleon and the setting of Prosper Mérimée's vendetta novel, *Colomba*. Puzzled, because so many aspects of the story were unexplained. Why had a boar hunt taken place at night? Why had Jean so readily inferred a correlation between the old man, the wounded boar and the nephew who had died of lung cancer? Why had he classed the old man as a *mazzere*? What exactly was a *mazzere*?

I went to Corsica with my husband as to a territory to explore, with little or no idea of what I should find there. The many things I encountered for the first time had a quality of the marvellous, the magical and extraordinary. When Jean came to join us, he told me at intervals more about the *mazzeri*. What he said opened fascinating new perspectives, while at the same time adding to my perplexity. Very many *mazzeri*, he told me, were women. They were usually armed with sticks or stones; in Corsica women rarely carried firearms. But how, I wondered, could anyone, let alone a woman, kill an animal – boar, pig, ox or cow – single-handed, with a stick or a stone? Or even a knife? I was incredulous. 'Have you ever seen a *mazzere* killing an animal?' I asked. 'How could I?' Jean replied. 'All that takes place in dreams.'

Everything he had told me, then, belonged to the world of dreams. Or rather, to the particular dream-world of the *mazzeri*; for their dreams present a bewildering combination of the possible and the impossible. Impossible, usually, are their methods of killing animals; yet their dreams usually take place in recognizable country close to their homes where they know by name every pasture, mountain slope or pool or stream. Very often they hunt near water. Water is thought to be the haunt of dangerous spirits, spirits of the dead who have not atoned their sins, and these spirits are in league with the *mazzeri*, agents of death. Water, giver of life, so prized in Mediterranean countries, universal symbol of purification and redemption, in traditional Corsica, surprisingly, was most often regarded as evil. To find any analogy to this belief one must look to more archaic societies. The Zulus, so the ethnologist Midi Berry related to me, tell many tales of river monsters. In Corsica, when crossing a stream, it is thought prudent first to throw in a pebble to dispel the spirits lurking there. A simple explanation of this fear is that streams can be dangerous. Almost every one of them is remembered for having consumed lives. During the autumn storms they swell in a matter of minutes; the pleasant trickle becomes a raging, roaring torrent, carrying on its current earth, stones, rocks, whole trees and the corpses of animals and human beings.

The *mazzeri* have a practical reason for lurking in such places. They hunt, as I came to learn, according to the techniques practised in Corsica in reality. They may hunt *a vardera*, that is, posting themselves in spots where they have detected the tracks of boar. These may be in orchards, or chestnut woods, and also on the edge of a ford of a stream. Or they may hunt, singly, or several together, *a l'abrettu*, that is, following their prey across country. They may even organize beats such as take place in the vicinity of innumerable villages during the boar-hunting season. The beaters drive their hounds across a valley with stirring, traditional cries; the hunters are posted at intervals along a path running along the opposite mountain side, waiting to shoot the boar head on as it breaks through the vegetation. One of my informants assured me that he often heard the *mazzeri* of his neighbourhood hunting at night and was kept awake by the voices of the beaters and the cry of the hounds as they scented the boar. *Mazzeri* living in large villages, on the other hand, may hunt in the streets like the urban guerrillas of modern war. A woman who grew up in one such village explained to me how the *mazzeri*, among whom were several of her close relatives, posted themselves at street corners to attack wandering pigs. Accounts of the *mazzeri*'s hunts are always circumstantial; I know of only one *mazzere* who discovered unknown landscapes, of whom I shall speak later.

The *mazzeri*, then, stay in their beds at night; their more or less incredible hunting tales are the matter of dreams. This statement is however too simple. When speaking of the *mazzeri* the usual arbitrary distinctions between dreaming and 'real life' must be laid aside. Roccu Multedo maintains that certain *mazzeri* really do go out at night, in a state of trance, as is confirmed by two of the words used to describe them: *nottambuli*, 'night-walkers', and more significantly, *sunnambuli*, 'sleepwalkers'.[3] Some *mazzeri*, then, go out into the maquis while others stay at home dreaming that they do so. Yet the supposition is not completely satisfying. Reliable witnesses have seen *mazzeri* walking abroad at night at an hour when they and their families swear they were sleeping in their beds. Jean dismissed the phenomenon with a disconcerting confidence as the *dédoublement de la personnalité*, the 'doubling of the self'. *Mazzeri*, it is implied, have the faculty of bilocation, one attributed in times past to witches and to saints. A young, well-educated woman of my acquaintance told me that one summer night when she was strolling with a girlfriend in the outskirts of her village, a well-known *mazzeru* of the community appeared striding along the road with the fixed expression of a sleepwalker. They called to him; but he gave no sign of having seen or heard them. The next day when they spoke to him of the incident he denied having set foot out of doors during the night. Another of my informants, a retired army man, told me that in his childhood he had lived with an elderly relative well known as a *mazzera*. Night after night he saw her creeping out of the house when she thought he was asleep, and returning just before dawn. She had no clear memory of how she had spent the hours, and was often dismayed to find her clothes torn by the maquis and drenched in dew. Such addicted *mazzeri* could not, of course, make a kill every time they went hunting. The death rate in the villages, though high until recently in relation to the rest of France, could not correspond with the number of dream-hunts experienced by the *mazzeri*.[4] Were they frustrated when they came home without killing an animal? Or did they find a satisfaction simply in wandering about the maquis? These questions have no answer: *mazzerisme* is irrational, and it is rooted in dreams.

The *mazzeri*'s supposed faculty of bilocation is the subject of a tale repeated with little variation in different parts of the island, as though it has become part of the repertory of Corsican legend. At Chera, the village where the *mazzeri* kill with knives or with their teeth, a man observed that his young, beautiful wife often left the house when she thought he was sleeping, to return in the small hours, visibly tired. He did not, apparently, suspect her of being a member of the hunting pack; he accused her of going out to meet a lover. She denied the charge and told him to go to a certain mountain cave, where he would find her bloodstained knife. It was the weapon she used when she went hunting, she told him: she was a *mazzera*. The husband knew the cave she mentioned, and also that it was too far away for her to visit on foot in a single night. He nevertheless went there, and found the bloody weapon.

Had she put it there in expectation of just such an eventuality? Had she a lover? Or was she really a *mazzera*? At all events, it does seem from collected evidence that *mazzeri* are believed to be able to travel further and faster in their night-hunting than they could possibly do in what is called 'real life'. Not that they are credited with the art of flying, as were the witches of European tradition. It was the evil witches of Corsica, who were quite distinct from the *mazzeri*, the *streie* or *streghe* of which I shall speak later, who according to Roccu Multedo travelled through the air by night astride an *aspa*, part of a spinning wheel.[5] But there is no valid evidence to show that the *mazzeri*, or indeed the *streie*, attended the witches' Sabbath. In fact, the dreams of the *mazzeri* present only limited deviations from imaginable reality.

Bradley Holway quotes another, no less enigmatic, story on the theme of a supposedly faithless wife.[6] Her husband, observing that she often left the house at night, suspected her of meeting a lover. He was no believer, it is said, in *mazzeri*, or rather *colpadori* as they are called in that region. One night, after pretending to sleep while she went out, he followed her into the maquis. He found her on a mountainside, standing over the bodies of three beheaded goats: 'real' goats. 'Beware of me,' she said, 'I am a *colpadore*!' The story presents a baffling confusion of the real and dream worlds. *Mazzeri* – *colpadori* – do not leave the maquis strewn with corpses of animals, because their hunting takes place in dreams. Did the woman slaughter the goats to prove her innocence, even though her husband did not believe in *colpadori*? Or did she enable him to share her vision, her dream?

Colpadori were once numerous in the village in question. Bradley

Holway reports that people known to be *colpadori* were often seen wandering about the mountains, haggard and exhausted, just before dawn. An elderly man of this same village told me that his grandfather had been a noted *colpadore*, and that he frequently left the house at night. A nephew repeatedly tried to follow him, but the *colpadore* always managed to slip out of his sight in the maquis. On one occasion when the nephew, particularly persistent, was walking beside him, the *colpadore* proposed that they should rest together under a tree; whereupon he mysteriously vanished. The nephew realized he had been sleeping when he woke up under the tree, alone.

Such reminiscences raise the question: who was dreaming? The *mazzeri* or *colpadori*, or their witnesses? The child who saw the old woman leaving her house at night and returning at dawn without any knowledge of how she had spent the intervening hours, the girls who watched the *mazzeru* walking abroad at night when he swore he was in his bed at that time, the jealous husband who saw his wife beside the beheaded goats, the *colpadore*'s nephew sleeping under a tree: were these people not dreaming, as well as the *mazzeri* or *colpadori*? Such experiences cannot be rationally accounted for. Perhaps some light may be thrown on the subject if one postulates a collective un-conscious of the village community in which both ordinary people and *mazzeri* participate.

The Corsicans, including the *mazzeri* – or *colpadori* – have their own explanation. The *mazzeri* do not go out at night in their physical bodies, but in their soul or spirit; the word spirit is more appropriate because free from Christian religious connotations. The spirit of the *mazzere*, when hunting, meets the spirit of his victim, a human being who has assumed animal form. When he kills the animal he severs spirit from body; the body may linger on for some time afterwards, but this life is only a reprieve and inevitably the body will sicken and die. The killing by the *mazzere* is therefore a symbolic act perpetrated in the realm of dreams, or what the Corsicans define as the 'other' or 'parallel' world, to which *mazzeri* have privileged access.

The sequel to dream and symbol is starkly, terribly real. The *mazzere* may avoid announcing the identity of his victim within that person's hearing, but in the cramped conditions of the average Corsican home news of the death sentence may be hard to conceal. Stricken, most likely, by an overpowering force of suggestion, the victim weakens, or sickens, while his relatives, barely able to keep up the pretence of ignoring his fate, cluster round him with small attentions, nurse him in his illness, waiting for him to die. Or the enormous weight of anxiety may drive the victim to reckless action, like riding or driving his mule over the brink of a ravine. I have however found no evidence of deliberate suicide.

When death at last strikes, has an appropriate *voceru* been composed? It is not at any rate likely to be the creation of a *mazzera*. *Mazzeri* do not play any specific role in the traditional death ritual. For them the death has already occurred; in the maquis, in the dark, days or weeks or months before. The care of the ailing victim is in their eyes bestowed on one who is already dead. Roccu Multedo esteems that the *mazzeri* are natural poets, and mentions a *mazzera* living at Guagno in the 1930s who became a celebrated *voceratrice*. The two functions are distinct, but sometimes, it seems, combined. The practising *mazzera* I had the good fortune to meet did indeed speak to me in poetic language, as I shall relate.[7]

The familiarity with animals apparent in the activities of the *mazzeri* is inherent in Corsican tradition. It is a prominent theme in the traditional tales.[8] The belief that human beings can take on the forms of animals is characteristic of archaic rural societies, which have retained an awareness of the animals hardly imaginable in the industrialized world of today. Surprisingly, it has endured in Corsica, as is illustrated in the following anecdote, that took place not more than a hundred years ago. A man was driving home to his village in his carriage, by night, on Christmas Eve, accompanied by his son's godfather. Towards midnight they saw a sow and her piglets swarm on to the road. The sow sprang up to worry the snout of the mule, and so brought the animal to a standstill. The driver left his carriage with his companion, carrying his gun, with which he belaboured the sow until she made off with her brood. They continued their journey after a considerable delay. Just before reaching their village they met a couple on horseback, a woman and a man. The woman congratulated the driver on his good fortune. Not far off, she explained, his mortal enemy, a bandit with his bodyguard, had been waiting to attack him. He had been saved by the delay caused by the sow. The man was convinced that the sow was the spirit of his mother, who had transformed herself in order to protect him.

The tale is astonishing in its context, for it is generally thought that only in the so-called savage countries of the world man and beast still cohabit on equal terms. According to Sir James Frazer, writing in *The Golden Bough*, the belief that a man's soul or spirit may temporarily inhabit an animal is, or was, current in Siberia, Melanesia, the New Hebrides, Malaya and central Africa. Certain peoples of Nigeria, the Gabon and the Cameroons believe, or did until recently, that every man has several souls or spirits, one of which may incarnate itself in a wild animal, known as his 'bush soul'. If the animal is killed, the man dies; if wounded, he falls ill. An African hunter may claim that he can recognize in a wild animal the 'bush soul' of a kinsman or friend and so avoid shooting it.[9]

The *mazzeri* hold the same belief, with this fundamental difference: whereas the African hunter's relation with the 'bush soul' is played out in real life, in Corsica it exists only in the dreams of the *mazzeri*. An African hunter may even believe that his own soul or spirit has left his body to enter an animal, and that if he inadvertently kills this animal he himself will perish. In Corsica, on the other hand, the spirits of the *mazzeri* are not thought to take on the appearance of animals, except that of dogs, animals that in general hunt and are not hunted.

The *mazzeri*'s relationship with dogs seems ambiguous. While certain people have assured me that they kill dogs just as often as other animals, dogs are evidently their allies in the hunting of wild boar. Moreover, it is believed that the *mazzeri* of Chera, there known as *culpadori*, change themselves into dogs to chase animals in packs and tear them to pieces with their teeth. At Levie, in the central south, the *mazzeri*, known as *mazzatori*, take on the form of dogs, so I was told, and leap onto the backs of horses or mules behind their riders at night. They are not however thought to hunt when so transformed. On the other hand, in a large village in the valley of the Spelunca, *mazzeri* are believed to turn themselves into dogs to act as beaters in the hunting of the pigs that roam the streets. According to a traditional belief, current in the south, a *mazzeru* would sometimes transform himself into a large white bull which would tear a man's spirit from his corpse when it was being transported to the cemetery.

Not all *mazzeri* are hunters. Marie-Madeleine Rotily Forcioli, author of a book shortly to appear with the attractive title *Le mazzere que j'ai connu*,[10] 'The *mazzeri* I have known', describes a man of her acquaintance in southern Corsica, who died some forty years ago, who was a practising *mazzeru*. Exceptionally gentle by nature, he hunted neither in real life nor in dreams. His dreams nonetheless often predicted malady and death. Animals were sometimes involved, but were not hunted. When he dreamed, for instance, of an old horse stumbling through the maquis until it fell dead to the ground, he foresaw the decease of the oldest inhabitant of the village, a man past ninety who in fact died the next day, quietly, of old age, 'like a lamp without oil', as the author puts it.

It was during the siesta hour that the *mazzeru* most often experienced his dreams, when he was lying on a couch in a downstairs room within sight of his family. One day, midway between sleeping and waking, he saw in a mirror the dead image of a cousin, a doctor living in Paris. Within three days his prediction was confirmed. The doctor, knowing himself to be seriously ill, sent for a sister living in Corsica to come to fetch him home. Like Corsicans the world over he wanted to die in the village where he was born. He failed to do so. During the crossing from Marseilles to Ajaccio he died on the boat, and he was carried back to his village in a coffin.

Some of the *mazzeru*'s dreams were violent. At the crisis of the dream he would make convulsive movements, cry out in distress. This was the moment, he afterwards explained, when he found himself killing a human being, or occasionally an animal, by striking down the creature with his bare hands. The gesture was symbolic, for he was never armed with a weapon. Though he could not always identify the animal – its shape was often vague – he always recognized the victim as someone known to him, usually a member of his village. That person invariably died within a year. The *mazzeru* awoke from such dreams physically exhausted.

They were the more disturbing because diametrically opposed to his waking character. By nature genial, frank, a man of his word, he was a good companion, a reliable friend and neighbour, an affec-tionate and cooperative kinsman. Riding and driving fine horses was his principal pleasure. Himself a landowner, he was skilled in the current agricultural techniques and was consulted by his neighbours on such matters as the building of haystacks, which in Corsica are conical in form, the hay being artfully twisted round a central pole. A fervent Catholic, he was solicited by the clergy to sing certain chants, in Latin, on the days of religious festivals, and, or course, at the Mass for the Dead.

How did it happen that such a man should be a *mazzeru*? What possessed him when, lying asleep in the afternoon, he was haunted by sinister dreams of death? One may moreover wonder: was he really sleeping? According to his biographer his eyes were only half closed, and he was aware of what was going on around him and even able to answer questions. Were his dreams not rather excursions into that state of semi-consciousness, described by the French as the *rêve éveillé*, or the *rêve dirigé*, the 'awake' or 'directed' dream? That experience of an interworld, somewhere between consciousness and unconsciousness, is known to many ordinary people, particularly the old. One has an experience that is in fact a dream, or one has a dream that is in fact an experience: either definition will do.

Roccu Multedo suggests that the *mazzeri* facilitate their access to this state by dosing themselves with certain hallucinogenic plants that grow in Corsica, such as mandrake, datura and belladonna.[11] I have found no evidence of this. Any idea that the *mazzeri* make use of imported drugs, the hashish, heroin or cocaine that now reach the villages, must be rejected. The drug trade penetrated into the interior only within the last twenty years or so, at exactly the period when *mazzerisme* was declining. Can the *mazzeri* in fact induce, summon their dreams? Evidence on the subject is inconclusive. While I have heard that some of them habitually did so, the two *mazzeri* I have met, a man and a woman, and the *mazzeru* known to Marie-Madeleine Rotily-Forcioli, experienced their dreams as imposed on them by a superior power. They were, to use the Corsican expression, 'called' to hunt, 'called' to kill; the order was absolute; they could not even choose their victims. *Mazzeri*, it seems, have no animosity towards the animal they have to kill, nor towards the human being it represents. They are unable to harm an enemy by this means and have played no part whatsoever in the vendettas.

Though they may be shunned or even hated by their fellow villagers because they are thought to bring death, they are peaceful enough in their daily waking lives. Aloofness from local affairs distinguishes them from their neighbours. Their attitude is shown in their particular expression: *mazzeri*, I have been told, look not at but through one, as though one were too insignificant to focus their attention. This I experienced when I eventually met a *mazzera*. They are uninterested in electoral and political rivalries; holding their own, marginal position in Corsican society, they set no store by worldly rank and power. Between themselves, men and women alike, they live, so I have been told, on a footing of equality, regardless of distinctions of sex or social status.

Mazzeri come from all walks of life. Roccu Multedo, drawing on a wide experience, maintains that the majority are shepherds, the people in Corsica who live most in harmony with nature. It can be added that they are said to have been the last converted to Christianity. Bradley Holway writes of a well-known *colpadore* of a village in the Alta Rocca who, around 1920, at the age of about sixty, handed over his land to his son and went up into the mountains with some goats so as to be closer to the other or 'parallel' world. The two *mazzeri* I have met, and most of those of whom I have heard, belonged to the class of small landowners that predominates in the villages. But I also have evidence of *mazzeri* born into the ranks of village notables, and of one who issued from a family bearing a distinguished name in the insular hierarchy. Roccu Multedo, on the other hand, knows a *mazzeru* who lives in French bourgeois style, and another who is a prospering truck driver.[12]

In the recent past a number of *mazzeri* were to be found in almost every village. In 1975 Roccu Multedo learned by the confession of a *mazzere* – or *culpatore* – of Figari, a little port in the extreme south, that he could recall a time when a dozen *culpatori* were operating in this community of less than seven hundred inhabitants; there were then only three; in 1981 all had disappeared.[13] Relations between *mazzeri* of the same village, I have heard, were friendly, if casual. They stuck together by day, conversing in a style that seemed rather brusque and unceremonious, like old drinking companions, I was told, who are inclined to argue and bicker when sober. The intoxication of the *mazzeri* was their night hunting; what happened by day was unimportant.

The relations of *mazzeri* with those of other villages were on the contrary hostile. Once a year, on the night between the 31st July and the 1st of August, the *mazzeri* of each village organized themselves into a '*milizia*', electing a captain, and went out to fight the *mazzeri* of a neighbouring village; or rather, they dreamed they did so. These phantom battles, known as *mandrache*, usually took place on a mountain pass separating the two communities. The *mazzeri* carried their usual variety of weapons: guns, the *mazza*, axes, lances, knives. According to Multedo certain *mazzeri* armed themselves with human tibias, while in two villages in western Corsica, Soccia and Guagno, and, it is said, elsewhere, they were equipped with the stems of asphodels.[14]

The asphodel holds an honoured place in Corsican tradition. Its name alone speaks for its antiquity. *Asphodelus*, its name in Greek, is considered to be a word of pre-Indo-European origin; linguists say the same of its Corsican names: *taravellu* or *taravucciu*. More explicit are the popular names it goes by in the island: *fiori di morti* – 'flower of the dead' – and *candellu* or *luminellu*, meaning a large or a small candle. The official name of the variety found in Corsica is in fact *Asphodelus ramosus*. Surabundant, the asphodels cover the Corsican landscape in spring. Growing on barren, sandy or rocky soil where no other plant can survive, they light acres and acres of land with their little pinkish star-shaped flowers sprouting from their stiff branches, like gawky candelabra. The bulbs, when heated, explode like fireworks, to the joy of the children who on the feast day of Saint John the Baptist hold them in the fire built in the village square and then knock them against stones to make them bang.

Today they appear to many people simply as an ubiquitous and rather ungraceful wild flower. But the asphodel bears a noble heritage which has been progressively discredited. The Greeks believed that it grew densely in the Elysian fields, resting place of heroes, and that it was a food agreeable to heroes and the gods. For centuries it was planted near tombs to nourish the dead. It also fed the living. The asphodel is edible: the substance of its bulb can be made into a kind of bread. But this food lost its importance with the advance of agriculture. Once valued as a plant to nourish animals and men, it was relegated to the status of a wild flower after the introduction of the potato. This occurred in Corsica not before the eighteenth century; Paoli, who actively encouraged it, was nick-named 'Generale patata'. After this the asphodel became known, rather scornfully, as 'the bread of the poor'.

The plant, however, continued to be esteemed for its medicinal properties. Concoctions made from its bulb and stem were used with more or less success to treat a large variety of ailments: indigestion, coughs, inflammations, ulcers, toothache, as well as the lethal disease that plagued Corsica until recent times: consumption, that is, tuberculosis. To be used in such circumstances, it must indeed have been considered magical. Sacred, restorative, beloved of the dead, the asphodel became a symbol of Corsica as a whole. 'He has forgotten the asphodel' was a popular saying meaning that a man had forgotten everything about his native land, had denied it. The choice of the asphodel as a weapon in the *mazzeri*'s battles can be accounted for by the plant's two-fold association with death. On the one hand, it possessed a force that resisted death, by counteracting maladies and flourishing on almost sterile soil; on the other, it nourished and honoured the dead, lifting them to the ranks of gods and heroes. Today it is no longer seen near tombs, unless it has grown there by accident. Its place has been usurped by the stately cypress, which points to a certain fairly recent prosperity, for the tree is not endemic in Corsica. The fashion for importing it developed in the last century; its exoticism is in tune with that of the cemeteries where it clusters like dark flames. Though it is sometimes planted to make windbreaks for houses and gardens, it is so generally connected with death that the expression 'he scents his cypress' has become proverbial for describing a person who is nearing his end. [15]

The outcome of the *mazzeri*'s battles on 31 July was premonitory. The *mazzeri* killed in combat were condemned to die within a year; sometimes they were found dead in their beds on the very morning of the next day. The village that lost most *mazzeri* would lose more lives in the coming year than the opposing village of the victorious *mazzeri*. The inhabitants of the villages were deeply concerned by these phantom battles, even participated in them. On the night of 31 July they would keep fires burning outside the houses and in the church squares. To encourage the *mazzeri*? To greet them when they returned after the night's fighting? Or to prevent enemy *mazzeri* from invading the community? Rather, it would seem that they were designed to ward off the spirits of the dead, just as cutting implements were placed, that night, on window ledges and above doorways.

The first day of August has been described as an unofficial feast of the dead, analogous to All Souls' Day, on 2 November. But in fact it had a contrary significance. On the eve of All Souls' Day the deceased of each family and community are welcomed to their former homes with food and drink, as has been described, and the fires are kept burning because the dead, it is believed, are always cold. But on the eve of 1 August the villages were thought to be invaded by the generality of the dead, swarms of angry unquiet spirits which had not found their resting places or atoned their sins. The fires and cutting implements were designed for protection, an expression of another facet of the ambivalent Corsican attitude to the dead. This primitive fear has a parallel in the myth of the 'furious horde' once current in northern Italy, as will be related.[16]

One may suppose that 1 August corresponds with a pagan festival, the significance of which has been forgotten. The Catholic Church has masked it, rather confusingly: now dedicated to Saint-Pierre-aux-Liens (St Peter of the Chains), 1 August was formerly the feast day of the Maccabees. This Jewish family raised a heroic rebellion in 167 BC against the Seleucid monarch, Antiochus IV, who attempted to impose Hellenistic religious practices on the Israelites. The temple of Jerusalem was desecrated under his fanatical rule, and thousands of recalcitrant Israelites were executed, including a woman and her seven sons, tortured to death after being forced to eat pork, a food forbidden by Mosaic law. The priest Mathathias, instigator of the uprising, is remembered in the Old Testament as a hero, as are his five sons, in particular the warlike Judas Maccabee who triumphantly continued the struggle. He and three of his brothers were killed before the survivor, Simon, concluded a treaty with Antiochus V in 143 BC guaranteeing the religious liberty of the Jews. Fighting against overwhelming odds to preserve their ethnic and cultural identity, the Maccabees have held a strong appeal for the Corsicans, who have so often found themselves in a like situation. James Boswell reports that the favourite reading of Pasquale Paoli, whom he visited in 1765, was the first book of the Maccabees which, with the second, is classed by the Protestants as apocryphal.[17]

The danger of enemy *mazzeri* was considered serious. An elderly woman told me that in her youth, in a village of the Spelunca, her cousin, a *mazzere*, confided to her one morning, 1 August, that he had not long left to live. The 'foreign *mazzeri*', as he described them, had 'committed a massacre'. 'We fought them near the chapel above the village,' he explained, 'it was the one-eyed *mazzere* who did me in.' His family was incredulous, for he was young and healthy. But soon afterwards he died of the 'Spanish flu' that ravaged the island at this period just after the First World War. His relatives went to the neighbouring village to seek out his enemy. They found him. There was only a single one-eyed man in the community and he was a *mazzere*. How they treated him afterwards I was not told.

It has been reported that at Salice, in the region of the Cruzzini, the inhabitants marched round the village on the night of 31 July braying like donkeys to scare away the enemy *mazzeri*. The whole population of the region banded together against them. When their own *mazzeri* announced their victory the people celebrated the occasion with public rejoicing.[18]

CHAPTER 5

The Unbaptized

A geography of *mazzerisme* – contacts with Sardinia
– names of the *mazzeri* – the foragers – women *mazzeri* –
heroism and servitude – initiation of *mazzeri* – *mazzeri*
and the Church

The battles of the *mazzeri* take place in dreams. But in *mazzerisme* there is no hard and fast distinction between dream and so-called 'reality'. Surprising as it may seem, the *mazzeri* name and describe the sites of their nocturnal battles, places well known to the local inhabitants, which can be located on a map. Nearly all are on mountain passes separating the territories of neighbouring communities. Most are some considerable distance from the villages where the *mazzeri* live: up to fifteen miles away. A Corsican friend in Guagno led me to the outskirts of the village so as to point out to me the Col de Manganello, site of the yearly battle. It could be seen on the skyline, a gap in the topmost trees of a forest that smothered a distant mountainside. 'One can get there in two and a half to three hours' walking,' he told me, 'it's rough going.' How could a *mazzere*, I wondered, particularly if elderly, walk there and back in a night, between fighting a battle? I had to remind myself, as so often when thinking about the *mazzeri*, that they act in dreams. The weapons of the warriors of Guagno, I learned, are the stems of asphodels.

Roccu Multedo has published a list of the battle sites, with the names of the villages concerned. Nearly all are in the *Au-Delà-des-Monts*, the northernmost being in the Niolo, the high central plateau where the shepherds pasture their flocks in summer, a region traditionally included in the *En-Deçà-des-Monts*, although in its economy and life-style it more resembles the *Au-Delà*. Multedo completes this geography with a map showing shaded areas where *mazzerisme* is practised or remembered.[1] They cover all the island south of the rivers Asco and Tavignano, about two thirds of the whole, with patches near the north-east coast and in the Balagne. My own findings are corroborative. Most of my knowledge of *mazzerisme* is drawn from my experience in southern Corsica, and reports from the Niolo; I have found no evidence on the subject in the north apart from some vague indications in the Balagne. This evidence, as well as that found by Multedo in the northeast, can be accounted for by the yearly migrations of the shepherds of the Niolo, who lead their flocks down to these lower altitudes in winter, taking their beliefs with them.

Multedo's map was published in 1975. Today the shaded area showing the *mazzeri* would be much smaller: a band running laterally across the extreme south of the island. *Mazzerisme* has progressively receded southwards over the years. One should not, I think, assume that it was never known in the north; indeed Roccu Multedo maintains that it was practised there until the beginning of the present century. An anecdote he relates, heard in his childhood, gives support to this view. A soldier returning from the First World War to his home at Sisco, in Cap Corse, shot a wild boar that was overrunning his land, without, he thought, killing it. Two days later he received a telegram from a friend living in a nearby village, Cagnano, announcing that he was seriously ill. The discharged soldier hurried to his bedside, arriving just before he died. He said nothing about shooting the boar, but his friend said to him: 'I was the boar you killed.'

The tale does not of course furnish a clear example of *mazzerisme*, but points to similar attitudes of mind. It seems likely that *mazzerisme*, perhaps the oldest surviving complex of Corsican beliefs, was originally shared by the two Corsicas, but that the relative prosperity of the north, the development of specialized sedentary agriculture, of craftsmanship, of trade with foreigners, gradually closed access to the 'parallel world' of the *mazzeri*, just as 'modernism' has done over a large part of the south in recent years.

The ethnological history of the two parts of the island appears to have been divergent. Customs of pagan antiquity are preserved in the *En-Deçà* that are unknown in the *Au-Delà-des-Monts*: most notably those pertaining to the *granitola*, a mysterious spiral procession, winding and unwinding on itself performed by certain *confréries* at religious ceremonies as different in character as those of Good Friday and those of the festival of the Nativity of the Virgin on 8 September. Its significance has been forgotten. Perhaps, as has been suggested, it was connected with the creation of life, or with the repairing of a natural cyclic harmony broken by death. This latter interpretation has also been applied to the *caracolu*, the death-ceremony dance violently opposed by the clergy, as I have already described. The *granitola*, however, seems not to have incurred any such condemnation.[2]

The *En-Deçà* was certainly exposed to the influence of the mega-lithic faith, but perhaps in an attenuated degree. The greatest number and the most spectacular of the megalithic monuments – the alignments of menhirs, the statues of Filitosa – are in the Sartenais, a region where the *mazzeri* have been particularly active. It would be tempting to suggest a correlation, but I think misleading. The geography of *mazzerisme* and of *megalithisme* does not coincide. *Mazzeri* are remembered, and until recently operated, in regions of the *Au-Delà* – the Cruzzini, the Fium'Orbo, the valley of Spelunca – which lack megalithic monuments, while traces of megalithic occupa-tion have come to light in the north, in particular in the Nebbio, where *mazzerisme* seems to have been unknown.

The two complexes of belief appear, moreover, discordant. Whereas the megalithic faith seems to have been focussed on the veneration of the dead, *mazzerisme* is less concerned with the dead than with killing. It is true that the *mazzeri* are thought to communicate with spirits of the dead, those, in particular, that haunt the pools and streams of their hunting grounds. But their main business is not to seek out the dead but to forestall death – physical death – by severing, symbolically, the spirits of the living from their carnal dwellings.

It must be added that no trace of *mazzerisme* has been reported from other megalithic areas of Europe, or indeed from anywhere outside Corsica. A question is however raised in connection with Sardinia. Bradley Holway affirms that *mazzeri* (or rather *colpadori*, as they are called in the village where he studied) exist, or existed, in the neighbouring island: this he heard from Corsicans of the south. I can add a small item of evidence, the more valuable for being unsolicited. I was walking one day in the southern Sartenais with Jean Cesari. We sat down to rest under a tree. As often happens in Corsica, a stranger came to join us. Without prompting he spoke to us of the *mazzeri*. A friend of his, he said, was a practising *mazzeru*; he hunted with others of his kind, all people of his village, save one, whom he had been unable to identify. Recently a Sardinian labourer had come to work in the district. The *mazzeru* at once recognized him as the unknown hunter of his dreams, while the Sardinian greeted him as the companion of his own hunting dreams whom he had never so far recognized.

It is by no means impossible that *mazzerisme* exists, or existed, in Sardinia. Contacts between the two islands date from prehistoric times. The Neolithic Corsicans must have traded with the Sardinians to procure obsidian, a substance then much valued for making cutting implements and weapons, arrow-heads in particular. This hard dark volcanic rock, which does not exist in its natural state in Corsica, is found on Monte d'Arci, in central Sardinia, whence it was exported in quantity from the sixth millennium BC to Corsica, southern France and northern Italy. In historic times, as is well known, Corsican outlaws took refuge in Sardinia; the speech of the Gallura, its northernmost province, is closer to the Corsican than anywhere else in that island. A polyphonic chant, similar to the Corsican *paghiella*, is heard there. Were some of the Corsican traders, adventurers and outlaws also *mazzeri*? Did they transmit to the Sardinians the secrets of their practices? Or did *mazzerisme* develop there independently, an analogous phenomenon of an archaic society? A programme of research is planned which in due time may bring answers to these questions.[3]

In the absence of proof to the contrary one may assume that *mazzerisme* is specific to Corsica. It must be noted that throughout Corsica the evidence on the subject is consistent. Little variety appears in the information about the *mazzeri* collected in the places where they are, or were, very active, and such differences as exist are minor, and usually concern language. The *mazzeri* are known in different places under various names. All express the notions of death, killing, knocking down and nocturnal activity. In the following list of names collected by Roccu Multedo and Bradley Holway I quote the Corsican words, with an English translation, from which each name seems to be derived. Since these words have been transmitted orally and have only recently been put into writing, their spelling in unreliable.

Terminations in 'i', indicating the plural, 'e', the singular, 'u', the masculine and the feminine 'a' are often disregarded. I therefore note the names as they were given to me, without comment; my suggestions for their derivations are based on consultation of a current Corsican–French dictionary.[4]

mazzeri (Multedo): the name most generally used; understood everywhere in Corsica where the phenomenon of *mazzerisme* is remembered; the only name of which the masculine and feminine forms are clearly distinguished: *mazzeru, mazzera*. Apparently derived from *amazza*: to kill, or *mazza*: rod.

amazzatori – mazzatori (Multedo), *mazzadori* (Holway), used at Levie (Multedo); derivations presumably the same as that of *mazzeri*.

culpatori, culpamorti (Multedo), *colpadori* (Holway); used in the central south – Alta Rocca, in the south-east – Chera, in the extreme south – Figari – (Multedo), and according to Holway in northern Sardinia; derived from *colpu*: blow.

murtulaghi, murtuloni (Multedo). Derived from *murtalaghju*: spirit of a dead person.

tombatori, or *tombadori* (Multedo). Derived from *tomba*: to kill.

lancieri (Multedo); *lanceri* (Multedo and Holway). Used in the extreme south (Multedo). Derived from *lancia*: lance. This weapon existed in prehistoric times.

acciaccatori, acciaccamorti (Multedo), *acciaccadori* (Holway). Derived from *acciaccia*: to break down.

nottambuli (Multedo). Derived from *nottambulu*: night walker.

sunnambuli (Multedo). Derived from *sunnambulu*: sleepwalker.

It is remarkable that reports of the activities of people who go by these different names, wherever they are found, are almost identical. What has been brought to light is a body of almost uniform belief of an extreme antiquity. It indeed seems likely that *mazzerisme* derives from a period of Corsican culture considerably older than the Megalithic faith; that of the hunting and food-gathering people, the first occupants of the island, as early as 7000 BC. The relationship between hunter and hunted was then impregnated with a dramatic intensity, because it was a factor of human survival. The mystic link between the *mazzere* and his victim echoes that of the pre-Neolithic hunter and his prey. Hunting, real-life hunting, is still endowed with an almost magical and sacred significance. The Corsican hunter is at one with himself, with his environment, and his tradition. He participates in what can be called an atavistic ecstasy, so that still, today, it is said of a person who is preoccupied, absent-minded, that his head is, not in the clouds, but in the hunt: '*avè u capu a caccia*'. Significantly, the ecclesiastical authorities forbade priests to go hunting, in particular boar-hunting, as though they detected its pagan heritage. Roccu Multedo has ascertained, by investigating the number of shooting permits issued, that hunters are more numerous in the Sartenais than in any other part of the island, that is, precisely the region where *mazzerisme* has survived longest.[5]

Its survival is nothing less than extraordinary. The *mazzeri* still distinguish themselves, by their spiritual endowment no less than by their day-to-day behaviour, as the inheritors of a pre-agrarian culture. Their easy-going egalitarian ways between themselves, with their lack of social and sexual discrimination, so alien to the attitudes of the sedentary, stratified peasantry, resemble those of the last hunting and food-gathering peoples now left in the world. Known as foragers, they inhabit, sometimes nomadically, extreme climates, in the Kalahari desert, in remote parts of Australia, and in the 'Great North' of Alaska, Lapland and Siberia. It is no accident if the majority of the *mazzeri*, as maintained by Roccu Multedo, are shepherds, for they are the Corsicans whose life-style most approximates to that of pre-agrarian societies. That *mazzerisme* stems from that distant world is borne out by the absence of any reference to crops or harvests or the fecundity of the soil. No suggestion of fertility rites, to my knowledge, has been detected in the practices of the *mazzeri*. In fact, the only plant mentioned in this context is the asphodel, mythical flower of antiquity, nourishment for gods and heroes, the living and the dead.[6]

Hunting and food-gathering remained important in Corsican economy long after other sources of food had become available. This is underlined by the Greek writers who described Corsica between the fourth and first centuries BC. Their accounts are compiled from considerably older texts based on the reports of traders and navigators. They reveal the Corsicans in their primal, untrammelled freedom, prior to the Roman conquest. Though the island was linked with the civilized world since the foundation of Alalia (Aleria) on the east coast by Greeks from Asia Minor in 565 BC, the interior was as yet little affected by foreign influence.

Theophrastus, in his *History of Plants* in the fourth century BC, remarks on the profusion of the natural vegetation and the lack of agriculture; Timaeus, quoted by Polybius, asserts that the Corsicans spent their lives hunting 'without knowledge of any other occupation'. Agriculture was still insignificant in the first century BC to judge by Diodorus Siculus in his utopian picture of the Corsicans at the dawn of their history. They were herdsmen, he writes, who lived on milk, meat and honey which their country provided in abundance. As proof of their high principles of justice he observes that they left their livestock to wander freely, without fear of theft, each animal bearing its owner's mark, and that a deposit of wild honey belonged to whoever found it, without dispute of his claim.

According to Theophrastus the honey was bitter, due to the prevalence of boxwood.[7] This is still true, even though boxwood is not so noticeable in the maquis today. While the honey from well-situated hives has a not unappetizing sharpness of taste, wild honey is to the modern palate almost uneatable. This I discovered to my cost when lunching with a shepherd family in the deep Sartenais. Happy to partake of this unaccustomed delicacy I allowed an ample helping of wild honey to be heaped on to my plate. I had to swallow it; I had no choice.

Women are the food-gatherers in the remaining foraging societies; their contribution to the diet of their communities has been estimated at 60 or 70 per cent of the total. Their supply of edible plants, fruit and nuts, berries and wild honey, and sometimes shellfish and fish, is more reliable than the product of the chase. This activity the men reserve to themselves, although among the Australian aborigines the women hunt small game and kangaroos with dogs which they themselves train.[8] A similar division of activities may have operated among the prehistoric Corsicans. According to archaeological research the animals most hunted were wild boar, and a small rodent known as the *lapin-rat* ('rabbit-rat'), *Prolagus sardus*, which became extinct in Corsica, as in Sardinia, in historic times. Perhaps this animal was hunted by the women, distant forbears of the feminine *mazzeri*.[9]

Women, so Jean Cesari told me, were numerous among the *mazzeri*; perhaps they outnumbered the men. They were drawn to *mazzerisme*, one may think, because it offered an escape from sexual discrimination, as well as a field for the exercise of their innate psychic gifts. The endowment of women in the spiritual sphere, as is well known, has been recognized in ancient and archaic cultures. Their role may be negative or positive, that of witch or vampire, or of priestess, prophetess or healer. The Greeks of antiquity attached a particular importance to the predictions of the sybils, whose feminine spirit was held to be more responsive to divine communication than that of the men. Why women should be, or have been, so distinguished I cannot venture to explain; such a discussion would be beyond the scope of this book.

Suffice it to say that women's occult gifts have been traditionally recognized in Corsica, at once respected and feared, and occasionally repressed with violence, as I shall later tell. They have been manifest in their activities as healers, by a technique of white magic which I shall describe, as *voceratrices*, the improvisers of deathbed mourning songs, and as *mazzeri*. When Corsican women entered the ranks of *mazzerisme* they assumed their natural place in a society heavily dominated by men. They were readily accepted by their fellows, who took no account of sexual distinctions. *Mazzerisme* operated as a catharsis, like that experienced by the *voceratrices*, but with a stronger compulsion, for whereas the *voceratrice* might seek revenge on a single person, or perhaps family, as I have explained, the *mazzera* revenged herself on society as a whole.[10] Whether women were deliberately able to develop their psychic gifts to this end I am unable to say. They certainly, at the same time, developed an extremely strong conscious power of the will.

By becoming *mazzeri* they were freed from many social restraints. While men could go out at night, congregate in cafés after work, smoke and drink and play cards, women were not allowed to enter cafés nor to go out after dark at all. More galling was their exclusion from hunting; the only hunts allowed to them were in the dreams of the *mazzeri*. The Sunday boar-hunt was – is still – the weekly high spot in the lives of men. The thrill of the early morning start with loaded guns, in groups twenty to thirty strong, the cries of the beaters and of the hounds, the culminating moment when one, at least, of the hunters shoots a boar charging towards him through the under-growth, the late midday picnic after the kill, with the hunters reclining round a fire in the maquis with the corpse of the boar lying beside them, the triumphal return to the village carrying the boar tied by its legs to a pole, the dividing of the meat between grateful householders: all this is the recurrent pleasure of men. More than a pleasure: the satisfaction of a fundamental need. It has always seemed to me cruelly unjust that women should be deprived of this fulfilment. Still, today, when they have emancipated themselves in so many spheres, they are seldom welcomed at the hunt. An English friend of mine, retired to Corsica, managed to get herself included in the weekly boar-hunt of her village because she was an excellent shot and completely indifferent to what people thought about her. I myself have joined in several hunts as a spectator, tolerated as an eccentric foreigner. Corsican women looked shocked when I related the experience, though in general they accepted my outlandish ways.

A Corsican shepherdess of the pre-First World War period is remembered for having braved public opinion to satisfy her love of the chase. Defying the social code, she refused marriage and set up house with another woman in the village of Venzolasca, in the En-Deçà-des-Monts.[11] Known as *La Mora*, she became a celebrity, and was photographed in man's attire leaning on her gun, a portrait that was sold as a picture postcard all over the island. Although the carrying of firearms was considered the prerogative of men, Corsican women were in fact not averse to handling a gun. A friend of mine in her fifties recalls how her great-aunts went out at night armed with guns to protect the family's hay harvest from human or animal marauders. Sometimes they slept the night through in huts roughly built on the land, with their guns beside them.

Warlike women apparently existed in prehistory. A statue-menhir found at Castaldu, near Ciamanacce in the central southern mountains, as I have described, is a headless figure with prominent breasts and a very clear representation of a large dagger carved in relief on the shaft of the body. Is it a portrait of a venerated female warrior?[12] It certainly accords with the reputation of women in historic times. Invading armies learned to dread their guerrilla tactics, when they rolled down rocks on troops passing through ravines, hurled missiles from the houses of beleaguered villages, wrenching the very beams from their roofs to fling them down on the assailants. Some have left their names in insular memory: Margherita Bobbia, who rallied the women to save Bonifacio in the last, desperate days of the siege of the king of Aragon in 1421; Faustina Gaffory, wife of a leader of the anti-Genoese rebellion, who defended their home in Corte when he was away at the war. Later Letizia Bonaparte joined her husband when he took part in Paoli's resistance to the French invasion, and, pregnant with Napoleon, followed him to the battlefields. Her sister-in-law, Geltrude, earned the praise of the shepherds in this campaign. Educated by the priests, who introduced them to the Italian classics, they were wont to chant verses from Tasso's *Jerusalem Delivered*, and they never failed to substitute the name of Geltrude for that of the heroic Clorinda of the poem.[13] The bandits, it is said, habitually carried volumes of Tasso with them on their wanderings. In modern times the figure of Danielle Casanova, who died at Auschwitz in 1943, towers above those of the many Corsican women who risked their lives in the Resistance, in the island as in mainland France. Several in Corsica acceded to positions of authority after the war, for brief periods before men reasserted their traditional monopoly of public affairs.

These were heroines. But so too, in my opinion, were the hosts of anonymous women who through the years and the centuries toiled in their villages, women who to an outsider might appear as serfs, were it not for their proud bearing. They carried. Often pregnant, they carried water to their houses from streams and fountains; they carried firewood from the maquis: when I first went to Corsica I could sometimes hardly distinguish their features under the huge piles of sticks balancing on their heads. Nor was this all. They were expected to carry stones and mortar to a site where a house was being built, so that the men, in the words of Georges Ravis-Giordani, had only to arrange the materials brought to them.[14]

They had little or no occasion to enjoy what draws thousands of feminine visitors to Corsica every year: sea bathing, mountain walks, were for them out of the question. Cooking, cleaning, bread-making, the care of children and old people kept them long hours at home; if they went out of doors it was to tend poultry, or vegetable plots, or join in the harvesting of grapes and chestnuts and olives. Their only excursions were walks to local markets in nearby villages, where they brought their products for sale. Defenders of the traditional régime point out that they thereby won power by controlling the family's finances. Perhaps, if the men refrained from squandering their gains at the card tables; but power, surely, means little without independence.

A professor of social anthropology once told me that the evolution of a society can be measured by the degree of choice it offers its members. Judged by these standards, Corsica has always been backward in the extreme. Men had few alternatives; women almost none. Until very recently their lives were dominated by men outside the narrowly domestic sphere. Fathers and brothers arranged their marriages, determined their occupations, with a view, always, to the advantage of the family as a whole. It was they who decided whom a daughter or sister should marry, and when, or that another, to save the expense of a dowry, should not marry at all; it was they who calculated that it was worth sending a clever daughter or sister to a university on the mainland, paying her board and lodging, or that another, less intelligent, should be kept to the tasks at home.

'My brothers kept me down. They put me under. It's not right to keep a woman under,' so declared a shepherdess with the unsuitable name of Rose whom I met by chance herding goats on a mountain-side. 'That's why I'm still here looking after their goats. If they hadn't kept me under I could have been free, like you,' she concluded, with a blithe ignorance of the troubles my free life could entail. All the same, Rose had detected one essential advantage in my life: choice. For why should I be there, a middle-aged Englishwoman on a Corsican mountainside, except by my own choosing?

Corsican women seldom had the right to choose. Many were trapped into unhappy marriages, forced on them by brothers or parents to avoid what was considered a scandal. Scandal could occur all too easily in a traditional Corsican village. If a man so much as spoke to a girl in the village street, or worse, touched her face or hands, she was compromised and he had to marry her immediately or a vendetta was declared. To kiss her, even on the cheek, was an outrage. An even more dishonouring gesture was to tear off her headscarf. Known as the *attacar*, it amounted to a symbolic rape; the girl, even if she had protested, was considered to be deflowered, and had to be married without delay. The *attacar* was a common cause of vendettas into the present century. If these compulsory unions were sustained by an underlying attraction they might work out well enough. But what is one to think about the woman, forcibly married to a man of inferior social status, who bore him three children but never, to her death, addressed him a single word?

It is safe to say that none of these miserable situations could arise today. Corsican women have emancipated themselves over the last thirty years, effectively, discreetly, without scandal or conflict. They wasted no time demonstrating, complaining or flouting public opinion, but realistically set about earning money, an activity that could hardly be disapproved since it benefited the family as a whole. They insisted on going to universities on the mainland, until the Université de Corse opened in 1981, a real boon to women who make up 60 per cent of the students. They pushed their way into the professions, not only of teaching, which has always been approved for women, but of medicine and the law. And like the men, they found places in various branches of the French civil service. Some have done brilliantly well; one woman I know has held a post some thirty years in the Council of State while at the same time successfully bringing up a large family.

Economic independence, coupled with the prestige accruing to certain careers, has demolished the old taboos. Corsican women now love, marry and unmarry as they please. In Corsica as elsewhere. No longer does talking to a man in the street entail the alternatives of marriage or the vendetta: the vendetta is out of date, and so, to some degree, is marriage, for unmarried couples no longer suffer social exclusion. Modern technology in the home – running water, electricity, drains – has brought unhoped-for leisure. With time to spare, and, quite often, a car to drive, women take advantage of the pleasures the island offers, ski, ride, climb mountains, sail and swim. Some even practise judo, taught in clubs in the towns. They make themselves felt in public life. When I arrived in Corsica only one mayor of the 360 *communes* was a woman; at the time of writing there are thirty-nine, thirty-one of whom are in Haute-Corse. Three women sit among the fifty-one elected members of the Corsican Assembly.

Such an evolution, when I first went to Corsica, was as unimaginable as the material innovations that have since transformed the island. On my first visits when I was invited to certain peasants' homes, with or without my husband, I was seated with the men, while the women of the household stood, served us, and from time to time went to swallow little snacks near the hearth where the food was cooking. At that period women seemed to me not so much ill-treated by men as treated as though they belonged to another and inferior species. I had no difficulty in believing Jean Cesari when he told me that women *mazzeri* were more numerous, and more attached to the dream-hunting than men. Being a *mazzere* meant release from domestic and social servitudes. Bradley Holway, writing in 1978, underlines the compensatory character of *mazzerisme*. It was a reaction, he suggests, to rigid family, social and sexual roles, a means whereby people the least able to cope with village life 'projected themselves into a transcendent, fantasy world' and 'downtrodden individuals could gain occult power over their superiors'.[15]

His arguments are persuasive, but they disregard one essential question: can anyone deliberately become a *mazzere*? *Mazzerisme* being an occult practice, dating, apparently, from prehistory, one can hardly hope to find any fixed rules in the matter. Nonetheless the available evidence indicates that admission, as to any religious association, depends on two factors: predisposition and initiation. To be a *mazzere* it is necessary to have a psychic gift that opens the door to the parallel world. The origin of the gift is mysterious, as is that of a gift for poetry or music, or the spiritual awareness that leads to the religious orders and the priesthood. Without such a gift no one can become a *mazzere*, for the initiation takes place in dreams. The postulant is co-opted by a practised *mazzere* who 'calls' him, as the Corsicans say, to join him in a dream-hunt. By this single experience he becomes a *mazzere*, for life; the engagement is virtually irrevocable.

One might suppose a more elaborate procedure, such as a period of retirement and fasting in the maquis under the guidance of an experienced *mazzere*, followed by a rite or ceremony of admission to the brotherhood. But no. There is no evidence of initiatory trials or rites, such as are imposed, for instance, on postulants to shamanism, with which *mazzerisme* has often been compared. To speak of a brotherhood of the *mazzeri* is moreover misleading. Roccu Multedo contends that the *mazzeri* all over Corsica use a secret password;[16] but the supposition is unconfirmed and no such word has been revealed. It seems indeed that the *mazzeri* have little awareness of *mazzerisme* as an insular institution, nor contact with *mazzeri* other than those of their own and neighbouring villages.

The initiated is likely to be 'called' by a relative, usually somewhat older: initiation seems to take place most often in adolescence. Corsicans insist on the hereditary nature of *mazzerisme* and speak of '*familles mazzeriques*'. I have indeed observed that *mazzerisme* runs in certain families: the *mazzeru* I met had originally been 'called' by an uncle; a *mazzera* confided to me that she had initiated her daughter: I shall later tell how I came to know those two extraordinary beings.[17] The *mazzeru* described by Marie-Madeleine Rotily-Forcioli was, one might say, born into *mazzerisme*: his father and aunt and a first cousin were all *mazzeri*. A family of the Spelunca counted several *mazzeri* in its household, women and men.

Roccu Multedo maintains that in certain places initiation is performed by a *mazzere* possessed of exceptional authority, known as a *capistregone* or *mazzerone*, and that the initiation may be designed to enable the *mazzere* either to kill, or to save lives. The latter privileged endowment permits the *mazzere* to stanch the blood of the wound he has inflicted, and so save a human being whom a superior power had marked for death. This category of *mazzere* is known as a *mazzere salvatore*; the killers are designated as *acciaccadori*.[18] I confess that I have been unable to obtain any direct evidence on the subject, for these distinctions are not operative in the southern areas where I have learned about the *mazzeri*. Those of whom I have close knowledge observed no hierarchy among themselves, and had no choice but to kill.

Whether or not the predisposition is inherited, it is undoubtedly stimulated by contact with practising *mazzeri*. *Mazzeri*, I have been told, are very insinuating, and will try by every means to win one's friendship. But any familiarity with them is dangerous, for inevitably they will draw one down to their realm of darkness and death. A retired military man told me that he was brought up in the home of a *mazzera*, to whom he was related. Increasingly, as a boy, he was subject to weird, disturbing dreams, usually connected with death. Eventually he went to some Franciscan monks in a nearby monastery and asked to be rebaptised. The monks performed the rite, after which he was freed of dreaming.

Mazzerisme, it appears, is transmitted by contagion, which may arouse faculties that have remained dormant. A story was recently brought to my notice of an adolescent boy who, some fifteen years ago, began to dream of night-hunting. He was repelled by it. When the dreams came he struggled and screamed in his bed, but could do nothing to prevent them. His parents remonstrated with an uncle, a powerful *mazzere*, a *capistregone*, who was no doubt the instigator of the dreams. They begged him at least to spare their child the obligation of killing. But the uncle, tied to his calling, did nothing to save him. He was a sad, withdrawn child, and he had only a single friend, a boy of his own age. His distress became unbearable when he found himself killing this very friend by striking down a pig in a dream. He tried, but failed, to stanch the wound. The physical death of the friend came a week later. In despair the child loaded a gun and shot down an old man and a little girl; in real life, or so he imagined. Did he hope thereby to exchange the sufferings of the 'parallel world' for those of the other, the world of police and prison and vengeance? He failed. When he examined his victims he saw the corpses of two pigs. He had been dreaming; he was still a *mazzeru*. This extra-ordinary tale, I should add, came to me by second hand, so that I cannot vouch for the authenticity of its details.

Parents did their best to keep children out of the clutches of *mazzeri*. Sometimes they were given amulets to wear as a protection: necklaces made from the teeth of hedgehogs. The hedgehog is an animal fairly common in Corsica, which is sometimes caught and eaten. Why it should be credited with magical powers seems to be now forgotten. In the ancient past, in western Asia, it had a mythical status; it was regarded as an instrument of civilization and was credited by the Turco-Mongols with the invention of sedentary agriculture. Did some echo of these beliefs inspire the Corsicans to credit it with a power able to overcome that of the pre-agrarian *mazzeri*? Or was it simply regarded as potent on account of its spikes, its wonderful natural protection? Teeth, moreover, have been generally regarded in primitive societies as a symbol of strength. The making of these protective necklaces may be a very ancient custom that originated before Christianity came into being to confront *mazzerisme*.[19]

In the context of a Christian society rebaptism would seem a more appropriate precaution. According to traditional popular belief a *mazzere* is a person who has been improperly baptised, the priest or the godparents having omitted some word or gesture of the ceremony. Untouched by the purifying rite, the *mazzere* was therefore accursed, enthralled to non-Christian influences.

Mazzerisme is very exactly a 'calling', in the sense that it is a summons from a supernatural power; but this power is not specifically Christian, and the *mazzere* who succumbs to it, however baptised, is likely to be burdened with tormenting mental conflicts. The boy who went to the monks for rebaptism was guided by a sure instinct in appealing to the one force which, in his system of values, could counterfact that of the *mazzera*.

By no means everyone called to the dream-hunt reacted in this way. Some took to it with glee. For certain women, Jean told me, it became an addiction, like drugs or alcohol. The craving increased with age. No doubt they felt the sinister fascination of the maquis known to the bandits described by the Corsican writer Marcaggi. Perhaps they even shared the bandits' 'mad desire to kill'.[20] 'There was one near here,' Jean told me, 'she went hunting at every full moon.' We were sitting in the maquis within sight of the old fortified town of Sartène. 'She ended by killing her poor husband,' Jean continued, 'I'll tell you how.'

They were strolling together in the maquis one evening at the hour of the Angelus; they were a very devoted pair. Suddenly the woman saw a large dog beside them; or rather she had a vision of it. 'What a fine dog that is!' she exclaimed to her husband. 'Give me your stick so that I can kill it!' Her husband was not a *mazzeru*, but he too saw the dog, perhaps because he was touching her at the time. According to a widespread belief one can share the vision of a seer by physical contact; in Scotland and in Wales this can be done by placing one's foot on his.[21] 'Don't kill that dog,' the husband protested, 'that dog is me!' But the woman was possessed by an irresistible impulse and before he could stop her she had seized his stick and cudgelled the dog to death. That very night her husband fell ill with pains all over his body as though he had been beaten, and a few days later he died. This happened in 1933.

The story well illustrates the elements of compulsion and guilt inherent in the practices of the *mazzeri*. This woman was an addict; she enjoyed hunting, enjoyed killing; yet she had not wanted to kill her husband, whom she loved. But she was commanded by a power stronger than love itself, when she was overwhelmed by her dream while she was walking about, apparently in 'real life', by daytime. The *mazzeri*, so the accumulated evidence goes to show, cannot avoid their dreams; the dreams come, welcome or no. Can the *mazzeri* invite them? Could the addicted women described by Jean enter their dreams at will, on the night of the full moon or whenever they fancied? There is no ready answer to the question; *mazzerisme*, I underline, is irrational.

If *mazzeri* can summon dreams, then they must surely have some share in the responsibility of the killing they perform and the human deaths that ensue. Certain people believed this to be so. The unbaptised *mazzeri* were to them essentially evil, allies of Satan who really caused the deaths they foretold. This opinion, surely, was that of people who had no personal knowledge of the *mazzeri* and who failed to distinguish between 'real life' and dreams. Acquaintances of the *mazzeri*, and the *mazzeri* themselves, insist that they are involuntary messengers of death, not killers, and that in daily life they are inoffensive and steer clear of hostilities. Often they are looked on with respect because possessed of exceptional gifts. A Corsican psychoanalyst told me that his patients were proud of having a *mazzere* in their families.

However they have been judged, the *mazzeri* have never, to my knowledge, suffered serious harm from the population. They may occasionally have been manhandled by crowds of frightened villagers, after deaths that caused great grief and for which they were held responsible, but violence stopped short of murder. 'No one would dare kill a *mazzere*,' a Corsican recently said to me, 'just think what the reprisals might be!' In the ambivalent attitude towards the *mazzeri* fear was often uppermost. Extreme antagonism was however the position of the learned churchman, S.-B. Casanova, author of a history of the Corsican Church published in the 1930s. He has no hesitation in describing the *mazzeru* as the priest of the Devil, a wicked individual who waited at night by streams to strike to death whoever passed by. Streams, as I have explained, were believed in traditional Corsica to be the haunts of evil spirits who had not expiated their sins. Casanova seems to have been unaware of the dream-state of the *mazzeri* and the symbolic nature of their killing. For him they were simply sorcerers, endowed with the powers generally associated with their kind. After rubbing their bodies with oil they could transport themselves, he writes, in a moment 'to the ends of the earth'. They had tails like animals, and they could transform themselves into pigs or dogs or giants; they could make themselves invisible, and so immune to attack. These assertions, for which I have found no confirmation, would be more convincing were they less charged with righteous hate. In his sweeping condemnation Casanova assimilates the *mazzeru* with the *stregone*, and the *mazzera* with the *strege*, words used in Corsica to designate human vampires, beings that existed in Corsican tradition, and of which I shall have more to say, but which were entirely distinct from the *mazzeri*.

His violent and, it must be admitted, superficial judgement seems, however, to have been exceptional among the clergy. I have found no trace of persecution of the *mazzeri* by the Church, and curiously enough they are not mentioned among the various wrong-doers, including practitioners of vampirism, condemned in the trials of the Corsican Inquisition in the sixteenth and seventeenth centuries, which I shall examine later. A possible reason for this is that the recorded trials took place in the bishoprics of Nebbio and Mariana, in the *En-Deçà-des-Monts*, areas where hardly any trace of *mazzerisme* has come to light. The trials, moreover, were instigated by accusations of sorcery from neighbours. The people were perhaps too much in fear of the *mazzeri* to denounce them.[23]

Today, the clergy maintains a neutral attitude to the *mazzeri*. No one any longer believes that the *mazzeri* actually strike human beings to death, and the Corsican priests, as one of them said to me, are disinclined to interfere with ancient insular tradition. In fact the Church has offered the *mazzeri* one incalulably precious benefit: liberation from their role by rites of exorcism. For just as no one can deliberately choose to become a *mazzere*, so a *mazzere* cannot abandon his vocation by a conscious effort of will. He is controlled by a supernatural power which may offend his basic nature. He may come to loathe his dreams, to suffer them in guilt and in anguish; but only the intervention of the Christian Church, to my knowledge, can release him.

Mazzeri, until very recently, could be exorcised by the clergy with certain rites that varied in the different communities. In the region of Sartene, I was told, the repentant *mazzere* had to go to the parish church before dawn and kneel in front of the altar. The priest then tapped him three times with the blunt side of an axe between the shoulderblades and covered him with his own vestment. Roccu Multedo wonders if any of the hooded penitents in the *Catenacciu*, the

Good Friday night procession at Sartene, were penitent *mazzeri*; a question that remains unanswered.[24] At Chera, the *mazzere* was required to attend Mass on Good Friday and, I have heard said, on the two days following or the two following Sundays, and make a public confession which can be translated as: 'Beware of me, I am one who strikes to death.' After which he covered his head with his own coat and the priest sprinkled it with ashes. At Palneca, in the central southern mountains, the priest in the course of the ceremony would shake the dust out of the penitent's coat.

These rites embody symbols that are ancient, universal, archetypical and issuing from areas of belief far outside the scope of Christianity. The axe, which cuts and divides, and is associated in many cultures with thunder, may symbolize anger and destruction, but also the breaking away from evil and spiritual elevation.[25] The Corsicans of Alta Rocca, until well into the last century, collected axe-heads of polished stones from various prehistoric sites scattered about their region, and valued them for supposed magical properties. They were hung on the necks of animals, and also placed on the stomachs of people suffering from pains of appendicitis or intestinal disorders. Three is a universally sacred number that contains the ideas of completion, illumination, transformation. In the Christian context it symbolizes the Holy Trinity and the Resurrection: Christ rose on the third day.

The covering of the *mazzere* with the priest's vestment symbolizes his re-entry into the matrix of the Church, the scattering of ashes on the garment he has placed on his head represents a symbolic death: he emerges from vestment or garment redeemed, reborn. Such ceremonies are remembered as having been performed as late as the 1930s. They ministered to a crucial need of certain *mazzeri* who, whatever they or other people thought they had done, preserved in their hearts an unshakeable allegiance to the Christian faith. This is demonstrated in Marie-Madeleine Rotily-Forcioli's account of a *mazzeru* who was also a practising Catholic, and confirmed by my own contacts with two *mazzeri*, as will be told.

The *mazzere* exorcised by the Church has need of courage, for it is believed that he who betrays his calling has not long to live. His fellow *mazzeri* will band together against him, in his dream, lynch him and tear him to pieces, and within a short space of time his body will die.

The *mazzeri* are loyal to each other only in so far as they remain *mazzeri*. But the drive to escape *mazzerisme* may be powerful enough to overcome such fears, and a *mazzere* who seeks redemption may face every danger. A Corsican may indeed be condemned to a perpetual, tragic pursuit of freedom; to escape the limitations of his society he welcomes *mazzerisme*; to escape *mazzerisme* he can only appeal to God. If he believes in God. Fewer and fewer people do; but then fewer people become *mazzeri*.

CHAPTER 6

Written in the Sky

A bard – a *mazzera* – Destiny – guilt – the Mother
Goddess – cannibalism – the *Odyssey* – funeral banquets –
a *mazzeru* – Redemption

I had heard much about the *mazzeri*; I wanted to meet one. At the time
when my wish became insistent Jean Cesari was not at hand to guide
me. His roving, adventurous nature had led him to Turkey. I thought,
rather naïvely, that I might meet a *mazzere* if I went to Chera, the
village in south-east Corsica where the *mazzeri*, so I had been told,
mostly women, hunted their prey to death in packs, like hounds.
What was I hoping for? Not, of course, to see a crowd of dishevelled
women wandering about the streets, their faces and hands smeared
with the blood of their last kill. The hunt, I had to remember, took
place in the 'parallel world'. But it had not crossed my mind that the
mazzeri of Chera might, after all, be but few in number, since the pack
was only an image of a dream.

In fact I met no *mazzeri*; instead I met the bard. A bard was a time-
honoured figure in a traditional Corsican village. Guardian of the
collective memory of the community, he recorded outstanding events
in verse and song and so bestowed on them an enduring existence. He
was at once public historian and entertainer. Jean-André Culioli, the
bard of Chera, was one of the last to follow this Homeric vocation. He
was there to meet me in the street when I arrived one morning,
unannounced, with a Corsican woman friend. He greeted us with a
song improvised in our honour. He belonged to the élite of the
Corsican bards, those who could improvise at once music and words
for any circumstance. So I was privileged to witness a spontaneous act
of creation.

After that there could be no question of meeting a *mazzere*. The

bard held me captive. He continued singing, tireless, exuberant, all
that day and well into the night. His songs echoed every mood: gay,
melancholy, ironic and caressing. He possessed the histrionic gift I so
appreciated in Jean Cesari, varying his tones of voice to accord with
his subject. With the dexterity of a ventriloquist he flung himself into
every role, spiteful and petty in a ballad about two women who
accused each other of stealing some washing, grave and plaintive in
the laments of the old wooden cradle that had rocked his grandparents, now relegated to the attic to make way for a white-wheeled
perambulator, and of the old metal oil-lamp, superseded by electricity. I shall have more to say about the oil-lamp, which was
indispensible to certain magic rites.[1]

Culioli was past seventy, and he knew that the Corsica to which his
art bound him was passing away. He knew, too, that his own days
were numbered; the earth itself speaks to him in one of his songs to
remind him that it will soon claim him as it has claimed many of his
kin. One of his most moving songs was chanted in the voice of the
oriu, guardian of Chera and of the Culioli, whom it had watched over
for the past two hundred years. *Oriu*: the word was strange to me;
what was the *oriu* that seemed to represent the life-force of Chera and
of the Culioli? 'The *oriu*? Why, everyone knows the *oriu*. Just look!'
the bard said to me. And he pointed to a large freestanding rock in the
centre of the village, higher than any of the houses. Like many rocks in
that part of Corsica, where the granite seems to have a particularly
friable, loose-grained consistency, it had been scooped by the
elements into a hollow form. A wall had been built to fill the cavity
between the overhang and the ground, leaving a square opening as an
entrance. 'What was it used for?' I asked. 'For storing fodder and hay,'
was the unromantic reply. The *oriu*, by the strangeness of its shape, the
skilful coordination of the work of nature and of man, as well as the
respect, almost reverence with which it was referred to, had suggested
to me a prehistoric temple or pagan shrine.

Originally, I learned, it had been the dwelling of the Culioli,
shepherds who came down from the mountains to settle there four
generations ago. It became the communal storing place after the
Culioli built their home, a stone house with only one window and one
door but which, so the bard proclaimed, he would not have
exchanged for the palace of Versailles. Chera is the village of the

Culioli; they fill and they possess it; their name is engraved thirteen times on the war memorial that bears no other name than theirs.

A little metal cross stood on the summit of the *oriu*, bent at a right angle. A religious procession, I was told, is made to it every year on the second day of Rogation, when the clergy lead their parishioners in a procession to invoke divine blessing on the flocks and fields. But the *oriu*, it is thought, resents the presence of the Church. A goat with iron hooves was often heard trotting over the rock by night, and it was the goat, it was said, that had deformed the cross. In Chera the goat seems to have had an arcane, perhaps totemistic significance. According to tradition a goat was killed whenever a house was being built and its blood poured on to the four corners of its foundations.

What the bard told me about the *oriu* intrigued me, and later sent me searching for others in that region. I found several: all extraordinary in shape, like breaking waves or cracked eggshells, shapes that recalled Walt Disney or Salvador Dali. All were then used for storage; the word *oriu*, it has been suggested, may well derive from the Latin *horreum*, meaning granary. None the less it appears that they also and simultaneously served as shepherds' dwellings. One I visited in the Sartenais is remembered as the home of a man who died there at a great age in the 1880s. The only opening is so low that one has to stoop to enter; but inside one finds a long space where one can stand upright, divided into three small rooms. A home that was very like a tomb. In fact archaeological research has revealed that the *orii* were used both as dwellings and as tombs in pre- and proto-historic times.

I returned from Chera to Ajaccio enriched by my experience, but frustrated. Would I ever meet a *mazzere*? I settled down to write and research on other aspects of the island. I discovered an inexhaustible source of information in the departmental archives where the director, Pierre Lamotte, initiated me into the sources of Corsican history. A person of very wide sensibility, he also invited me to collaborate with him in a study of the *mazzeri*. Our article in a Corsican learned journal aroused some readers' curiosity, and stimulated my own.[2] Pierre Lamotte had actually met a *mazzeru*; would I have this experience?

Then one day Jean Cesari returned from his travels. 'Be ready to come out with me tomorrow,' he said, 'we shall go to visit a *mazzera*,' just as some years before he had announced to my husband and me that the next day he would take us to see the stone heroes of Filitosa. We drove down into the deep Sartenais, that mild November afternoon, to the village where lived the *mazzera*. We had no means of warning her of our arrival and Jean admitted to me that she was old and that he had not seen her for several years. 'Shall we find her?' I asked him. 'Do you think she's still alive?' Jean reassured me; the day before he had met a schoolmistress who had just returned from that same village and she had reported that the *mazzera* was alive and well. 'But will she speak to me, a foreigner?' I asked. 'I think so,' Jean answered. 'I'm very fond of her, and I've always been kind to her.'

The *mazzera*, he told me, had been harshly treated by the villagers. Once she had prophesied that two coffins would leave a certain house together within eight days. This happened: a week later two brothers died almost simultaneously of Spanish flu. 'Their relatives were mad with anger,' Jean told me, 'they thought her responsible.' They had dragged her to a pool fed by a spring of natural warm water where people sometimes stop to bathe, and there they had ducked her, so Jean told me. 'She might have drowned,' he said, 'but she managed to fight herself free.' They had not, it seems, adhered to the appalling practice inflicted on witches in European tradition, whose feet and arms were tied before they were plunged. 'They say too,' Jean added, 'that she foretold her own husband's death. That means, to their way of thinking, that she killed him. Everyone avoids her; she must be very lonely.'

The *mazzera*'s village was aligned on a mountain spur, small, bleak and poor: half a dozen houses facing each other across a patch of bare earth where the road ended. The few visible inhabitants fled indoors at our approach. 'You see,' I said to Jean, 'we won't find her.' 'Yes we will,' he replied, 'she's outside, over there.' She was standing alone, beyond the houses, at the edge of the escarpment dropping to the valley. She was not as I had expected her to be. An old woman *mazzera* had conjured in my mind the image of a bent, beak-nosed, crunched-up old hag. This woman was certainly old, in her seventies I thought, and she was shabbily dressed in black and scarecrow-thin. But she was erect, imposing as a statue.

The account of our meeting that follows is quoted, with little alteration, from my book *Granite Island*; any change of expression would, I think, diminish the immediacy of the impact it made on me.

When the *mazzera* caught sight of us she came towards us with a springing tread. And then I saw her face. A black kerchief covered her hair, falling almost to her eyebrows, and she held one end of it across the lower part of her face with her teeth. It made a frame for her high-bridged nose and huge, amazing eyes. 'She wears it like that to make her gaze the more impressive,' Jean later explained to me.

I was encountering the notorious piercing look peculiar to the *mazzeri*. But it was not only intimidating; it fascinated. Her eyes, immense and deep-sunken, were a clear sky blue: a young girl's eyes, ageless, unveiled and brilliant as though lit from within. They looked not at but through me, as though fixed on some private vision. She knew their power. A white tape, to which was attached a little gold earring, circled her brow. 'It's to ward off evil spells on the eyes,' she said, fingering the earring; 'I have need of my eyes.' Those seer's eyes that can perceive in dream-animals the doomed spirits of the living are the essential instrument of the *mazzeri*. They see beyond appearance, they magnetize. According to recent Russian research the eye emits a measurable electro-magnetic ray.

Contrary to what I had anticipated, the *mazzera* told us about herself, without prompting or questioning. Do *mazzeri* habitually speak of their activities, fearlessly, sustained by the authority of their calling? Or was she so communicative because she was meeting Jean, of whom she was fond, after a lapse of years? No sooner had she embraced him, and greeted me without any sign of distrust, than she began to speak of her life-work.

At that time I could understand a good deal of the Corsican language if it was spoken slowly, and without the excess of harsh guttural accent sometimes affected by card-players and others in cafés and bars. The *mazzera* was not difficult to understand because her accent was exceptionally pure. Moreover, her speech was a kind of chanting, a mode that is sometimes affected in southern Corsica when serious matters are under discussion. By her voice and delivery she compelled one to grasp her meaning; she spoke in magic intonations, like a great actress, or as the sybils must have uttered their oracles. After we left the village Jean and I stopped in the maquis to record her words, which I reproduce here. Some of her statements, cryptic, cast in trenchant imagery, require amplication which I give, noted under Jean's supervision, in parentheses.

'It still happens that I go out at night,' she began, 'over there, on that mountainside.' (She was pointing across the valley.) 'I tear my flesh and my clothes.' (Her clothes were in fact torn, and there was clotted blood on her legs and hands.) 'It is stronger than I' (the need to hunt), 'the blood wills it so. I have rendered my daughter exactly as I am' (turned her into a *mazzera*). 'Often we see the night complete its span and the day come without closing our eyes' (because we are hunting). 'When my master' (my husband) 'was taken by something in the night' (was taken ill), 'he did nothing but cry aloud. The others' (the villagers) 'wanted to fetch a doctor. I opposed them, saying that what God has destined those madmen and liars' (the doctors) 'can do nothing to prevent. They took him away to the Continent, but before they put him in the boat he died. He came back in a closed coffin and I never saw him again. They' (the villagers) 'have harmed me. But nevertheless what God has written when man is born on the sheepskin, that is recorded and none can avoid it.' (In these remote regions sheepskins until recently served as bed coverings.) 'It is better,' she concluded, 'to die in my way than like those they cut down in the wars.'

She had been speaking almost without pause, in melodious, rhythmic phrases, verging on music; now she passed naturally into song. In that high thin poignant voice in which Corsican women mourn the dead, she began to chant, her hands clutched together, her eyes turned to the evening sky, repeating: 'May the Blessed Mercy hold me as witness, I spoke only what was written, what was written!' We were standing on the extreme edge of the cliff; her black vibrating figure silhouetted against the vast backdrop of mountain and sky was spellbinding. This was an authentic prophetess, proud of her calling. Clearly she had never thought of herself as a killer, nor wanted nor needed to kill. Her role was that of a world-crier of an unseen power, that of God Himself. I sensed no harm in her, but extraordinary gifts.

She had reached the apotheosis of her monologue. She was telling Jean where she hunted on the mountain slope, pointing across the dark chasm of the valley with a magnificent hieratic gesture. Then, abruptly, she disappeared. With the dynamic vitality that characterized all her movements she suddenly strode away, into the maquis, out of sight. 'I think she's gone hunting,' Jean said. 'You saw how tense and restless she was, and how she was hovering on the edge of the village when we arrived. I think she's been called.' So by an amazing accident of fortune I was privileged to hear the confessions of a *mazzera* at the very moment when she was about to execute her mission. Or so I imagined. I had forgotten that we were not dreaming, neither I, nor Jean, nor she.

What most struck me about this woman was her elevation of mind, a nobility that expressed itself in her words, her looks and her bearing. Yet she was totally enslaved to her calling, and she had thereby suffered both physical brutalities and social exclusion. Her situation was the more unhappy because it could never change. Had she felt herself to be manipulated by some sinister non-Christian power she might have hoped for release by an appeal to the Church, by some rite of exorcism. But no; she felt, with an absolute conviction, that God ordained all she did, all that happened to herself and to others, the Christian God of her ancestors, to whom she owed obedience. It was He, she believed, who determined the day of the death of each one. She had been chosen to convey this news; she could only submit to His will.

Though persecuted, she was also privileged, for she was spared the sense of guilt that has tormented many *mazzeri*. Paradoxically, her Christian faith preserved her from any feeling of wrongdoing. Her creed, which might be described as 'fatalistic Christianity', is adhered to by many Corsicans. The Christian teaching of freedom of choice and personal responsibility has made little imprint on the Corsican psyche; the majority are convinced, like the *mazzera*, that every life is programmed from birth to grave by a supreme power variously defined as God, as Providence or as Destiny.

It was once my job to write a study on the Corsican concept of Destiny.[3] As a preliminary I questioned many people on the subject, in every rank of society. Almost all believed in Destiny as an active, transcendent force that governed their lives. Practising Catholics confounded it with God, described as Providence; for others it was a force distinct from God and more powerful. The Christian God, described by such people as '*le bon Dieu*' – 'the good God' – may be influenced by repentance, contrition, prayer; but there is no good-ness in Destiny: its decisions are without appeal. Only a few intellectuals I spoke to were of the opinion that Destiny can be interiorized: one carries it within oneself and one can modify its decisions, except, however, in such serious matters as accident and death.

The image of the incontrovertible written word evoked by the *mazzera* is traditional, and perhaps contains an idea of the magical authority of writing. When Napoleon's father, Charles Bonaparte, who according to his son was inclined to mock at religion, made a famous speech to urge his countrymen to resist the French invasion, he used the words 'if it be written in the book of destinies that the greatest monarch in the world shall combat the smallest people on earth, we can only be proud . . .' I here translate from the French rendering of the speech. But the expression is more vivid in the original Italian: '*se e scritta in cielo* . . .' – 'if it be written in the sky . . .' or 'in heaven'.[4] Destiny, written in the sky, has been the Corsican Bible.

The most independent-minded individuals were not above believing in it. Napoleon, writing to Josephine, declared: 'All my life, I have sacrificed everything, tranquillity, self-interest, happiness, to my Destiny.' Accustomed from his youth to the dangers of the battlefields, he had realized the futility of taking precautions and 'abandoned' himself to his Destiny, so he said to Las Cases at Saint Helena. But Destiny, he knew, had deserted him in the fatal campaign of 1815; if he occasionally wrenched from Destiny some advantage, Destiny lost no time in taking a revenge on him.[5]

It might be thought that Pasquale Paoli, man of the Enlightenment, would stand aloof from Destiny. But no; he merely substituted for Destiny the concept of Providence, as do many Corsicans today. Providence, he was convinced, intended to bring about the liberation of Corsica. When his visitor, James Boswell, ventured to ask why Providence had not intervened sooner, Paoli replied that its ways were inscrutable. True to the Age of Reason, Boswell was dismayed and slightly shocked when he learned that Paoli often had prophetic dreams. In spite of his rational principles, his avant-garde culture, Paoli, in the depths of his being, remained very close to Corsican tradition.[6]

A generalized respect for Destiny (or Providence) has developed certain traits in the Corsicans, prominent in their history no less than in their daily living. Most strikingly: a recklessness valuable in war and often damaging in other circumstances. A firm belief that the result of any action depends not on the actor, but on Destiny, has inspired the Corsicans to pit themselves against great powers, to stand up to the armies of the Romans and those of the French monarchs. Leaving the outcome of the engagements to Destiny, they fought with the mad courage of the pre-defeated. Reliance on Destiny, too, has encouraged respectable Corsican heads of families to stake their lands, their flocks, their homes on the gaming tables, in the back rooms of cafés, and until recently in the booths set up at religious festivals. The celebration of the Nativity of the Virgin, on 8 September, at Casamaccioli, in the Niolo, occasion for a majestic procession of a much revered statue of the Virgin known as *La Santa*, is accompanied by a fair at which outdoor roulette has always been a major attraction.

A passion for gambling has operated as a counterweight to the wary calculations of the peasants; a gesture of defiance to a monotonous routine. In the same spirit young men today perform acrobatic stunts on their motorbikes that often end in disaster to them and to anyone who happens to be nearby. Belief in Destiny leads to a revolt against Destiny, and this usually takes the form of irresponsible or violent action. On the other hand the weight of Destiny may crush its disciples into apathy, immobility, despair.

It has been said and written that the Corsicans' fatalism is a reaction to their political history. During two thousand years and more they have repeatedly been invaded, repeatedly resisted – 'to exist is to resist' is a Corsican proverb – and have always been defeated, always failed. The conquest of their country has been felt by some as a physical mutilation; in the words of Guerrazzi, an Italian novelist deeply in sympathy with the Corsicans, the 'strangers' – the French invaders – 'penetrated Corsica as painfully as the nails penetrated the blessed flesh of Jesus Christ'.[7] Without going to such lengths of dramatisation it can be said that strangers – various strangers – have always governed Corsica, and that the Corsicans, unable to make major decisions for their own country, have always had to submit, endure.

Yet to me this interpretation is less than satisfying. The Corsicans' sense of Destiny seems to be carried within themselves, not imposed by political factors, and the Corsicans most oppressed by it are those who are least involved in political affairs. One must look back to classical times, I think, to find a parallel to the place held by Destiny in Corsica, past and present. To the period of Homer, when Destiny challenged the gods. But the concept of Destiny was then already ancient, and its personification in the three *Moerae* (the three Fates or *Parcae*) issued from dateless popular tradition.[8]

The activities of the *mazzeri*, as I believe, stem from an epoch anterior to that of Homer, from the Corsican hunting and food-gathering peoples of pre-Neolithic times. No personification of Destiny, as distinct from God, has come to light in connection with their practices, nor indeed of any other supernatural being. The Corsicans, as has been shown, venerated their ancestors in the megalithic period and earlier; but the *mazzeri*, belonging to an even more archaic layer of culture, are apparently unconcerned with the ancestor cult, or indeed with any other. There is no tradition in Corsica of a pre-Christian divinity, such as are preserved the names of Thor and Odin in Germanic memory, or of Diana the huntress, who for centuries haunted the peoples of central Europe, as I shall later tell.

When I wrote of the *mazzeri* in *Granite Island* I postulated their submission to an aboriginal Mother Goddess, giver and taker of life, believed by archaeologists to have presided over the Megalithic faith. I here modify this statement. Evidence of her cult in Corsica is too scarce to warrant such an assumption. It amounts to a small figurine of a fat woman, dated to the third millennium BC, in the conventional style of images of the goddess, and five or six, only, of the eighty-four statue-menhirs classed as female on account of indications of breasts, in relief or incised. These interpretations have however been contested. In fact only one statue-menhir, at Castaldu, which I have already described, is unmistakably female. She is the figure not of a mother goddess, but of an Amazon, carrying below her prominent breasts the representation of a dagger. The Mother Goddess, patroness of fertility, of agrarian abundance, can have had little appeal to a country where agriculture played so small a role. The hosts of the statue-menhirs, triumphantly male, speak of another form of fertility: observers see in their prevalent conic shape a phallic symbolism. In Corsica increase was identified with human lives.

None of the presumed female statue-menhirs have any affinity with the obese Mother Goddess figures found elsewhere in the Mediterranean. One, known as Santa Maria, stands close to the Pisan church of that name near Cambia, in the southern Castagniccia, a slender schist pillar, over six feet high, with small indentations to mark the breasts. She suggests not a goddess of plenty, nor yet a warrior, but a prophetess. The sculptor, working in a stone less obdurate than the granite of the south, was at pains to represent the mouth, a feature little emphasized in the statue-menhirs of Filitosa and elsewhere. The mouth is shown wide open above a salient chin, as though she were speaking. Or prophesying? Is she a portrait of a *mazzera*? Were certain *mazzeri* commemorated by the devotees of the Megalithic faith, then the dominant religion? Conceivably they were the objects of an ancestor cult without being its practitioners.

The local inhabitants must have set up this figure, not necessarily on the spot where it first stood, and placed it close to the Pisan church so as to include it in the aura of the Christian religion. They also incised a cross on the body, and a date, unfortunately illegible, after the word *Anno*. Various legends are attached to the image, Christian in colouring, none of which have any links with the Mother Goddess or with *mazzerisme*. They tell of a young girl who was petrified in punishment for her transgressions. According to one tale she accepted a challenge from a man to enter the nearby burial ground at midnight and poke a stick into a grave. In punishment for this sacrilege she was turned to stone. Another tradition, likewise reported by the archaeologist Roger Grosjean, maintains that the girl, again in response to a challenge, entered the church at midnight to confront a vampire, but that instead she found a man hiding there who so frightened her that she died on the spot and was turned to stone. Yet another legend relates that the girl, taking up a challenge made to her at a *veillée*, poked a skewer into the keyhole of the church door, pronouncing the words '*Ci chi ci cio*', which have been translated to me as 'You are here, it is me', to which a voice replied, '*Si chi ci so*', 'Yes, I am here.' Terrified, she was turned to stone.[9] All three tales point to the same moral conclusion. Impudence, desecration, meddling in the sacred without due reverence, or braving dangers to impress rather than to help other people, incur the terrible penalty of permanent paralysis: petrification. By trying to do too much this girl was condemned never to do anything again. And contained in at least two of the tales is a lesson in modesty. A sexual significance surely underlies the anecdote of the keyhole and the skewer; the answering voice was no doubt that of a man. Men, it is shown, are dangerous to young girls. So, of course, are vampires; young girls should steer clear of sex and the occult.

Search for a prehistoric Corsican divinity has so far proved fruitless. Extremely archaic peoples do not necessarily acknowledge any definable, anthropomorphic divinity, and this may have been true of the early Corsicans. The arrival of the civilized peoples of Antiquity from the middle of the sixth century BC brought a galaxy of gods and goddesses to the island. Classical scholars and archaeologists have detected a proliferation of religions in the Greco-Roman settlements; but there is little to show how much they were heeded in the interior. The poet Seneca, unhappily exiled in Corsica from 31 to 49 AD (it is not known exactly where), describes the Corsicans with disgust as a people given to vengeance, plunder, lying and denying the gods. The classical archaeologists Jean and Laurence Jehasse, however, postulate an inter-penetration and mingling of foreign and indigenous cults. The Corsicans, they suggest, recognized in the Roman settlements a cult of the dead and of the family not alien to their own, while the foreigners saw in the statue-menhirs images of familiar divinities, such as Mars and Herakles who, according to an ancient legend, landed in Corsica on his return from the Hesperides and left his son Kurnos to rule as king.[10]

Place-names in widely separated spots of the interior point to the practice of Graeco-Roman cults: the Col de Mercujio, and the village Santa-Lucia-di-Mercurio, where the name of the Christian saint was simply added to that of the pagan god, were surely sites of the veneration of Mercury, one of whose attributes was to protect shepherds. And no doubt Minerva was worshipped in Cap Corse, on Monte Minervio and the site of the village Minerbio. But concrete evidence on these subjects is lacking.

The Greco-Roman myths have left little mark on Corsican tradition; in fact I know of only one that is reflected in a popular tale.[11] A beautiful young girl, Mariuccia, was betrothed to the handsome young lord Matteo. Just as they were proceeding to the church with their families to celebrate their marriage, the dreaded sound of the conch shells was heard. The shells, which in Corsica served as bugles, announced a raid by the Saracens. Outnumbered by the invaders, the Corsicans were soon defeated, their village burnt, their women captured as slaves. Among them was Mariuccia, who attracted the notice of the Saracen chief. Her fiancé, Matteo, was dying of his wounds under a tree when he saw her being led into captivity. He offered his soul to whoever would save her.

The Devil promptly appeared and shook the tree, from which fell, like fruit, more than a thousand well-armed warriors. They rapidly defeated the Saracens. Matteo recovered; he rescued Mariuccia and new arrangements were made for their marriage. But during the church ceremony the candles emitted sparks, an odour of sulphur filled the air, and at the very moment when Matteo was placing the ring on his bride's finger the Devil arrived, dragged him three times round the altar and out of sight.

Mariuccia was in despair. But her fairy godmother offered to help her retrieve Matteo from hell. She gave her a cross which would protect her from every danger, provided she refrained from speaking or from answering any of the voices that would call to her in the course of her journey. After passing through a dark forest, assailed by many voices but refusing to reply, Mariuccia reached a wide river, identifiable as the Styx, in which were drowned and drowning many of the damned. The magic cross interrupted its flow so that she was able to pass through it unharmed. She then entered the infernal regions where she recognized relatives and friends and saw many people condemned to appalling tortures. The Saracens were chained to the ground while vultures fed on their hearts which were reconstituted as soon as consumed. In a place where fell a rain of boiling water she found Matteo, bound by chains. She released him with her magic cross and made sign to him to follow her. They walked together until they reached a door guarded by a seven-headed monster roaring and vomiting flames. Here Mariuccia's courage failed; she cried out to Matteo to save her, flung herself into his arms. She had disobeyed her fairy godmother. The couple was swept away in an eternal storm.

The myth of Orpheus and Eurydice is easily recognized, if in a brutalized form. Orpheus, in the Greek myth, penetrates into Hades to rescue his wife Eurydice, overcoming by the mere sound of his music the monsters he meets on the way. His magic notes enchant the terrible Pluto who consents to restore Eurydice on condition that he never turns to look on her face as he leads her back to earth. But Orpheus fails to respect the injunction, and he reaches the world broken-hearted, alone. His only consolation is to play music in the forests. There he meets a wretched end when some Bacchantes, enraged by his refusal to give them a cheerful tune, tear him to pieces and throw his remains into a stream, while the trees echo the plaintive notes of his lyre. This at least is one of several accounts of his manner of death.

The poetry and humanity of the Greek myth is lacking in the cruel Corsican version, which seems to indicate that the love between Matteo and Mariuccia was in itself reprehensible. It belongs to the Middle Ages when the Christian God and his opponent, Satan, were firmly established in the Corsican belief system. But it also conveys a notion of Destiny as a supreme destructive force in human affairs. Destiny twice, at critical moments, prevents the young couple from marrying. It sends the Saracens to the island. It tempts Matteo to make a pact with the Devil. The pact is not explicit, and Matteo appeals for help only for the praiseworthy purpose of liberating Mariuccia; but the Devil seizes him all the same. Destiny breaks Mariuccia's courage at the critical moment of her journey through Hell. The young couple is thereby condemned for all eternity.

Destiny takes no account of merit; it strikes the innocent with the guilty. Omnipresent in Corsica, it has no anthropomorphic image. Corsican belief, as I have explained, acknowledges various supernatural powers: the Christian God, sometimes referred to as Providence, the Devil, Destiny, *falcina* – death, she who carries the scythe; but are they not all facets of a supreme, overriding authority, that which controls all men and all things? Neither male nor female nor good nor bad, but simply existing, it is sometimes described (and for this I have the confirmation of a Corsican psychoanalyst) as '*qualcosa*' – 'something'. A similar concept is expressed in the words '*quello quasso*' – 'that which is above'.

This, then, is the force that dictates the span of human life and all that happens. The *mazzeru* known to Pierre Lamotte maintained that all great events, such as revolutions, epidemics, wars, are enacted in the parallel, spirit world before they take place in material reality. According to this view man, or rather his conscious part, is no more than an actor in a shadow drama, the original of which has already been played, elsewhere. He has no future, only a timeless, eternal past.

Mazzeri are so much aware of being governed by an unseen power that they may feel guilty for what they have done although not responsible for doing it. This was brought home to me in a conversation with a middle-aged man I recently met in a bookshop. I was signing copies of a work I had written on the youth of Napoleon.

The stranger was evidently not interested in Napoleon, nor, I thought, in me: he looked not at but through me with a peculiar penetrating stare that reminded me of the *mazzera* I had met with Jean Cesari. When I asked him if he was a *mazzeru* he seemed unsurprised. He was not, he said, but his great-grandmother had been a reputed *mazzera*; perhaps he had inherited something from her. He had heard about her from his grandmother. One morning the *mazzera* informed a female member of the family that she had killed her child, that night, in a dream. She regretted what she had done; but it was not she who had committed the act, but something that had entered into her. She would make amends. A vain regret, I thought, for what amends could she make since she could never restore life to the condemned child? The unhappy predicament of the *mazzeri* is their inability to repair what they have done, or rather, what they have been compelled to do.

Such was, is still, the role of the *mazzeri*: to transmit to their villages warnings of deaths that have already been inflicted by an unseen power. Death, as in many archaic societies, was not regarded as the outcome of physical causes, but as imposed by an occult agency. The *mazzeri* explained death by the killing of dream animals; their own deaths were accounted for in their yearly phantom battles. Their role, neither good nor evil, serves only to lift a fragment of the veil that covers the mystery of dying. They act always in the service of their communities. This seems to be confirmed by a rather horrifying detail of their practices, of which I have received reports from three places where they operated: two villages in the valley of Spelunca and another near Sartene. There, it is said, the *mazzeri* habitually cooked their prey in cauldrons and feasted on it after the hunt. My informer from the Spelunca remembers that the *mazzeri* of her family (several members of which followed the calling) complained one morning that they had been unable to eat the animal that had been killed because it represented a person known to be dying of tuberculosis. Its bones were all rotten, they declared; they had to throw them to the dogs. Needless to say, this person soon died of his disease.

Should one suppose a far-distant memory of cannibalism? Evidence on the matter is inconclusive. Classical scholars who are of the opinion that the ports of call mentioned in the *Odyssey* represent real places believe that Bonifacio was the fortress of the Laestrygonians, giant cannibals who killed and ate many of the fellow-mariners of Odysseus.[12] The subject will be discussed later. The supposition, however persuasive, hardly justifies the assumption that cannibalism was current in Corsica in ancient times, and no other evidence, to my knowledge, points in that direction. Should one not rather suppose that the *mazzeri* consumed the spirit of the person who was to die in order to keep it within themselves, and so within their village community? A spiritualized form of cannibalism, if cannibalism it can be called.

But perhaps the nocturnal meal, or rather picnic, was merely a rehearsal for the *manghjaria*, the enormous traditional funeral banquet that took place after a burial in the home of the deceased. All his or her relatives were present, some of whom had travelled considerable distances. A member not only of every family in the village, but of neighbouring villages was invited; as many priests as possible were included among the guests. The menu was substantial: a meat broth with vermicelli was followed by two successive stews of meat and carrots, olives and dried beans; the meal was concluded with cheese, cakes, coffee and *eau de vie*, a white alcoholic spirit. Fruit was banned in sign of mourning.

These huge meals were designed not so much to feed the guests as to honour the dead. Often they were supplied by the dead themselves, who made provision for them in their wills, a custom particularly common in the south of the island. Presumably the banquets were attended by *mazzeri*, although for them the death and burial ceremonies were but pale reflections of what they had already enacted by night. The peoples of northern Siberia, where dwell the shamans, foregather after a death for such a banquet, accompanied by ritual offerings to the deceased, food and drink which is thrown into the fire. They believe he will not leave his home until these ceremonies have been performed. While venerating their ancestors, they fear those who have recently died. The Corsicans may well have held the same belief in accordance with a similar ambivalent attitude to the dead. The custom of the banquet apparently dates from prehistoric times. The archaeologist François de Lanfranchi has detected traces of a funeral feast in an Iron Age burial site in the Alta Rocca.[13]

Judgements of the *mazzeri*, as I have said, vary. *Mazzeri* may exist as sinister as talk of cannibalism and pacts with Satan might lead one to imagine, creatures whose mere expression is so terrible that just to encounter one is a searing experience. I can only say that the two I have met, a man and a woman, as well as the *mazzeru* portrayed by Marie-Madeleine Rotily-Forcioli, were people of a superior cast of mind, inherently Christian and genuinely distressed by the nature of their calling.

The *mazzeru* I met did not, in fact, impress me by his expression, but this, I learned, was because he had recently renounced *mazzerisme*. He lived in a small village in the central southern mountains. The landscape, though not the most imposing in Corsica, was spectacular; the slopes blazed with the autumn tints of beech and chestnut leaves as though on fire. The *mazzeru*'s home was spacious and well-furnished in the typical Corsican rural style. He was middle-aged, sturdy and welcoming; his wife was gentle and attentive.

Nothing about him seemed out of the ordinary. Until, that is, he began to speak. He spoke to me, in a deep rich poetic voice, all that afternoon and far into the evening, without restraint, as though, like the *mazzera* I had met with Jean Cesari, he was relieved to confide his memories. He had constantly hunted, he told me, during the past twenty years. Each time he had entered a landscape familiar to him only in his dreams. Whereas the other *mazzeri* I knew of hunted, if they hunted at all, in recognizable places close to their homes, and sometimes in the very streets of their village, this *mazzeru* entered another country. It was grander, he said, than Corsica; the mountains were higher; there were no trees. Huge rivers crossed the land; one he followed until it disappeared into a tunnel through a mountain. He walked round the mountain – no such feat was impossible in his dreams – until he reached the spot where the river issued from the other side of the range. He straddled it, planting a foot on either bank. He saw a hundred children floating on its current; floating to their deaths. One he recognized as René, a boy in his own village. He stooped and rescued him from the water. There was an epidemic in the village and René was the only child not to die. An epidemic of smallpox perhaps, such as are often suggested by the sudden deaths in Corsican tales. Until recent times the Corsicans were notoriously negligent in vaccinating their children; in the last century it has been estimated that on average less than half were so treated.[14]

The *mazzeru*'s dreams were full of unearthly wonders; but they were also terrifying. This *mazzeru* had no taste for killing and he tried if possible to save his victims. His situation was the more painful when members of his own family were concerned. 'Once I had to kill a bull with a knife,' he told me. 'Imagine my horror when I recognized the animal as my poor father! I did no more than strike it, and I withdrew the knife immediately. My poor father broke his leg. He was very ill, but he recovered.' Not all his dreams were of hunting; but those in which no hunting took place might be equally disturbing. Once he saw a close member of his family, for whom he had great affection, surrounded by a group of fellow *mazzeri*. Did they intend to kill him, even though his spirit had not assumed animal form? Before he could discover their intentions he was abruptly woken by an accidental noise in his house. It is said to be dangerous to wake a *mazzere*, that harm will ensue. This was indeed what occurred. When the *mazzeru* returned to his dream he saw the same gathering of *mazzeri*; but without his beloved relative. That person died within a few days.

After this the *mazzeru* determined to free himself from his dreams; they had become too oppressive, overwhelming him with anxiety, guilt and remorse. He felt a strong urge to reintegrate himself into the Christian religion: 'I preferred Jesus Christ,' was how he defined his attitude. But the Catholic rites of exorcism were no longer performed. In great distress he appealed to a Christian sect established in a suburb of Ajaccio. These people, accused of excessive militancy and little appreciated by practising Catholics and the clergy, none the less showed him charity. They re-baptised him, according to his wish, and thereafter he ceased dreaming. They continued to care for him, visited him in his far-off village, brought him illustrated books of Bible stories which he showed me with pride. He was free. Redeemed. When his time came he died quietly, comforted by his faith.

CHAPTER 7

Forbidden Ground

Vampires – the Inquisition – accusations of
sorcery – the Franciscans – the Giovannali – the
benandanti – the Sabbath – the wild hunt – the furious
horde – magic healing

I was tempted to entitle this chapter 'What the *mazzeri* were not', so
often have they been likened to other practitioners of the occult. Their
uniqueness is something that many people, Corsicans among them,
have been unwilling to allow. The isolation of Corsica with reference
to the centres of civilization, its poverty, its status through the
centuries as a colonized country, are factors that have led certain
Corsicans to undervalue their culture, just as others have adopted the
extreme opposite view. To be included in a European or worldwide
movement or organization is for many Corsicans reassuring: links
with the medieval Papacy, with the empire of Charlemagne, with the
ideology of the Enlightenment introduced by Pasquale Paoli have
been valued as life-savers in the stormy seas of history. The French
conquest, offering a partnership with a wealthy powerful nation-
state, was a source at once of humiliation and pride, provoking mental
conflicts which have remained unappeased to this day. The impact of
the illustrious French culture for a time threatened to crush that of
rural Corsica almost out of existence, until the reaction, charged with
insistence and violence, of recent years.

Attitudes to the *mazzeri* reflect these contradictory views. For
some, the *mazzeri* represent a base superstition unworthy of serious
attention. Others have classed them among evil-working witches and
sorcerers; such, as has been shown, was the over-simple opinion of
S.-B. Casanova, historian of the Corsican Church.[1] Roccu Multedo,
on the other hand, has devoted several books to demonstrate the

similitude of the *mazzeri* and the shamans, the so-called 'masters of ecstasy' operating in the Great North and some other little-civilized areas of the world, the subject of an important body of study, of which I shall speak later.[2] Meanwhile well-informed ethnologists, the Italian Carlo Ginsburg and the Corsican Georges Ravis-Giordani, point to resemblances between the *mazzeri* and the *benandanti*, who pursued an occult calling in the sixteenth and seventeenth centuries in the Friuli, in what is now northern Italy.[3]

These comparisons are valid, as far as they go, but they take too little account, I think, of the fundamental, distinguishing characteristic of the *mazzeri*: their submission to a supernatural power. The *benandanti*, though subject to occult influences, acted deliberately, to ensure the prosperity of their communities; the shamans use their occult faculties to protect, or occasionally damage, members of their tribes. The *mazzeri*, on the contrary, do not act with good or evil intentions, or indeed with any intentions at all; they simply carry out orders. Unlike *benandanti* or shamans they take no part in the struggle between good and evil, but stand aloof from this cosmic war.

The involuntary nature of their activities precludes any affinity with the malignant witches and sorcerers of European tradition, or with those specific to Corsica. Such creatures did exist in Corsica, or are thought to have existed there: but they are quite distinct from the *mazzeri*. Men and women, they are known as *stregoni* or *surpatori* (the men) and *streghe* or *streie* (the women). Their principal activity was to enter houses, usually at night, disguised as cats or weasels, and suck the blood of human beings, usually babies and small children, until they fell fatally ill and died. They were supposed to fly, invisibly, by night, bestriding, not a broomstick, but an *aspa*, a vertical component of a spinning wheel. They were considered to be partly responsible, but only partly, for what they did. Georges Ravis-Giordani draws a convincing contrast between them and the *mazzeri*: whereas the *mazzeri*, he states, bring deaths that are inevitable, the bloodsuckers cut short the lives of potential survivors. They represent the forces of evil and destruction, while the *mazzeri* represent 'the law of death'.[4]

These vampire-beings seem to have been less numerous in Corsica than the *mazzeri*. Did they in fact exist in reality, or were they only figments of popular imagination? Evidence on the subject is scarce.

Although *streghe* were believed by some to be the spirits of women who had died in childbirth, and so inevitably infected by envy, they were not, surprisingly, thought of as the principal authors of the Evil Eye, of which I shall have more to say.[5] According to Roccu Multedo they faded out of public consciousness at the end of the last century.[6] Yet belief in them lingered on. The word *strèga* continued to be used to designate any woman suspected of witch-like proclivities. When I first went to Corsica I heard of a *strèga* (not a *mazzera*) who had managed to enter a house in the Niolo and killed a child by sucking away its blood. Her tooth marks, I was told, were found on either side of a vein in the child's arm.

Such tales can be understood in the Corsican context. The infant mortality rate, until recently, was alarmingly high; one of the highest of any *département* in France, it was estimated in the last century at 10 to 20 per cent.[7] On my first visit to Corsica I met a man in his seventies who had lost all the fifteen children given to him by two wives, who had also died. He proudly introduced me to his third wife, and to the heir she had borne him who had survived to adulthood. Popular thinking no doubt sought an explanation for the terrible death-toll of the very young; an agent had to be found. The *surpatori* and *streghe* were perhaps thought to perform the same function in relation to infants as did the *mazzeri* in relation to adults and adolescents, people who could incarnate themselves in the forms of animals, as was impossible for infants, and roam about in the maquis by night.

But belief in human vampires may also have masked real infanticides. It does seem possible that in pre-contraception days women, bound as they were to unremitting physical labour, did occasionally leave unwanted children to die of hunger and neglect, just as they are known to have abandoned – 'exposed' – infants by roadsides, in churches and on doorsteps. This was a common practice in the eighteenth century, when the French authorities showed a certain charity to the foundlings. One of them, it is reported, was dumped on the doorstep of Lucien Bonaparte, Napoleon's ecclesiastical uncle, who did not however take it into his home.[8] On the other hand, real human vampires did perhaps exist, and, astonishingly, still do, though not in Corsica. Only a few weeks before writing these lines, in August 1993, a middle-aged man was arrested in Latvia for sucking the blood of infants; he had been addicted to this, he confessed, for many years, ever since acquiring in his youth a taste for human blood.

In the trials of the Corsican Inquisition that took place between the mid-sixteenth and mid-seventeenth centuries women were accused both of vampirism and of infanticide by occult means. The documents, published and analysed by Francesca Lantieri, provide a valuable if incomplete insight into certain hidden aspects of Corsican life during the Genoese régime.[9] No *mazzeri* are mentioned or described. Their absence may be attributed to the fact that all the trials recorded took place in the dioceses of Mariana and Nebbio, in the north of the island, where *mazzerisme* may have been virtually unknown. No records of the Inquisition are available for the diocese of Ajaccio, which covered the greater part of the south, with the Sartenais, so that one cannot ascertain if the *mazzeri* were ever pursued there by the Church. Possibly the population, there as elsewhere in Corsica, feared and respected them too much to denounce them, the means by which suspects were habitually brought to the notice of the ecclesiastical authorities. But had the Inquisitors proceeded in the south with due diligence the *mazzeri* could hardly have remained immune. To visit the dead, to 'go with the dead', in the expression most often used in the trials, was the fault most often held against the unfortunate victims of the Inquisition. The *mazzeri*, one knows, had contacts with the spirits of the dead, albeit without seeking them, but their nocturnal wanderings could not have failed to excite the animosity of the Inquisitors.

One reads the trial of a certain Catarina of Bastia, a widow, who in 1617 was accused by her lover of visiting the dead at night and returning 'blackened all over' by what they had given her: to eat? To smear on her body? This is not explained. Here one finds an example of the horror that so strangely alternates with reverence in the ambivalent Corsican attitude to the dead. Catarina also promised a certain man that she could make him see the dead provided he held a piece of iron in his hand: iron, a substance with protective magical properties that is a recurrent theme in popular Corsican belief. She had in fact earned a reputation as what would now be called a medium, foretelling deaths, communicating with the dead and offering to show them to their bereaved relatives, and she was often consulted in such matters. Once she dreamed that she met a dead man who begged her

The baroque campanile dominates
the mountain village: la Porta
d'Ampugnani in the Castagniccia

San Michele de Murato,
Pisan-inspired masterpiece in
polychrome locally-quarried stone

Proto-historic hero; bust of a statue-menhir at Filitosa

Statue-menhir near Tavera; an ogre turned to stone

Shepherds of the Niolo preparing cheese

A goatherd at milking time

Jean–André Culioli, bard of Chera,
in the shadow of the *oriu*

An *oriu* in southern Corsica

Barbara de Benedetti,
voceratrice

La Mora, the hunting shepherdess

The *incantesimo*: a son dispels
the Evil Eye afflicting his
mother

Catenacciu, Good Friday
night: the penitential
procession at Sartene

The Devil's sculpture in the red cliffs near Piana

Rockscape in southern Corsica

The 'Bridal Veil' near Bocognano

Bonifacio, stronghold of the Laestrygonian giants

to bring him one of his living children; when this child died soon afterwards she was held responsible. Her own two children also mysteriously died, and she was accused of sucking the blood of others with blasphemous incantations.

Her three companions in this trial, also widows, were likewise accused of frequenting the dead, and the four of them were put in prison; what happened to them is untold. The records of the trials are fragmentary and mention of the penalties inflicted are often missing. They were likely to be excessive, to judge by the case of a certain Lucrezia, another widow, convicted in 1661 of suspected sorcery and notorious sexual licence – 'making abundance of her body' – and sentenced to five years' banishment (presumably from her parish of Furiani, in the northeast of the island) and flagellation if the terms of the sentence were not respected.

In seeking to frequent the dead these people were considered guilty of a kind of sacrilege, as though they had trespassed on forbidden ground reserved to the Church. Only the Catholic Church, by the celebration of masses and by authorized prayer, had the right to commune with the dead, a claim that has been maintained to this day. At the time of these trials the upper ranks of the clergy, the inquisitors and the bishops, were Genoese, and they commanded the collaboration of the Genoese police. This was precisely the period when Genoese rule lay most oppressively on the island, after the defeat of the rebellions led by the feudal lords and then by the man of the people, Sampiero Corso, and before those which erupted in the century of the Enlightenment. In such circumstances the obsessive urge to visit the dead, so evident in the trials, appears as a spontaneous expression of Corsican resistance. The Corsican cult of the dead, dating from prehistoric times and reinforced by the Megalithic faith, was undestroyed. It was in fact stimulated by repressive Genoese rule, as were all the specifically Corsican traditions, including the vendetta.

Albert Memmi, in his provocative little book *Portrait du Colonisé* (Portrait of the Colonized), in which he analyses colonial conditions in French-ruled North Africa,[10] observes that a colonized people resorts to its indigenous traditions, '*valeurs refuges*' ('refuge values') as a safeguard against subjection and servitude. The most important are the family structure and the inherited religion. The basic religion of the Corsicans, intertwined with Christianity, was the cult of the dead, and it sanctified the family, the supreme social bond. The family consisted not only of its living members, but of all those who had died. The combined mass of the living and their ancestors, of the whole Corsican people, present and past, was thus ranged against the tyrannical foreign overlords, who, being instinctively aware of the strength of the alliance, persecuted it without scruple or mercy.

Not that the Inquisition was worse in Corsica than elsewhere. This is clearly enough demonstrated by the records of the Inquisition in northern Italy, which at this same period victimized the *benandanti*, with whom the Corsican *mazzeri* have been compared. It exercised a similar brutality, as will be described. The Inquisitors in Corsica were merely following the instructions in *Le manuel des inquisiteurs*, diffused throughout Catholic Christendom, where it was stated that the main object of trials and condemnations was to 'terrorize' the people so as to ensure public order, without regard for individuals.[11] The status of the Inquisitors in Corsica as foreign colonial rulers may have exacerbated their contempt for the population. They attacked those least able to defend themselves: the poor. And among the poor the poorest: that is, women. And among women the poorest of women: widows. The death of a husband, chief breadwinner of the family, might mean near-destitution for his widow, especially if she had no able-bodied sons or relatives to work for her; this desperate situation is echoed in a well-known *voceru*, which I have quoted earlier on.[12] Catarina was in just such a terrible plight. She was a bastard, one reads in her trial, and so without family protectors. She was living with a married man; to save expenses she shared a lodging with him and his wife. Free lodging seems to have been all she received from this particularly odious individual who denounced her to the Inquisition; in the record of her trial one learns that she earned a living 'carrying sacks', that is loads; no doubt the hardest and most humiliating labour that existed.

She also collected wild herbs for medicinal purposes, and went out at night carrying a knife, presumably to dig them up; for she was not accused of killing animals, she was not a *mazzera*. But seeking to cure by the popular methods of the time was condemned by the clergy as witchcraft. Just as death was by many people regarded not as a natural happening, but the result of evil machinations, so was illness, and, conversely, attempts to cure it. Nearly all the women who feature in the trials were accused of this activity; it was one that brought them a little money as well, no doubt, as a modicum of social consideration.

It must have been extremely prevalent. In a recently published work on the Corsican flora fifty-eight plants, out of a total of a hundred and twenty, are noted as having curative properties. Not only the asphodel, which was supposed to cure, among other illnesses, consumption, but a multitude of less spectacular flowers and shrubs were used to alleviate all too common complaints: rheumatism, urinary disorders, indigestion, stomach ache, headache, earache, toothache, chilblains, warts, worms (apparently very frequent among children), eczema and various skin diseases, as well as some more serious maladies: 'seasonal fevers' – malaria? – whooping cough, and, optimistically, typhoid, which was treated with a compress made from a plant known as *pariétaire officinale* (*Parietaria officinalis L.*).[13] Finding, collecting and preparing this wide variety of plants and administering them in infusions and compresses was perhaps the most valuable of the many forms of work that devolved on women. One at least of the plants was taken seriously and purchased by pharmacists: a variety of nettle, *Urtica spp.*, which dispelled rheumatism. Gathered into bunches, it was used for beating the afflicted part of the body until blood appeared. Catarina, the supposed sorceress, was not however accused of any such drastic behaviour, but merely of having placed a compress made of flour mixed with honey on the stomach of an ailing woman. It can have done her no harm and may even have brought relief; Corsican women knew, by experience as much as by intuition, what present-day doctors have come to appreciate: the powerful influence of the psyche in medical treatment. In fact the Corsicans, from an early period, evolved an elaborate technique for dealing with psychosomatic disturbances which includes secret magical incantations learned on Christmas Eve. But these healers, so far as I know, have never been harassed by the Inquisition, perhaps because their rites are outwardly Christian in style. Tolerated, albeit grudgingly, by the clergy, they still practise all over Corsica, men and women, known as *signadori*, of whom I shall have more to say.[14]

The Inquisition was hard on women just because women they were. The psychic awareness that had brought them respect in the era of antiquity now weighed against them. The Church had not forgotten that Eve tempted Adam and so brought about the irretrievable fall of the human kind. Catarina was actually accused of giving a bewitched apple to a man, who paid her for it. Another man, a certain Angelo, was accused of giving an apple infected with sorcery to a woman so as to bring her under his control – his sexual control, it is implied. He even tried to make himself invisible, apparently to facilitate his sexual exploits. To this end he dug up a skull in a graveyard and planted it in his garden filled with beans. When they grew and ripened, he would eat them so as to ensure his invisibility.

This procedure was attuned to very ancient, widespread beliefs that had filtered into Corsica. Beans in antiquity were sacred, magical, force-giving. According to Pliny they contained the souls of the dead. Their appearance in spring represented the first gift of the underworld to man. While the disciples of Orpheus and Pythagoras condemned the eating of beans as equivalent to cannibalistic consumption, others considered the act as an essential means of communicating with them.[15] This was no doubt the intention of Angelo, who perhaps hoped that they would confer on him their invisibility, while allowing him to stay alive.

Using sorcery for sexual purposes was the principal accusation made by the Inquisition against the few men brought to trial. One was convicted of entering a house by night with a false – magical? – key and attempting to rape a girl. For this misdeed, so strangely classed as sorcery, he was condemned to five years in the galleys; by default, for he evidently managed to escape in time. Men were condemned for making magic potions for seducing women. In 1610 no less a person than a parish priest fabricated a concoction of duck's excrement, sugar of grenadine and barley water for one of his parishioners, and made him pay for it.

Women might take advantage of the sexual greed of men. Several are accused of prostitution, and of encouraging other women to follow their example, acting as intermediaries. Widows might be sexually obsessed and deprived: this was surely true of the woman who in 1588, in Rogliano, in the north of Cap Corse, climbed on to the roof of the church and there stripped herself naked. The village must have been seriously perturbed, for it is reported that the priest thereupon abandoned it for a couple of weeks, taking with him his gun. Priests were in fact forbidden to carry firearms, just as they were forbidden to go hunting; they were allowed only knives, or if their lives were threatened they could equip themselves on journeys with lances or swords.[16] The exhibitionist woman seems to have incurred no more disapproval than she who was found reading a book in a church at midnight, or on another occasion in a cemetery; in the eyes of the Inquisitors women who read books could only be studying black magic inspired by Satan.

The overall impression made by the trials is of the abject poverty of the supposed culprits. It is shockingly revealed in the records of searches made in their homes. The objects listed, being without utilitarian value, were automatically classed as the apparatus of witchcraft. There was indeed no mistaking the nature of a wax figurine found in the house of two sisters denounced for inciting women to prostitution. Wax, but unmodelled, was also discovered in the homes of the four accused widows, Catarina and her friends, besides scraps of paper, dried grass, human hair, teeth and bones, powdered stones, unidentified greasy substances, a snake's skin, and little sachets of variously coloured material. These, it was known, were surreptitiously slipped under altar-cloths in churches, filled with an assortment of such things; they were believed to acquire magical virtues by the celebration of Mass and were worn as talismans against misfortune. One such sachet, containing the consecrated host, was offered for sale as a protection against violent death.

None of these people brought to trial, obviously, had abjured Christianity; all believed in its miraculous power. The worst they could be accused of was seeking to direct that power to their own advantage, and by their own means. The Church claimed a total monopoly of human relationship with the sacred. This bishops and Inquisitors declared in no uncertain language. The bishop Castagnola, in 1615, published an inventory of forbidden occult practices, some of which have now been forgotten. Among the people to be pursued were those who captured the Devil in a ring or medal, those who made use of 'young virgins' or sacred objects or the sacraments to cast spells, those who wrote or recited prayers not approved by the Church, who claimed to read the future in the shoulderblade of a lamb, or who held a lizard in the flame of a lamp to bring about the death of an enemy. The bishop Carlo Fabrizio Giustiniani, in a diocesan synod in 1665, observed that 'superstition and incantations' issued from a 'disordered appetite' to achieve certain ends by enlisting the aid of Satan and perverting ceremonies instituted by the Church. It was he who poured scorn on the traditional Corsican funeral rites, as has been told.[17] With the same vigour he indicted the magicians and witches who recited superstitious prayers, made use of signs, letters, words or images or rings, or procured the consecration of herbs or stones by means that belonged to the Holy Mother Church. No doubt he was referring to the placing of such things under altar-cloths. Attempts to arrange marriages or to cure illnesses were equally sinful in his eyes; those guilty of any of these faults should be immediately denounced to himself or to '*la Sainte Inquisition*', the Holy Inquisition.

Such people had intruded into areas reserved to the clergy. The wearing of talismans and amulets was not in fact reprehensible provided they had been previously blessed by a priest or member of a religious order. Sacred talismans – *scapulaires* – are still worn in Corsica by some practising Catholics. They are usually composed of small pieces of material cut from the robes of monks or nuns in which are placed pious pictures, sacred words, or fragments of olive or palm branches that have been blessed by the Church on Palm Sunday. A sliver of the wax of the 'candle of the *Miserere*', the candle set on the summit of a triangular candelabra during the ceremonies of Good Friday, was thought to be particularly efficacious.[18] Chips of red coral were often given to children to wear for protection, and, as has been told, necklaces made from hedgehogs' teeth to ward off the *mazzeri*. The latter do not, however, seem to have been previously blessed, the hedgehog's magic being apparently considered self-sufficing.[19]

Bandits were among the people most given to wearing talismans, and who were indeed the most in need of them. On their wanderings through the maquis they carried not only volumes of Dante, Tasso and Ariosto, but, attached to their bodies, a variety of crucifixes, holy medals, wooden rosaries and *scapulaires*, whether blessed or not. The most highly prized was the consecrated host, which many wore stuck to their skin in the belief that it made them invulnerable. It could be obtained only by theft at the moment of taking communion. This practice was so frequent that the clergy adopted the rule of placing the wafer straight into the mouth of the communicants, for fear that they would otherwise secretly slip it into their clothes later to give or sell to friends and outlaws.

The action of the Inquisition in Corsica was intermittent. Only once, in the mid-fourteenth century, did it condemn what could be judged a heresy: the sect of the Giovannali, which was in fact a revolutionary movement in the Third Order of Saint Francis directed against the material prepotence of the Church and the feudal lords. The Franciscans were then numerous in the island and much respected. Poverty, the creed of their founder, constituted a valid bond: the Corsicans trusted the Franciscans because they were poor; the Franciscans sympathized with the Corsicans because Saint Francis loved, above all, poor men. Perhaps his communion with nature and the animals endeared him to a population composed largely of shepherds and peasants. According to tradition, the saint visited Bonifacio in 1214 on his journey between Italy and Spain, driven into the harbour by a storm. He camped, it is said, in a rock shelter not far from the town, where his followers later established a monastery.

By the end of the century there were eight such foundations in the island; by the eighteenth no less than sixty-four. 'Franciscanism' became a powerful force among the people. The Franciscans sided with them in their struggle against tyranny and oppression; during the national rebellions they welcomed innumerable patriotic gatherings within their walls and hoarded rebels' arms under cover of their large baroque altars. Faithful supporters of Paoli, they taught the principles of the Enlightenment at the university he founded in Corte.

Today they are far less numerous; not more than twenty dispersed in four monasteries scattered across the island. That of Bastia upholds their tradition of scholarship by caring for the Corsican Franciscan library and adding to it microfilms of thousands of original documents. In Sartene, the cult of the saint is celebrated with genuine devotion when a statue of the 'Poverello', as he is called, is carried in procession of his feast day on 4 October. Here, close to the town, a handful of monks maintain a small monastery: they who every year prepare the *Catenacciu* for the penitential procession of Good Friday and who, not long ago, sheltered the dying bandit Muzarettu, as I have told.[20]

The mid-fourteenth century was one of the most troubled and confused epochs in Corsican history. The Pisans, defeated by Genoa, had abandoned the island; the Genoese, frustrated in an attempt to occupy it by the Black Death, held only Calvi and Bonifacio. Left to themselves, the Corsicans were subjected to the domination of their own feudal lords, whose record of exploitation always equalled that of any colonial power. Deep popular resentment is echoed in semi-legendary tales.[21] In these unhappy circumstances the foundation of a congregation of the Third Order of Saint Francis by a certain Ristoro, a Corsican living in Marseilles, met with an enthusiastic response. In the little village of Carbini, in the central south of the island, a third of the population immediately joined: forty men and sixty women. The predominance of the latter probably reflects their reactions to social constraints.[22]

The Third Order of Saint Francis was a lay association open to both women and men, who took no vows but engaged themselves to observe certain moral and religious disciplines. Much valued in Corsica, it enabled the Franciscan doctrine to permeate the mass of the population. At the time when Ristoro came to the island, two Franciscan monasteries existed in and near Bonifacio, and six in the *En-Deçà-des-Monts*, but there was as yet none in the Sartenais. The population of Carbini spontaneously welcomed the establishment of a centre of Franciscan teaching in its midst. But the congregation soon ran into trouble, for it adhered to an extremist tendency among the Franciscans which Ristoro had brought with him from Marseilles. The Order had split into two factions after the death of its founder: the 'Spirituals', known in Italy as *Fraticelli*, who advocated absolute 'evangelical' poverty, and the 'Conventuals', who sought to mitigate the austerity of the rule. The former were soon classed as heretics and persecuted wherever found. At this period they had nonetheless attracted an ardent following in Provence, where the self-styled 'Poor Brothers of Penitence' practised their ideal at the risk of being burnt at the stake, as many were.

This, then, was the creed Ristoro introduced to Corsica; it corresponded at once with the basic conditions of the country and the prevailing convictions of its inhabitants. The congregation of Carbini inveighed vigorously against the riches of the Church and the power of the feudal lords, preaching the doctrine of the equality of men and the community of possessions. Like other groups devoted to this ideal, before and since, the Giovannali were violently opposed. A Corsican chronicler accused them of holding their women and children in common and of indulging in outrageous orgies in the church of San Giovanni, the superbly austere Romanesque church of Carbini from which they probably derived their name.

The bishop of Aleria hastened to excommunicate them, although he had attended their inaugural meeting in person. Ristoro appealed to the archbishop of Pisa, who lifted the sentence; but at the end of 1353 he was re-excommunicated both by the Pope and the Franciscan Order. Undeterred, the Giovannali elected as their leaders two illegitimate brothers of the local lord of Attala, who no doubt nourished their own grievances against the feudal régime. Armed and militant, they advanced northwards across Corsica until they seized and occupied a Franciscan monastery at Alesani, in the heart of the chestnut forests. They were welcomed by the bulk of the inhabitants, for at this same period a certain Sambocuccio d'Alando of the Bozio, one of the grand popular heroes from time to time thrown up by Corsican history, had mobilized the people of the *En-Deçà-des-Monts* in a revolt against their feudal lords. The Giovannali offered them an ideological inspiration.

The rebellion triumphed; the feudal lords of northern Corsica were dispossessed for good. Their rule was replaced by the so-called 'popular régime', according to which the communities elected their own chiefs and exploited their natural resources in common. The system accorded with a primeval Corsican social pattern which had already been established in certain areas despite feudalism. To consolidate his victory Sambocuccio appealed for Genoese protection, no doubt as a safeguard against possible intrigues of the Corsican nobles with other foreign powers. But this move merely resulted in the exchange of feudal for colonial oppression, one which was to last four hundred years. The Giovannali also failed. In 1362 the Pope sent troops to the island which combined with conservative forces in Corsica to exterminate them; their bodies were burnt on enormous funeral pyres. A rugged peak at Carbini, surmounted by a cross, marks the spot where the last of the resistants died. Franciscan and other inquisitors were sent to the island by order of the Papacy at intervals over the next three decades to stamp out every vestige of their beliefs. Yet their sacrifice was not altogether useless; their doctrine of equality cut deep into the Corsican collective psyche, while the contemporary rebellion, leading to the independent organization of the rural communities, marked a step in the evolution of primitive democracy to the more modern expression of the same principles embodied in the constitution of Pasquale Paoli.

This was the only occasion when the Inquisition in Corsica came to grips with a body of opinion that could be interpreted, justly or not, as heretical. Thereafter the Inquisitors had apparently nothing more serious to deal with than the squalid little faults of such pathetic figures as Angelo and Catarina. These people never formed a movement or group; they acted individually without any aim beyond the satisfaction of their needs, sexual and material.

Curiously, no evidence has come to light in Corsica of accusations of more serious matters, such as attendance at the witches' Sabbath, a subject that elsewhere in Europe obsessed Inquisitors and public well into the seventeenth century. Innumerable descriptions extorted at trials and consigned to treatises on demonology depict the ceremony. All describe in more or less detail the same scene: the gathering in some wild spot at night, reached by flying on a broomstick or magically transported in the guise of a small animal, a mouse, a hare, even a butterfly. There homage was paid to Satan in person, seated on a magnificent throne, while his adepts desecrated the Christian symbols, trampling on the cross and defiling the sacraments. Partaking of ample food and drink, they indulged in sexual intimacy with Satan; singing, leaping and dancing was followed by public lovemaking on couches. The orgy took place amid a glittering display of riches: the participants wore jewelled bracelets and necklaces, and swilled down wine out of gold and silver goblets.

Accounts of these imagined joys and atrocities fill pages of books and manuscripts. But not in Corsica. Alone Roccu Multedo speaks of the Sabbath, stating that the *mazzeri* attended it on Saturday nights, and pointing to certain spots, near water or on hilltops in Cap Corse, as the sites of these unholy gatherings, as well as threshing floors in the agricultural regions of the *En-Deçà-des-Monts*, notably in the Bozio. These are circular paved areas, delimited by small upright stones, where oxen or mules dragged a segment of a rounded stone over the stooks of corn. They were still in use when I first went to the island, beautiful in themselves and seemingly fitted for some less utilitarian purpose. But Multedo's assertions about the Sabbath are unconfirmed, even hotly denied. The dream of the Sabbath seems not to have haunted Corsica.

The ethnologist Margaret Murray has advanced the much disputed theory that the Sabbath was a survival of a widespread pre-Christian religion, a collective celebration associated with fertility cults.[23] Perhaps; but if so it had receded into the realm of dreams in historic times. Many of its features, such as the transformation of the participants into small animals able to travel long distances, are incompatible with physical reality. Confessions of visitors to the Sabbath do not, moreover, pretend that the experience took place in 'real life'. According to those quoted by Carlo Ginsburg, the visitor fell into a deep sleep during which his spirit left his body to assume the form of an animal, or to bestride an animal, such as a hare, and thus reach the gathering by magical means. He was careful to warn whoever stayed in his house not to shift his body before he returned at dawn, otherwise the spirit would be unable to reintegrate with the body and the body would die. Such people, like the *mazzeri*, had the faculty of entering a state of dream that had the quality of reality, which they shared with certain *benandanti* as well as others of their kind. The *mazzeri*, on the other hand, have never been seriously accused of visiting the Sabbath, and indeed this whole complex of beliefs seems alien to them.

The *benandanti* of the Friuli, with whom the *mazzeri* have been compared, were repeatedly accused by the Inquisitors of visiting the Sabbath and consistently denied the charge. Their name, translated as 'good walkers', speaks for their high intentions. Their principal function was to go out at night, 'in spirit' and in groups, to protect the harvests of their communities from the witches and sorcerers who would otherwise destroy them. The battles took place during the four 'ember seasons' of the year, periods of four days each dedicated by the Church to abstinence and prayer. They corresponded with crucial epochs in the traditional agrarian calendar: Wednesday to Saturday after the first Sunday in Lent, and four-day periods that included Whitsunday, Holy Cross Day on 14 September, and Saint Lucia's Day on 13 December. The *benandanti*, so they proclaimed, sought to protect the wheat and other cereals, the livestock and the vines: 'If we are victorious that year there is abundance, but if we lose there is famine,' one of them declared to an Inquisitor in 1580. The weapons of the *benandanti* were bunches of fennel, those of the witches and sorcerers sorghum stalks.

The Inquisition pursued the *benandanti* relentlessly: if they knew where to find the witches and sorcerers and joined them in battle, then, in the minds of the Inquisitors, they must belong to the same category of evil beings. It was useless for the *benandanti* to protest, as they often did with dignity and serenity, that they went out 'in the service of Christ', that they were 'called' by an 'angel of God', that they left pronouncing the words 'May God and the saints be with us'; the Inquisitors refused to credit their innocence. Year after year through the 1570s to the 1640s they were harassed by the Inquisition, which strove to make them confess what it wanted to hear; its methods were those of the totalitarian states of our time. Small wonder if some of the *benandanti*, worn down by unremitting interrogation and in dread of torture, ended by saying that they had visited the Sabbath. It is comforting to know that their self-respect was not completely broken, and that several insisted that they had attended the Sabbath only as spectators, without taking part in the defilements and orgies. This, of course, did not satisfy the Inquisitors, who contested the basic function of the *benandanti*. The protection of the harvests was the business of the Church, performed on the three days of Rogation, when the clergy invoked divine blessing on the flocks and fields; in claiming to perform the same function, but more aggressively and more often, the *benandanti* were treading on forbidden ground.

If the belief in the witches' Sabbath was so generalized and supported by such a wealth of circumstantial detail, it must surely have corresponded with a deep-rooted human need, one that is unashamedly tolerated today: the need quite simply for pleasure, to enjoy eating and drinking and dancing and sexual adventures, casting off restraints, defying taboos. The so-called civilized societies of our time provide for such indulgences; even unrich people in a country as unluxurious as Corsica can let off steam on the Saturday night outing to the local *discothèques*, with their cars conveniently parked outside. But in times past nothing of the sort was available to the mass of the people; in the intervals between religious and family festivals their lives were unmitigatedly cramped and dull. Lords and ladies might entertain in their castles, give banquets with musicians and ample food and wine, perhaps flowing from gold and silver goblets, while they turned a blind eye to the sexual indiscretions of their guests. Common people could only glimpse such scenes, as servants or purveyors of supplies, and dream of them afterwards. Dreams of pleasure and plenty in which were mingled images of the precious objects they had seen in churches, the gold and silver crucifixes and chalices and candelabra; dreams that were stained with guilt. The belief in the Sabbath, was it not a collective wish-fulfilling dream?

If it had no place in Corsica, this was perhaps because there were fewer models for it than existed in more prosperous lands. The feudal lords might relish deflowering brides on their wedding night; but their life-style was harsh and bare. Their castles, perched on peaks which may need an Alpinist's skill to scale, were designed less for comfort than for war. Such means as their owners possessed were often bestowed on the Church; some gave proof of a generous piety in founding monasteries and donating to them valuable works of art. So Rinuccio della Rocca, the last of the feudal lords to make war on Genoa, in 1492 founded a monastery for the Franciscans at Sainte-Lucie-de-Tallano and gave to their church two magnificent paintings, an altarpiece and a crucifixion, which I have been able to attribute to the school of the master of Castel Sardo, an artist, probably of Catalan origin, working in 1501 in Sardinia, where Rinuccio went to seek reinforcements. But such treasures were reserved to the churches; the dream of the Sabbath could hardly take shape in Corsica because there was too little in the island's life to encourage it.[24]

The *benandanti*, by their own acount, were predestined to their vocation by being born with a caul – the amniotic sac – on their heads. According to an old belief of which I found no echo in Corsica, such people were endowed with exceptional powers: soldiers went through battle unscathed and lawyers always won their suits if they had been born with the caul. Witches and sorcerers were distinguished in the same way. The Inquisition was thus not altogether mistaken in connecting the *benandanti* with witchcraft and sorcery. When asked to give the name of the practitioners of the black arts they refused, just as they refused to betray the identity of their fellow *benandanti*. They had engaged, they said, in a lifelong pact not to reveal secrets about one side or the other; the order had been given by their 'captain' whom they were bound to obey, on pain of being beaten black and blue. Similarly, the witches, if betrayed, would come to beat them with sorghum stalks.

The *benandanti* formed a closely organized society; each group or 'company' was controlled by a 'captain' who summoned its members with the sound of a drum. They entered the company at the age of twenty and resigned at forty. They were co-opted, like the *mazzeri*, in a state of dream; one of them related to an Inquisitor how he had been mobilized for the first time on the Thursday night of the ember period of December, when he was summoned by his captain during his first sleep. Or rather his spirit was summoned and thereupon went out into the night, leaving his body behind. The *benandanti* inhabited relatively well-peopled areas, so that their armies might be imposing: 'At times we are five thousand and more,' one of them asserted to an Inquisitor. Most seem to have been of humble origin: shepherds and peasants or artisans.

Resemblances to the *mazzeri* – apart from the numbers involved – readily come to mind. The *benandanti*, like the *mazzeri*, constituted a distinct category of the population; they frequented each other in both the 'real' and 'spirit' worlds. They were initiated by co-option, in dream; but they had to possess occult gifts. These were given to them in consequence of something that occurred at the start of life, by God's will. Or by the agency of Destiny, '*qualcosa*' or '*quello quasso*'? The *benandanti* were born with a caul; the *mazzeri* were improperly baptised. Thereafter *benandanti*, like *mazzeri*, were bound to follow their calling, and like the *mazzeri* they were compelled by their own admission to go out at night by an irresistible arcane power.

Both *benandanti* and *mazzeri* had an ambiguous relationship with Christianity; deeply attached to the Christian faith, they were often at odds with the Church. The *mazzeri*, however, escaped persecution. Both operated in the mysterious inter-world between sleeping and waking: 'It seemed to me that I was both sleeping and not sleeping,' one of the *benandanti* told an Inquisitor when describing how he had first been summoned. The *benandanti*, like the *mazzeri*, believed that their spirits left their bodies to travel long distances. Both acted in the service of their communities, or imagined themselves to do so. Both went out at night to fight enemies, equipped with wild plants as weapons.

But the resemblances are not more significant than the differences between them. The *mazzeri* did not – do not – go out at night to fight witches and sorcerers, but people of their own kind; they were – they are – entirely free from any association with practitioners of the black arts. They fight only once a year, and their object was not – is not – to defend harvests, but human lives. Their activities belong to a pre-agrarian epoch of society; they were, and are, essentially hunters, and no plant is mentioned in connection with them except the wild though edible asphodel. In that distant period there was no counting of crops or perhaps even of herds; life was lived from day to day almost without property, as it still is among the remaining hunting and food-gathering peoples of the world. Nothing was then so precious as a human being; the wealth of the community consisted in having sufficient members to pursue the chase with success, to wrench survival from nature.

The world of the *mazzeri* seems at once freer and more limited than that of the *benandanti*. Individuals had more liberty of action as *mazzeri* than was allowed to the *benandanti*; they went out, they go out, often, and sometimes singly, without any order from their fellow beings; there is no hierarchy among the *mazzeri*. They have never been oppressed by the constant menace of imagined witches and sorcerers; in fact, they seem to have been remarkably little aware of evil. On the other hand the *benandanti* had access to areas of experience unknown to the *mazzeri*. Vestiges of ancient cultures lingered on in the Friuli that never prevailed in Corsica. Not only was Satan revered, but the pagan goddess Diana, as well as popular female divinities of uncertain origins: Abundia, Satia and Perchta, all of them connected with the cult of fertility. They led their disciples, who were always women, in nocturnal wanderings across country during the nights of the ember periods, followed by hosts of the dead made up of those who had prematurely perished: soldiers, children, victims of violent deaths who were condemned to roam without respite until the end of their allotted time on earth. Did the *benandanti* join in these mysterious excursions? It seems that some female *benandanti* did take part in them, in spirit, and that their main object in so doing was to contact the dead.

Women, who might be *benandanti*, were constantly accused by the Inquisition of frequenting the dead, as were the poor women of Corsica at the same period. Those who claimed to have seen the dead in nocturnal processions were condemned out-of-hand as witches. Some pathetically told how they had seen dead people, and offered to bring them to their living relatives, in return for minute rewards: five *soldi* for supporting a husband and children, or 'a few mouthfuls of bread'. The Inquisition of the Friuli was no more charitable to the poor than was that of Corsica, and reading their trials, it is difficult not to believe that the women really thought they had seen the dead. On Fridays and Saturdays and, particularly, on the eve of All Souls' Day, the vision was generalized: beds were made up in the houses and food prepared for the dead who walked through the streets on the night of 1 November carrying lighted candles to guide them to their former homes.

A more alarming vision of the dead was embodied in the belief in the 'Furious Horde' or 'Wild Hunt'. Led by a male figure who seems to have been Satan, and followed by a crowd of men and women, on foot and on horseback, it charged through towns and villages followed by malignant, menacing spirits of the dead. They were the hostile dead of primitive belief, unredeemed by the Christian doctrine of salvation, beliefs that have lingered on in Corsica, as has been shown.

Nothing resembling the 'Wild Hunt' or the 'Furious Horde' has however come to light in the island, unless it be the wild women of Chera who hunted their prey in packs, like hounds. But these *mazzere* were fulfilling a precise prophetic function, and Charles-André Culioli, who grew up in the village, remembers many of them as beautiful, blameless young girls. The goddesses Diana, Abundia, Satia and Perchta had apparently no following in Corsica. Classical archaeologists have found evidence of the cult of Diana in the antique city of Aleria; her name was given to the great lagoon that sheltered the Roman fleet; but, so far as I know, there is no trace of her cult in the interior, even though her attributes as goddess of the chase would seem relevant to a society that depended largely on hunting.[25] Presumably she was dethroned by the Christian Church, so that her very name was forgotten. The *mazzeri* recognize only the Christian God, and the undefined *qualcosa*, or *quellu quassu*: that which is above. Sinister processions of the unquiet dead did sometimes take place in Corsica, the '*Squadra d'Arrozza*' and the '*mubba*'; their message was simply that of impending death.[26] Corsican traditional beliefs spoke boldly and implacably of death: they were much less polluted by the concept of evil than those of the sixteenth-century Friuli. And they endured much longer; they were still alive after the Second World War whereas, according to Carlo Ginsburg, interest in witchcraft had died out in the Friuli before the seventeenth century.

The *benandanti* had also a reputation as healers, and this too was held against them by the Inquisition. Wild herbs were used, as in Corsica, where healers were likewise suspect. In 1621 a little boy was cured when on the advice of a *benandante* garlic and fennel were placed under his pillow. Fennel, the plant that served as weapons in the fights against witches, was naturally thought to have magical powers. It was also drunk in a *tisane* in Corsica to cure stomach aches. But the *benandante* was obviously counting on its occult rather than strictly medical properties, seeing that neither the fennel nor the garlic – a plant also used in popular Corsican medicine – would be consumed by the child. This attitude was appropriate, for the child's illness was attributed to an evil spell, as were all those treated by the *benandanti*. Illness and cures were thought to be equally contaminated by witchcraft; in the mind of the Inquisitors 'he who knows how to heal knows also how to destroy.'[27] It has been shown that popular healing in Corsica was liable to similar condemnation. The *mazzeri* were however never attacked on these grounds. Yet heal they did, in purity of heart, using the techniques of a parallel category of people known as *signadori*, as will now be told.

CHAPTER 8

The Shadow and the Light

Signadori – the Evil Eye – rites and prayers – past and
future – Christianity from overseas – miraculous Virgins –
shepherds' divination – love and marriage

Corsicans, when writing about the occult phenomena of their island,
tend to accord as much attention to the *signadori* as to the *mazzeri*, if
not more. Roccu Multedo, in his first work on the subject published in
1975, *Le mazzerisme et le folklore magique de la Corse*, devotes the first
half of the book to the *signadori*, as though they were to him more
significant than the *mazzeri*, of whom he nevertheless has much to
say. Pierrette Bertrand-Rousseau, who grew up in the island, is the
author of a university thesis published three years later that gives a full
account of the *signadori*, while making only a passing reference to the
mazzeri. Her title, *Ile de Corse et magie blanche*, indeed excludes the
mazzeri. Practitioners of an art that might appear dark rather than
white, they do not in fact perform magic of any kind, if magic be
understood as the influencing of persons, situations and events by
occult means. The *mazzeri* do not influence: they can only announce a
death that has already been decreed by a superior power.[1]

A reason for a certain reticence in connection with the *mazzeri* is no
doubt their relative inaccessibility. While they cannot be said to form a
secret society, they are few and diminishing in numbers and inclined
to keep themselves to themselves. I count as a major reward of my
years in Corsica to have been privileged to meet two of the last
practitioners of *mazzerisme*, and to hear them speak so freely of their
calling. But meeting *mazzeri*, even if they are communicative, does
not necessarily imply a complete understanding of them; various
aspects of their activities are enigmatic, obscure, belonging as they do
to the world of dreams. The *signadori*, on the other hand, much more

numerous at the present time, perform their function openly, in 'real life', in their homes, and are still to be met with in almost every village. They are generally regarded as antithetical to the *mazzeri*; while the latter may inspire fear or loathing because they are linked with death, the *signadori* are reassuring, proclaimed allies of health and happiness and well-being. They are held to represent the element of light in the Corsican occult world, while the *mazzeri* are shrouded in shadow. Yet on close examination this opposition is neither so clear nor so convincing as it at first appears.

Many, though not all the *signadori* cure natural illnesses. Knowledge of the medicinal properties of plants is part of the Corsican tradition, as has been told.[2] In the treatment of common ailments such as stomach-ache or worms the ministrations of the *signadori* may overlap with popular medicine. But the *signadori*, and they alone, can allay a malady against which plants are of no avail: their most valued function is to dispel the Evil Eye.

Belief in the Evil Eye is worldwide: according to a specialist on the subject, it is 'one of the hereditary instinctive convictions of mankind', the origin of which is 'lost in the obscurity of prehistoric ages'. Everywhere and at all times technicians of the occult have laboured to combat the Eye; the Corsican *signadori* have parallels the world over; incantations similar to theirs are remembered from Scotland to Ethiopia.[3] In speaking of them one is not therefore presenting a category of people specific to Corsica, like the *mazzeri*, but describing the particular Corsican reactions to a universal fear.

In Corsica the Eye, '*l'occhiu*', manifests itself in persistent head-aches, nausea, lack of appetite, unaccountable tears, while at the same time cruelly depriving its victim of the vital energy needed for resisting it. A person afflicted with the Eye slides into a state of physical and mental depression. It attacks for preference those who are in themselves weak, especially children. It may also assault domestic animals: cows and sheep and goats stricken by the Eye give no more milk, donkeys and mules waste away and become useless. It is thought of as an influence, or 'fluid' – the word is often used in this context – transmitted by the eye of a person motivated by jealousy: envious old women are the stereotyped authors of the Eye. Yet it is not specifically attributed to the *streghe* or *surpatori*, the human vampires who for so long lingered in Corsican belief.[4] Nor is the

Evil Eye associated with the *mazzeri*. It may however be projected by the angry dead, ever-present in the deeper layers of the Corsican psyche. In this instance it is described as the *imbuscada*, literally 'ambush', as though the victim were waylaid by a hostile wandering spirit in one of the danger spots of the Corsican countryside: near a river, a cemetery or an isolated tomb.

Archaeologists have postulated a belief in a primeval Mediterranean Mother Goddess who was also the author of the Eye; but evidence of her cult in Corsica is limited, as has been shown.[5] '*L'Occhiu*', in Corsica, is either more human or less personified. It may be deliberately cast by wicked old women, but also by otherwise harmless individuals who are unaware of doing so. According to Roccu Multedo, the affliction of the Eye, is hereditary in some families of the Sartenais, and for this reason incurable.[6] It may also, I have heard, exist without reference to any being, human or supernatural, something floating in the atmosphere, ever ready to destroy health and happiness. Precautions must constantly be taken against this lurking enemy. It is unwise, for instance, to compliment anyone for fear that the words will attract the notice of the Eye. Such remarks as 'What a beautiful baby you have', or 'How well you are looking' must immediately be followed by a protective formula: 'May God bless it', or 'God bless you'. Until not-so-distant times it was thought that spitting on the person concerned, or close to that person, ensured his immunity, in the belief that saliva repelled the Eye. Another gesture, still seen, is to *faire les cornes*, 'make the horns' (of the Devil), by pointing a clenched fist downwards with the first and little fingers extended.

Envy, *invidia*: the besetting Corsican sin. Envy it was that in times past instigated damage to property and, just as seriously, to reputations, provoked unforgivable acts and words that set family against family in interminable bloody vendettas. Its impact is no less violent today. Rival firms blow up each other's premises; money is extorted by armed threats and kidnappings; political extremists blow up visitors' holiday homes. Local political conflicts, inherent in democracy, traditional or modern, sometimes lead to murder: two mayors have been killed in recent years. José Gil, in a perceptive analysis of Corsican society, speaks of '*la lutte des envies*': 'the struggle of envies'.[7] Envy he defines as a natural lust for power, innate in individual Corsicans, which paradoxically establishes an equilibrium between them in communities that are essentially egalitarian and cooperative. Until, that is, envy, or rather envies, erupt into action, destroy the social harmony, and with it the warring individuals and whatever they have gained.

The prevailing Corsican attitude to success is indeed dangerously ambiguous. Those who achieve it, especially in political and administrative spheres, are adulated for the sake of the benefits they can bestow, but also severely criticized if they fail to meet expectations. Conspicuous wealth is resented as an aggression. Money, in Corsican thinking, is suspect, probably ill-gotten. Rich people are thought to be proud and heartless, a recurrent theme in popular tales.[8] The Corsicans were thus predisposed to welcome the Franciscan cult of poverty that penetrated the island from the lifetime of the saint. Yet envy, un-Christian envy, remained unsubdued. Curiously, it is less reproved by the Corsicans than pride, the opposing attitude in the same complex of behaviour, as though pride were the excuse for envy, its justification.

The *signadori* exert themselves against envy and the Eye by invoking the mystic forces of Christianity. Their intervention, though differing in detail from one person and one locality to another, conforms to an established rite practised all over the island. The *signadore*, who is likely to be a woman, pours cold water into a white soup plate and makes the sign of the cross above it three times with her right hand. She then lets fall into the water, again making the sign of the cross, three drops of hot olive oil from the little finger of her left hand. The oil was traditionally taken from the glass or metal lamp that stood on the mantelpiece; today it is scooped from any receptacle of heated oil. The *signadori* are so-called because their function is to sign, in Corsican *signa*, the particular signing that consists in pointing to the four extremities of the holy cross.

The plate containing the water and oil is sometimes held over the patient's head, sometimes laid on top of a lock of his hair on a table, or placed on a table where he clasps it between his hands. The rite is performed in a ceremonial silence during which the *signadora*, her eyes half-closed, seems to be entering a state of trance. In fact she is inaudibly reciting one of the appropriate prayers. These must be learnt at or near midnight on Christmas Eve, that sacred night when God comes to visit men and evil influences are inoperative. They may also, I have heard, be transmitted on the eve of New Year's Day. Taught by grandparents to grandchildren, they are thought to be inspired by the spirits of ancestors. If divulged by the *signadori* they lose their power.

The pattern made by the oil in the water reveals the patient's condition, his physical and mental health and whether or not he is suffering from the Eye. The Eye is shown when the oil disperses in little blobs and refuses to coalesce in spite of the prodding of the *signadora*'s finger. If it is the consequence of an *imbuscada* the oil flows all over the plate. The rite sometimes operates in such a way as to transfer the ill from patient to healer. The *signadora* is suddenly stricken with headache, nausea, tears: she is infected by the Eye until it is captured in the oil and water and expelled after she has broken the pattern with her finger and thrown the contents of the plate out of doors, or into the hearth.

When I first met a *signadora*, guided to her by Jean Cesari, I expected to be faced with a sinister old hag similar to those who cast the Eye. I found instead a fresh-looking middle-aged woman with trim modern clothes and the manner I associated with an old-fashioned English governess. 'You believe in God of course?' she said briskly; for the rite to take effect it is necessary that the patient should participate in the same area of belief as the person who performs it. At that time I thought my well-being was menaced by a persistently hostile individual; I could hardly pursue my career as a single woman freelance journalist without exciting *invidia*. I however said nothing of this to the *signadora*. But she confirmed my fears. 'May such a thing never come into the home of any family,' she cried as she scrutinized my plate, and thereupon flung it out of the window to break on some stones. Jean restrained me when I wanted to offer to replace it: the *signadori* function without thought of material reward and are indeed embarrassed by any show of gratitude. This one calmly took another plate from the dresser and twice repeated the rite; after the third time she judged that the danger had been exorcised. The change had perhaps been wrought on me rather than on my enemy; forewarned, I took extra care to avoid trouble.

Women are numerous among the *signadori*, as among the *mazzeri*. Pierrette Bertrand-Rousseau, while bringing to notice the activities of male *signadori* in the shepherds' communities, lists ninety women in the total of the hundred and eighteen *signadori* she met in Corsica, prospecting in Ajaccio, Bastia, Corte, Cap Corse, the Sartenais and the Niolo. My own experience suggests that women predominate as *signadori* in the villages. This must surely be attributed to the same factors that have drawn women to *mazzerisme*: being a *signadora* has offered them escape from the restricted, subordinate role allotted to them by society as well as an opportunity to exercise innate psychic gifts. The possession of such a gift is generally considered indispensable to a *signadora*, and judging by results some *signadori* are better endowed than others. Only one I consulted denied having any gift whatever: learning the prayers, she maintained, sufficed, the magic issued from the words. In so saying she was underlining, I think, the intensity of her inner life.

According to Roccu Multedo the postulant must be a practising Catholic, the mother of a family and over forty. The great majority of feminine *signadori* are indeed middle-aged or elderly, as though they had adopted their profession after their children had grown up and left home. Of the ninety interviewed by Pierette Bertrand-Rousseau, all but seven were over forty. All those I have met, men as well as women, belonged to this age group, while displaying widely different personalities. One I consulted, an elderly woman in a mountain village, moved with difficulty about her home. She had been a victim in her youth of infantile paralysis, she confided to me, and this had deprived her of marriage and motherhood. She had found her fulfilment in becoming a *signadora*. Another, who came to visit me when I was staying in a small seaside resort, was the owner-manager of a successful local hotel. She may have been over forty, but she was wearing a slinky low-necked scarlet cocktail-party dress and high-heeled gold sandals. Yet I was impressed by her qualities of sincerity and concentration. Perhaps her professional life had left underlying, half-conscious tendencies unsatisfied. These she may have inherited. The gift to dispel the Eye, like the proclivity to suffer from it, is said to run in certain families, the members of which affect each other by daily contact, by contagion, as also happens among the *mazzeri*.

The *signadori*, most evidently, are one and all devout Catholics. To judge from the available evidence they were not persecuted by the Inquisition that operated in Corsica between the mid-sixteenth and mid-seventeenth centuries, even though it had no hesitation in condemning women for trying to heal. The Christian emphasis of the *signadori*'s rites cannot, however, have ensured their immunity. On the contrary: the ecclesiastical authorities were particularly hard on anyone other than the clergy who made use of Christian symbols and formulae to achieve specific ends. Were not the *signadori* among those who recited prayers unauthorized by the Church whom Monseigneur Castagnola, in 1615, branded as adepts of Satan? Were they not alluded to in the diatribe published by Monseigneur C. F. Giustiniani forty-six years later, in which he urged the population to denounce to him or to the Inquisition whoever presumed to cure illness by means of 'superstition and incantations'?

Yet the *signadori* survived, and continued to perform their mission; perhaps precisely because, like the *mazzeri*, the were too well respected to be denounced. The clergy has tolerated them, if with a certain disdain. The Church historian S.-B. Casanova, though far from indulgent towards the *mazzeri*, as I have told, is lenient in his judgement of the *signadori*, or rather the *signadora*, whom he refers to as '*La Mammina*', a Corsican expression current in the Sartenais. Though she is addicted to superstition of a minor kind, he admits that she endeavours to remedy harm and to heal, and goes on to give an accurate, unprejudiced account of her techniques.[9]

The *signadori* I consulted, men and women alike, gave me a sense of security, and fortified my determination to deal with current problems. None of them, however, undertook to predict the future; *signadori* are not fortune-tellers. They can read thoughts and see into the present, but only a very few of the most gifted can see the future, and then only the general drift of the patient's life, without circumstantial detail. A young woman suffering from a fatal disease recently consulted a *signadora*. She did not pretend to be able to cure her, but true to her role of emanating light she foretold that this woman would live several months longer, as in fact happened, while saying nothing about her death.

Corsicans other than *signadori* tend, on the contrary, to see only death in the future, albeit without seeking that knowledge. The *mazzeri* foresee death in a symbolic act performed under compulsion, in dreams. Ordinary people may foresee death in dreams and in what might be called unsolicited visions. A man on his way to work one morning in Ajaccio glimpsed in the marketplace a cousin who, he thought, was then living in mainland France. He was, and that night he died. A woman I know dreamed of her sister, who was likewise living overseas; the dream was realistic except that the sister's face appeared as a blank white oval, without features. Soon afterwards she died. I met a young man in a mountain village recently invalided out of the army for tuberculosis; I was struck by the transparent pallor of his skin. He told his friends that his sister, who had been many years dead, came down from the cemetery situated on an upper slope and took him by the hand. Not long afterwards I learned that he had died. A cultured town-dwelling friend of mine detected in an eggshell the outline of a crucifix and of a funeral wreath; news of the death of a relative came the next day. Many people claim that the future can be seen in the shell of an egg laid on the day of the Ascension, which is supposed to keep fresh for a year and to possess a protective magic against illness and accident. Magic is likewise attributed to a certain herb – *Sedum stellatum L.* – which must be picked on that morning before dawn and nailed to an inner wall of the house, where it will remain forty days in flower. It is often seen in shepherds' cabins.[10]

The shepherds are the people in Corsica most given to predicting the future, and who deliberately practise this art. Their technique consists in holding up against the sun the shoulderblade of an animal, preferably a lamb, stripped of its flesh and skin. The pattern made by the sun shining through the bone offers a vision of the future. This procedure, which may be of very ancient origin, is mentioned by a Corsican chronicler of the sixteenth century; condemned in the seventeenth by the heresy-hunting bishop Castagnola, it nonetheless survived into the nineteenth. The shepherds' visions were grand in scale and impressed their fellow-countrymen. They predicted the shattering treaty of Cateau-Cambrésis in 1559, at the conclusion of the national rebellion led by Sampiero Corso, when his French allies traded back the island to the detested Genoese. And they foresaw the tragic death of the hero on the very eve of the day, 17 January 1567, when he was assassinated in the maquis. Later they predicted the whole epic story of the rise and fall of Napoleon. By such means unlettered herdsmen read their country's history in advance of the events. Yet they might as well have been reading it in a book. They never attempted to intervene in the dramas they foretold: while they could hardly have changed the treaty of Cateau-Cambrésis they might have detached a guard to protect Sampiero, murdered by his best friend with the complicity of the Genoese on the day after the prophecy. But for the shepherds what they prophesied was inevitable; it already belonged to the past because it was pre-ordained.[11]

The occult faculties of the Corsicans, paradoxically, tend to wipe out their awareness of the future: what will happen has for them already occurred. A traditional attitude that goes far to explain why the Corsicans, even today, have difficulty in envisaging new developments in their island and in taking steps to bring them about. The past weighs on them heavily, the present they endure: what will happen is inescapable; they simply wait for what comes. Until, unexpectedly, they react, rebel in a fury of pent-up resentment: Sampiero and others against the Genoese, Napoleon against the mediocrity of his family's condition, the resistants against the Fascist occupation, the nationalists against a centralized non-Corsican government. Not to speak of the innumerable individuals who at all periods, having endured harassing neighbours, domineering superiors, uncooperative relatives, faithless lovers and marriage partners, suddenly protest and kill, without concealment, in fact commit social suicide. Violent death by vengeance, years in hiding or in prison, may be the consequence of the act; but not necessarily remorse. Many Corsicans feel justified in their crimes; candidates for the penitent's role in the procession of the *catenacciu* may be booked up ten years in advance; but there is always more than a single murder in a single year.[12] The Corsicans have as scant respect for the sixth commandment, 'Thou shalt not kill', as for the tenth, which prohibits covetousness. Covetousness: the root of envy, of the Evil Eye.

The *signadori* do much to appease conflicts, unobtrusively, using their own chosen methods. They take no part in local quarrels, even when they well know what is going on in their communities. Their action is not directed against individuals, but against the Eye, the envy that is working through them. Their aim is to restore a harmony, psychic or physical, broken by the forces of destruction, by invoking those of Christianity. Roccu Multedo reports that in a certain prayer of the Sartenais an illness is referred to as a *miracula*: a supernatural happening. The *signadori* strive to induce a counter-miracle.

Their prayers appeal to the great figures of the Christian religion: '*Le père Sauveur*', God the Father; '*Le Saint Sauveur*', Jesus Christ; John the Baptist; the Virgin Mary; Saint Joseph and Saint Anne. In spite of the rule of secrecy quite a few have found their way into print, usually translated into French from the original mingling of Corsican and Italian. Those I quote here are doubly degraded, by being published, and in a language other than that in which they were composed, for as Roccu Multedo observes, their magic is in the sound of the words rather than their meaning.[13] In fact the meaning is often evasive:

> When Mary travelled across the sea
> Picking flowers of marrow
> She was measuring a garment for the Holy Saviour
> The pain leaves the eye and heart.

It is useless to look, here, for a rational sequence of sense. A description of a situation, the details of which are more or less incomprehensible, is interrupted by a declaration of the efficacy of the words: the affliction under treatment has been cured. Similarly, a prayer to stanch blood is cast in a sequence of declarations which pay tribute both to the Virgin Mary and to the magical quality of the number three:

> Mother Mary came by sea
> She held three lances in her hand
> One cut, the other wounded
> And the other stopped the flow of blood.

As Pierrette Bertrand-Rousseau remarks, the prayers are misnamed because they are recited in expectation of immediate results, whereas true prayers to God are not automatically granted. Certainly they are wanting in qualities of humility and supplication. The holy personages are abruptly ordered to effect the desired cure: 'Jesus, Mary, Joseph / Cure this ache of the head and heart.' The ache of head and heart, often mentioned, must surely be the Evil Eye, which is however never named. If the Eye has been cast in an *imbuscada*, then the saints are not appealed to, as though the hostile spirits of the dead were beneath their notice, and the so-called prayer is simply an injunction to depart: *'Fore ogni male'*, 'Get away all harm!' In an incantation against violent death, presumably composed in a time of war, the tone is even more peremptory:

> Stop, bullets, shot and cannon fire!
> As we saw Christ
> In the house of Anne
> If bullets, shot and cannon fire do not stop
> Then Christ does not exist!

Rather than prayers, the words recited by the *signadori* should be termed incantations, as is indicated by a Corsican expression describing their rite, *incantesimo*, while the *signadori* may be called '*incantatora*'. It cannot really be said that the incantations form a body of oral literature comparable to that of the *voceri* and *lamenti*, for they lack literary quality. Lines rhyme and scan, but the resources of literature are neglected. Adverbs and adjectives are seldom used; descriptions are bald if not incomprehensible. Their bareness and incoherence are somewhat surprising when one reflects that the Corsicans have an innate talent for verbal expression. In Latin, in Italian, in French and in their own language their output of literature, written or oral, is uninterrupted from the Middle Ages to the present day; an impressive performance of a small population living in rough circumstances.

The chroniclers, beginning with Giovanni della Grossa in the fourteenth century and continuing to Ambrogio Rossi in the time of Napoleon, are both invaluable to historians and make good reading, as do the memoirs of Sebastien Costa, Grand Chancellor to the precarious monarch Theodor von Neuhoff during the eighteenth-century rebellion. Churchmen in the entourage of Pasquale Paoli, C. Rostini, P. Guelfucci, are important witnesses of their time, as is the historian Renucci, contemporary and partisan of Napoleon. Napoleon, who had the originality of writing in French while his countrymen were still using Italian, after a youthful false start as a romantic but not uninteresting fiction writer, proved his talent in his letters and proclamations. In the late nineteenth century a movement analogous to the *félibrige* of Provence sought to give Corsican the status of a written language: the bishop de la Foata, then Santu Casanova and Maistrale left noteworthy verse. Meanwhile Jean-

Baptiste Marcaggi, writing in French, outstripped Mérimée in the horror of his true story of vendetta and banditry, besides producing one of the best-informed existing works on Napoleon's youth, *La Genèse de Napoléon*. He also carried out the valuable task of collecting and publishing traditional *voceri* and *lamenti*, as did Frédéric Ortoli, as well as a selection of traditional tales.

Corsican writers of the present day, in French and in Corsican, are far too numerous to be listed here. More than a hundred and twenty books are published every year in the island, while other Corsican authors find publishers in mainland France. Paul Silvani, chronicler of the insular resistance in the Second World War, Xavier Versini, champion of Charles Bonaparte, the often underrated father of Napoleon, are outstanding in the tradition of Corsican historians. Two Corsican fiction writers, Angelo Rinaldi and Marie Susini (deceased in 1993), hold a place in the limelight of French letters. Though residing in Paris, both have written exclusively of their island, to which they have been bound by anguishing hypnotic ties. Whenever she found herself in a plane approaching Corsica, writes Marie Susini, and the island 'brutally' appeared, 'harsh and sinister', she longed to get away without setting foot on its soil. So she concludes *La Renfermée La Corse*, a magical evocation of her loved-hated homeland, where even the sun, she observes, is tragic in its implacable presence. More recently a young poet and novelist, Patrice Franceschi, adventurous world-traveller and explorer of New Guinea, has created a spellbinding picture of rural Corsica in *Quelque chose qui prend les hommes*. Corsica keeps its hold on its writers, even after they have chosen to leave the island, even after they have denounced it.[14]

If the so-called prayers of the *signadori* are wanting in grace and coherence it is surely because they were composed by simple people, in desperate circumstances, and long ago. Conceived as magic, not as art, they were designed to bring specific results, not to charm or even to be understood since they were to be known only to a few initiates. Their bleak style, or rather non-style, is in fact characteristic of prayers and spells designed for like purposes the world over; an international mode of esoteric expression. Roccu Multedo has found incantations almost identical with the Corsican in Lunigiana, in Italy, midway between Genoa and Pisa. More surprisingly, incantations used in the Scottish Highlands resemble those of Corsica both in their lack of adornment and their form. So the Holy Trinity is pitted against the Evil Eye:

> Seven pater Maries will thwart the Evil Eye
> Whether it be on man or on beast
> On horse or on cow
> Be thou in thy full health this night
> In the name of the Father, the Son and the Holy Spirit.

A similar cry rings from distant Coptic Ethiopia:

> In the name of the Father and the Son and the Holy Ghost
> Deliver her from the sickness of the slave and the Eye.

The 'sickness of the slave' was epilepsy. Hymns and incantations of the Siberian shamans, of whom I shall speak later, though said by specialists to have a high literary quality, are marked by the same abruptness of manner.[15]

If the incantations of the *signadori* seem, as a whole, to emanate from medieval Christianity, it is hardly possible to determine their date. One may note that very many refer to Christianity as having come from across the sea, as though this were a recent happening. Mary arrived by sea carrying three lances, or a golden apple, or a robe for the 'Divine Saviour'; God himself came by boat as is stated in an incantation that also recalls the coming of the Franciscans:

> God arrived in a boat on the sea
> He held in his hand a golden lance
> Saint Francis cut and sewed
> The clothing of our Lord
> Holy Saviour rid me of the pain of this head and this heart.

Insistence on the sea-borne origin of Christianity surely derives from a collective memory of historical events. Christianity reached Corsica in Roman times. A firm tradition that Saint Paul preached there is not disproved: he may well have stopped in the island in the course of his missionary journeys between Rome and Spain, which were supposedly undertaken around 67 AD. Christians fleeing persecution in Rome and North Africa took refuge, it is thought, in the island. The recorded martyrdom of Saint Devota, a young girl brought up as a Christian, occurred in about 202 in the Roman settlement, Mariana. Her ascetic fortitude throughout her ordeals has led certain classical scholars to link this first phase of Corsican Christianity with a current Judeo-Greek mysticism. The martyrdom of other women followed; women seem to have been outstanding among the early Corsican adepts of the faith: Laurina at Aleria, Amanza near Bonifacio, Julia in Cap Corse, Restituta, whose remains lie in a fourth-century marble sarcophagus discovered in the parish church of Calenzana, in the Balagne. All are now revered as saints.[16]

The slow, painful penetration of Christianity was later threatened by Vandal and Saracen invasions, which must have left deep scars on the Corsican psyche. The urgency and violence of the *signadori*'s incantations might suggest that they derive from such heroic times. But in fact those for which any date can be suggested are more recent. The invocation against bullet and cannon fire cannot be prior to the sixteenth century, when firearms appeared in the island; perhaps it was composed during the wars of Sampiero Corso. Those that speak of Saint Francis may belong to any period after the lifetime of the saint.

The coming of the Franciscans revitalized Corsican Christianity, almost like a second conversion. Their influence increased through the centuries with the number of their foundations, generously supported by the population. Though sometimes centres of revolutionary activity, they were also, and above all, havens of security and spiritual serenity.[17] It was the Franciscans, seeking to mitigate the harshness of island life, who propagated the cult of the Virgin Mary, so often appealed to by the *signadori*. She is honoured all over Corsica in works of art of different periods that are credited with miraculous powers. All are supposed to have come from the sea, and several are believed to have been found by fishermen, who play a privileged role in these legends in the likeness of Christ's disciples. At Lavasina, on the eastern seaboard of Cap Corse, a sixteenth-century painting of the Virgin and Child in the manner of Perugino was apparently offered as an ex-voto by shipwrecked mariners. It is still believed to protect seafarers. How exactly a beautiful painting of the Virgin and Child reached the Franciscan monastery at Alesani, the base, for a time, of the militant

Giovannali, has been forgotten. Attributed to the fifteenth-century Sienese artist Sano di Pietro it was presumably the gift of a wealthy benefactor. This image, too, is thought to possess miraculous powers.[18]

A baroque wooden statue of the Virgin in the parish church of Fozzano, the vendetta-wracked village that inspired Prosper Mérimée, was found, it is said, by fishermen in the Gulf of Valinco, floating on the waves. She was so heavy that no one could lift her until two old men, come down from Fozzano, raised her without effort on to their shoulders and carried her back to their village, where she has remained in the parish church, author of many miracles. In fact, there is documentary proof that the statue was commissioned from a sculptor of Ajaccio in 1635; but the legendary tale is preferred.[19] Another statue of the Virgin, of white marble, found washed up on the east coast sands, was miraculously conveyed to a mountaintop where she is still venerated by the people of Cervione; I joined in their pilgrimage on 15 August to attend Mass in her chapel at dawn. Yet another figure, the celebrated 'Santa', a large painted wooden statue of the Virgin and Child, paraded at the fair of Casamaccioli on 8 September, was mysteriously transported from the west coast to this village in the heart of the Niolo. Following the procession I watched the men crowded round the roulette tables doff their cloth caps and wide-brimmed black felt hats as the venerated figure was carried by.[20]

The Virgin was upheld in opposition to the aggressive forces of male-dominated custom. Very many churches in Corsica bear her name. Two Pisan masterpieces, the cathedrals of Mariana and Nebbio, now stranded on the sites of vanished Roman towns, were dedicated to the Assumption of the Virgin (Santa Maria Assunta).[21] Later the elegant Renaissance cathedral of Ajaccio was named for Notre Dame de la Miséricorde (Our Lady of Mercy), revered as the city's guardian. Her statue, known as 'La Madonuccia', now standing in a niche of a building in the Town Hall square, is thought to have saved the inhabitants by miracle from an epidemic of plague brought from Genoa in 1656, as well as protecting them from bombing by an Anglo-Corsican fleet which in 1745 made a clumsy intervention on behalf of the Corsicans in their anti-Genoese rebellion.

A decade earlier the patriot leaders had in fact placed their nation under the patronage of the Immaculate Conception. The deeply stirring chant, 'Dio vi salvi, Regina' ('God save you, Queen') became the national anthem and is still sung at Corsican ceremonies, religious and others, with a mingling of exaltation and awe. Tradition maintains that it was spontaneously created on 25 August 1720 by a certain shepherd, Sauveur Costa, in a chapel at Corscia, a remote village high up in the Niolo. Perhaps he did sing it there, on that day, and it was previously unknown to his audience; but scholars have ascertained that it was composed in the seventeenth century by the Neapolitan Saint Francis of Geronimo, who adapted it in Italian from a Latin chant dating from the Middle Ages. Brought to the island, it seems, by itinerant churchmen, or by anti-Genoese rebels who had taken refuge in Naples, it was adopted by the Corsican patriots with a small but significant change of words. 'Give us victory over your enemies' ('Voi dai nemici vostri / a noi date vittoria') became 'Give us victory over our enemies' ('nemici nostri'), so that this hymn, originally imbued with tenderness and humility, was transformed into a war cry and the Virgin was officially mobilized into the national resistance.[22]

She had become not only queen but goddess of the island. No prehistoric forerunner paved her way; evidence for the cult of the Mother Goddess in megalithic Corsica is limited, as has been shown. Her victory was that of tenderness and light in a society overshadowed by violence and war, and so it was fitting that she should become the ally of the signadori. It would however be imprudent to assume a Christian origin for their practices. The Evil Eye is much older than Christianity. Their rites and prayers may well mask others, invoking forgotten pagan nature-spirits or divinities. The image of the sea-borne goddess is archetypal, and features in various ancient cultures: Aphrodite-Venus in the Greco-Roman, Isis in the Egyptian, Syrian Astarte, Sumerian Innana, Tiamat of the Enuma Elish, the Babylonian epic of creation. The sea, universal symbol of the source of life, offered the Corsicans an alternative to their rock-bound warrior-worshipping insular mythology.

The signadori may have been active for as long a time as the mazzeri before they Christianized their rites; in fear, presumably, of the Church, ever ready to persecute those who sought to heal or uttered incantations. The technique of divination with oil and water, widespread in the Mediterranean, is supposed to date from the Chaldeans.

It may not, however, have been originally used by the *signadori*. One may bear in mind that the olive tree was introduced to Corsica by the Greeks of antiquity. *Signadori* of an earlier period may have employed other substances. Today, some throw into the water grains of wheat, or scraps of heather, or salt, reputedly magical, or melted wax or lead.[23] One can also note that the berries of the lentisk, common in the Corsican maquis, can be crushed to produce oil, the so-called 'oil of the poor' which was still sometimes resorted to when I first reached the island. Certain *signadori*, moreover, can operate without any apparatus, *a secca*, literally 'dry', by making the sign of the cross on the patient's forehead, or in the air, standing in front of him so as to indicate his entire physical configuration. Analogous methods and signs may have been used by *signadori* contemporary with the prehistoric *mazzeri*.

Observers of the Corsican scene, and notably Pierrette Bertrand-Rousseau, regard the *signadori* as antithetical to the *mazzeri*. The *mazzeri* bring death, the *signadori* health; the *mazzeri* act surreptitiously, by night, in the maquis, the *signadori* openly, by day, in their homes. One can add that whereas the *mazzeri* act in a state of a dream, and under compulsion, the *signadori* act deliberately, of their own free will. Yet in view of the available evidence the contrast seems less conclusive. I heard of a woman of the southern Sartenais who some twenty years ago practised as a *mazzera* by night and as a *signadora* by day, to rid herself, she admitted, of a sense of guilt. Guilt such as not infrequently torments the *mazzeri*, as has been told.[24]

Signadori may temporarily assume the role of *mazzeri*, to judge by the following story reported by a reliable informant. The events took place in the inter-war years. Three young men were returning to their village by night, by car. They saw two women in white barring the road, whom they took to be spirits, and therefore dangerous. They turned back and reached the village by another route. The next day they called on a local *signadora* in the hope that she could deliver them from the danger by which they felt themselves to be threatened. However, they told her nothing of their experience. 'There were two waiting for you on the road last night,' she said. 'If I had arrived in time you would not have got away unharmed.' A healer by day, she was apparently a killer by night. A *mazzera*? Was the harm she spoke of symbolic or what is called 'real'? The confusion of the 'real' and 'parallel' worlds in this tale forbids any coherent interpretation.

The overlapping of roles suggests that those of the *signadori* and the *mazzeri* are not so incompatible as supposed. It seems possible that they both once shared a body of occult knowledge and skills that has since been fragmented, dispersed and in part forgotten. This is also the thesis of Jérôme Pietri and Jean Victor Angelini, authors of a recent work entitled *Le Chamanisme en Corse*, in which they assimilate the *mazzeri* and the *signadori* with the shamans, practitioners of the occult such as are still active in northern Siberia and some other archaic societies, which I shall discuss later. In Corsica it can be supposed that both *signadori* and *mazzeri* once possessed much wider powers than they now exercise. When I first arrived in Corsica I met an elderly man in the far south who remembered that certain *mazzeri* were also rainmakers. Their technique was to lay sheaves of corn in the bed of a stream. Charles-André Culioli of Chera spoke to me of a celebrated *mazzeru* who could raise and quell rain and storms. It is remembered that the people of Cauro, not far from Ajaccio, would place a skull in a dry river-bed to induce rain. One such skull was said to be that of the patriot hero Sampiero Corso, who was murdered in that neighbourhood. It worked so efficiently that it was swept away in a torrent brought on by an instantaneous cloudburst.[25]

Mazzeri and *signadori*, it seems, once collaborated as weather-controllers. The technique of the *signadori* in this matter is perpetuated by the shepherd-practitioners of the Niolo, whose art has been brought to notice by Pierrette Bertrand-Rousseau. The incantations she presents are not, strangely enough, designed to bring rain, but to avert it, rain storms being more dreaded in that mountain area than drought:

> Rain not
> Do not rain.
> Saint Joseph has fallen asleep
> Beneath the arms of Our Lord
> Stop, water! And shine sun!

Certainly the storms that hit Corsica with the break up of summer are terrifying. The old houses seem to shudder under the impact of booming thunder and slashing rain; the tall *laricio* pines sway and groan. Alone in the open, one feels oneself to be the condemned victim of the elements. The experience is of course the more dramatic in the mountains where the shepherds may be overtaken by a spell of bad weather in September, just before leading their flocks to lower areas for the winter.

Their main preoccupation is naturally the welfare of their livestock, as is expressed in the following all-embracing prayer pronounced once a year, in spring, after the sheep-shearing. It is the moment for the blessing of the flocks, sometimes performed with a priest assisting:

> White sheep, black sheep
> Which leave in the morning and return to you in the evening
> Go without harm
> Graze the good grass, leave aside the bad!
> Grow and multiply
> Fill the earth where you pass.

Water is then sprinkled over the animals, an acknowledgement of the beneficent quality of water unusual in a country where it is, by tradition, and so surprisingly, regarded as the abode of evil spirits. But this water has been blessed, so that it has a holy virtue akin to that of baptism.

The shepherds possess a variety of incantations against the destructive forces of nature that environ them: rain and lightning and storm, fire (the maquis and forest fires of Corsica can be devastating), illnesses peculiar to livestock and which can also afflict men, marauding dogs, and the eagle that swoops down to batten on new-born lambs.

> O little eagle
> Accursed bird
> May you be accursed by God
> And by the saints
> And by the crowing of the cocks
> And by the grand Mass of Christmas Eve.

So the humble ordinary cock is brandished as a counter-force to the majestic *aigle royal*, the royal eagle which is officially protected: thirty pairs of that bird, according to the Parc Naturel Régional, still inhabit the Corsican skies. It may be noted that for the shamans, practitioners of the occult in the Great North, the eagle is sacred.[26]

Animals gone astray can be traced and recuperated by the appropriate formulae, just as Saint Anthony is appealed to all over Corsica for finding lost objects, with or without the aid of the *signadori*. Cures can be invoked for the bites of poisonous insects; scorpions, and the *zinefra*, a venomous spider. Sunstroke, a prevalent mountain malady, conjunctivitis and bronchitis are all subject to the treatment of the *signadori*. In fact, the Corsicans have inherited an arsenal of magical cures designed to combat every ill that can befall them, natural or supernatural. But for the *signadori* all are supernatural, and therefore vulnerable to their rites and spells. Only one misfortune is not susceptible to magic: against death there is no appeal.

Roccu Multedo nevertheless remarks on the absence of prayers to remedy unrequited love: this terrible tribulation is apparently outside the scope of the *signadori*. Perhaps it was never brought to their notice. Corsicans, as has been described, brewed potions and indulged in occult proceedings to facilitate sexual adventures, but for the sake, it seems, of rapid physical conquest rather than what could be termed love. In fact romantic love, which looms so large in English life and letters, seems to have played little part in Corsican tradition. The social code left small place for it. Young people were married young, and often under pressure of their parents, to consolidate the position of their families or to avoid scandal if they had shown the least preference for each other in public. Personal sentiments were considered less than the interests of the families concerned. Status, rather than money, was the aim in view. Money was scarce; what counted was an alliance with a large number of upstanding men, able to produce food for their families and defend them in the all too frequent times of danger. Letizia Bonaparte was said to have been escorted to her wedding by more than fifty handsome male cousins. The story may be apocryphal, for no authentic account of her wedding has come to light; but it serves to illustrate a dominant attitude.[27]

Once married, the young couple was bound to its role of producing producers and protectors. 'Marriage is two people harnessed to a sledge dragging it up a mountainside,' a Corsican explained to me.

'The children are sitting on the sledge and it gets heavier and heavier with the years.' Yet this man was not complaining of his lot, nor thinking of abandoning his wife and children. Corsican husbands seldom do. Even today, when the sledge is lightened by the pill, they are steadfast if not always physically faithful partners. The fidelity of wives has always been taken for granted; exceptions are well concealed to avoid dramatic sequels.

In such conditions Corsicans have not been much given to pining for love. Confronted with obstacles they either renounced their feelings for good, or acted on them and took the consequences. These might be tragic. A Corsican girl was seduced in the inter-war years by a man of a neighbouring village on promise of marriage. To prepare for their conjugal life he went to continental France to find work. It seems his intention was not to prepare for marriage but to avoid it. When the girl discovered she was pregnant she wrote to him, but received no answer. She gave birth to her child in humiliation and shame. When he returned she arranged to meet him at a crossroads between their two villages. They met; without discussion she shot him dead. She was tried and acquitted.

Many tales of violent death could be told in connection with unhappy love. One that occurred fairly recently involved both partners. The daughter of a country magistrate loved a young man without prospects or property, the son of a refugee from a foreign country. The girl's father, furious, sent her to continental France to forget her love. She did not. She returned in secret and went to live with him in a nearby village. They existed in extreme poverty, ostracized by society. When need and exclusion became too hard to bear they went to a rock outside the village and there killed each other. In these suicide pacts the man first shoots the woman and then turns the gun on himself. Such solutions are not contrary to Corsican principles.

Divorce and the pill, which have reached Corsica only within the last fifteen years, have certainly alleviated the intensity of love's dramas. Strangely enough, the pill was more readily accepted than divorce, which has become current only within the last decade. At the same time, the authority of the family has dwindled; the young have left the land; parents no longer arrange marriages or are not listened to if they attempt to do so. Young Corsicans, congregating in the towns, have discovered new ways of loving. And also new forms of unhappiness. Suicides, carefully concealed from the media, have become increasingly frequent. Are they caused by unrequited love? Or rather by economic frustration? Of the 13,500 Corsican unemployed, the majority are young.[28] Loneliness consequent on the breakup of village life, reassuring in spite of all its severity, is another element in despair. Road accidents, the punishment for the new thrill of fast driving, take their toll of victims crippled, maimed or dead. The Evil Eye is replaced by new forms of suffering, less mysterious, perhaps, but no less overwhelming.

CHAPTER 9

Magicians of the Chase

Shamans of the Great North – initiation – journey
to the underworld – to heaven – shamans and *mazzeri* –
Murngin shamans – Azande witchcraft

Are the *mazzeri* shamans? Can *mazzerisme* be termed a Corsican shamanism? These questions have been much debated by specialists of the Corsican occult. The answers depend very much on how shamans and shamanism are defined. The name was first given to practitioners of the occult, so-called 'technicians of the sacred', men and women of the Great North, in Siberia, Lapland and Alaska; later it was extended, rather confusingly, to more or less similar categories of people known as 'medicine men' in North, Central and South America, as well as Indonesia, Oceania, black Africa and aboriginal Australia. Can it now be applied to Corsica? Roccu Multedo maintains it can, even though this implies classing the Corsicans among the most primitive peoples existing in the world today.[1]

Travellers from the Great North, since its exploration in the fifteenth century and especially in the nineteenth, have brought back a wealth of evidence about the magico-religious activities of the shamans, now the subject of fascinating full-length studies.[2] For fascinating these people are, and fantastic. Like the *mazzeri* they operate in the world of dreams, dreams which like those of the *mazzeri* pass for reality in the minds of both the shamans and their fellow tribesmen: the phenomenon of a collective unconscious is discernible in this context as in rural Corsica. The function of the shamans is to procure the well-being of the tribal groups; in this they less resemble the *mazzeri* than the *benandanti* of the Friuli three centuries ago.[3] In the words of Mircea Eliade, a leading authority on the subject, the shamans defend life, health and abundance against death, disease, sterility and the 'world of darkness' by intervening with the gods and supernatural beings. It is they who cure illnesses, read the future, control the weather and, most important of all, ensure the success of the chase.

The shamans belong to societies that live mainly by hunting, fishing and food-gathering, with stock-breeding as a subsidiary activity. Agriculture, at least in the Great North, for climatic reasons, is minimal. Such conditions, one may suppose, were those of the prehistoric, pre-Neolithic *mazzeri*. Eliade believes that shamanism dates back to 25,000 BC, and observes that representations of the shamanistic trance can be detected in a celebrated Paleolithic relief in the cave of Lascaux. The shamans, in common with the *mazzeri* and other prehistoric Corsicans, acknowledge no supreme Mother Goddess, the divinity which throughout the Mediterranean presided over the fertility of the crops. Spirits of ancestors, as in Corsica, were revered by the Siberian shamans, as well as an ill-defined supreme celestial being comparable to the Corsicans' *qualcosa* or *quellu quassu*, 'that which is above'. Erlik, lord of the dead and the dark underworld, is his counterpart. Between humanity, dead and living, and the gods of above and below is a host of gods and goddesses and spirits often associated with the forces of nature. I should perhaps add that the shamans inhabit areas that are in theory Christian, but where the influence of the various churches is slight or negligible.

The shamans act as intermediaries between the people and the unseen powers. Their communities rely on them to remedy every misfortune. Shamans may also be harmful. Black shamans exist who cause disease and death; but in the Great North, at least, they are much less numerous than those who help and heal.[4] Candidates for shamanism are impelled by a mingling of inclination and contagion, as is also true of the *mazzeri*. Heredity, and the proximity of family life, as in Corsica, play important roles. Given the public, indeed spectacular nature of shamanism, it is hardly possible for a shaman's son to resist following his father's example. But he may also be drawn to shamanism by innate psychic gifts that cannot be denied. These are supposed to be derived from the spirits of dead shamans, but they may also be personal and spontaneous.

Shamanistic tendencies manifest themselves in early years, as may happen in the development of the *mazzeri*. A child becomes taciturn and withdrawn, he has strange, alarming dreams or hallucinations, he is subject to convulsions or epilepsy. Later, at the age of around thirteen, he retires into the forest, lives there alone for days on end in the terrible Arctic cold that may be seventy degrees below zero, feeding himself on the bark of trees. He may commit apparently demented actions, like leaping into iced water, or stepping into fires, or slashing himself with knives. By such signs his destiny is proclaimed; his family will call upon an elderly, expert shaman to instruct him in the techniques of what will be his calling. Thereafter he will bear its mark. Like the *mazzeri*, the shamans are distinguished by their peculiar, penetrating gaze.

The initiation of the *mazzeru*, as has been related, is accomplished in a single night's hunting, when he is 'called' in a dream by a practised *mazzeru*, who may be an older relative.[5] His experience of the compulsory killing or harming of an animal representing a human being may be traumatic, but it is mild indeed compared with what is endured by the postulant shaman; or rather, what he dreams he has endured. The ordeal, which lasts from three to nine days, follows the cycle of suffering, death and resurrection, an archetypical pattern that is enshrined in Christianity. Suffering occurs when the demons, who inhabit the densely populated mythological universe of the shamans, set upon the postulant and hack his body to pieces, gouging out his eyes, chopping off his head, tearing out his inner organs and cutting them into slices. He will then be exposed to the exalting shock of a brilliant light pervading his whole being: the light of knowledge that will enable him to see the future and rescue souls drawn down by demons into the underworld.

But now it is he who is assaulted by demons, or by the spirits of hostile ancestors which drag him to the realm of darkness and death. He cannot avoid them; indeed, he must not do so; on the contrary, he has to encounter and master them in order to possess himself of their vital energy, which he will subsequently use for his own ends. Finally those which have dismembered him repair him. His skeleton is reconstructed: his bones are joined together with clamps of iron, a substance believed by the shamans, as in Corsican popular tradition, to have protective qualities. The bones are then covered with new flesh; new organs are placed in his body into which new blood is poured. A shaman cannot cure illnesses unless he has been submitted to this physical dismemberment.

The trials imposed vary in different tribes. According to another programme, the postulant is taken up into the sky by the spirits of the ancestors to be instructed by the assembled gods before being cut up and roasted over a fire during seven days and nights. Yet another tradition maintains that the spirits of the ancestors cut him up, eat his flesh and drink his blood. A woman shaman reported that she was initiated when a band of strange men carved up her body and boiled it in a cauldron, a procedure that recalls the dream-banquets of the *mazzeri*.[6] Women are numerous among the shamans, as among the *mazzeri*; certain tribes indeed believe that the first shaman to appear on earth was a woman, and that woman is the origin of all magic. The shamanistic mythology includes many feminine divine or semi-divine beings, all associated with animals or with the forces of nature: a goddess of the sun, of fire, a 'Lady of the Waters', a 'Lady of the Young White Horse' and a 'Lady of the Animals': an Arctic Diana? The 'Gentle Lady of the Nativity' suggests a parallel with the Virgin Mary, but the 'Mother of the Seal' seems to be a more powerful divinity, patroness of the animal on which depends the main nourishment and so the survival of the tribe. A 'Celestial Bride' is also mentioned among the spirits that can assist the shamans.

The candidate to shamanship emerges from his trials transformed, regenerated. He can never disavow the experience; like the *mazzeri*, he cannot abandon his calling without putting himself in jeopardy. By his initiation he has become a consecrated person, able to converse with the gods. So he believes, and so believe all those surrounding him. The shamans, like the *mazzeri*, have the faculty of convincing others that their dreams are reality. In fact, during the initiatory period, the future shaman has all the time been lying in his yurt, the tent made of felt that is his family's home. He has existed in a state of coma, without food or drink. If it lasts too long his relatives may conclude that he has died, and make preparations for his funeral, so that he risks being buried alive. But most often he is welcomed back in time to the land of the living as a superior, privileged being.

Described by Mircea Eliade as a 'specialist of the human soul', the shaman enjoys immense prestige. He is not however a priest. Shamans do not form a religious sect, they do not propagate a dogma or follow a calendar of rites. Nor do they attend those performed by the official clergy, such as weddings and funerals, although they may be summoned to the latter if it is esteemed that their presence may serve to scare away spirits of the deceased unwilling to leave their earthly environment. Occupying a marginal place in society, like the *mazzeri*, the shamans live and practise alongside the clergy of the established churches; apparently without friction: I have found no report of a persecution of the shamans.

The dream of dismemberment is only the beginning of the shaman's training; he has much to learn, now that he is thought to have acquired the ability to do so. The elders of his community instruct him in the traditions of the tribe. He must acquaint himself with the spirits that will become his guardians and guides. The shamanistic world is crowded with spirits, spirits of the ancestors, spirits of nature – of the trees, of the water and the winds – and spirits of the reindeer, bears, wolves, fish and birds. All the birds, including the eagle, accursed by the Corsican shepherds but for the shamans the emblem of the Supreme Being.[7] He must learn their language, or rather recapture the language that in the beginning of time was given by the lord of the universe so that men and animals might live together in harmony and exchange identities – a widespread myth which has actually lingered on in Corsica, not only in many popular tales but in the existing beliefs of the population in connection with their own experience, and those of the *mazzeri*.[8]

To summon the spirits the shaman must learn to play the drum. This primitive instrument is significant in Corsican tradition: the drum which heralds the march of the phantom funeral procession, the *Squadra d'Arrozza*, or which announces an imminent death.[9] For the shamans it is sacred and indispensable: it summons spirits and supernatural beings, creates a link between the invisible world and man. It acts as a drug, on shamans and others; according to reliable reports shamans perform 'real' surgical operatons on patients anaesthetized by the beating of a drum.

The completion of a shaman's initiation is usually marked by a public ceremony in the presence of the assembled tribe. On this occasion he may perform no less a feat than ascending to heaven. Shamanistic society holds to the ancient, once worldwide belief that the universe exists on three levels: the earth, inhabited by men, the sky, abode of superior beings, and the underworld where dwell evil spirits and the dead. The shaman has the power to travel at will from one level to another. At his consecration ceremony an older shaman plants a birch tree cut from the forest in his yurt, its roots in the hearth, its summit piercing the roof. The tree symbolizes the Axis of the World, and is also sometimes planted in the centre of the shaman's community, crowned with the image of one of the celestial birds: eagle, wild goose or diving bird. Only a shaman has the right to climb it; its sacred qualities enable him to reach the sky.

The shaman climbs with ease the tree planted in his yurt, raises his hand above the roof and calls aloud to the gods to give good hunting to the tribe. A male goat is sacrificed; he is smeared with its blood while the onlookers beat their drums. Eight attendant shamans follow his example. The drum induces a state of trance that prepares them for their cosmic journeys. The shamans believe that by communicating with the gods and demons of above or below they can change the lot of their fellow beings. What is even more strange is that their audiences believe they can do so. A shaman's first duty is to heal: if he neglects to exercise this power he himself falls ill. The tribes of the shamans, in common with many primitive peoples, regard illness not as a natural happening but as the work of hostile agents, a belief that underlies the practices of *mazzeri* and *signadori*. Minor ailments can be treated, as in Corsica, by popular remedies concocted from wild plants.[10] But a serious illness implies that the spirit of the sufferer has been seized by a demon, and in these situations only a shaman can effectively intervene.

To recover the stolen spirit, the shaman must travel down to the realm of darkness and wrest it from the great god Erlik. The journey is preceded by a complex sequence of rites and ceremonies in the presence of the shaman's family and tribe. An animal is sacrificed, a cow or a reindeer; its flesh is consumed by the assembled company and its blood poured into a wooden bowl to be offered to the demons. But first it is imbibed by the shaman, who then spits it out with a torrent of imprecations. Blood is important in shamanistic ritual; one may note its absence in the practices of the *mazzeri* who may strike with axe or knife or lance yet never, to my knowledge, speak of an effusion of the blood of their prey.

On such occasions the shaman will apostrophize the demons in verse. Shamans, like *mazzeri*, are natural poets. A specialist on the subject, Mario Mercier, emphasizes the richness of their language: the shamans of the Yakouts, he reports, use a vocabulary of 12,000 words, whereas their tribesmen limit themselves to 4,000. Some of their chants have been recorded, translated into French and published; they are distinguished by an imperative style that also characterizes the incantations of the Corsican *signadori* and various practitioners of the occult in other parts of the world, as has been shown. A shaman of the Yakouts addresses the demons at a healing ceremony:

You have caused this harm
With your flesh you have created this illness
With your blood you have fed the pain . . .
So I insist
So I abuse you
By the blood of a bluish mottled cow [literal rendering from the French]
I inflect your thoughts
I am quits with you.

On the evening following the sacrifice the shaman dons his ritual costume, a gown falling to his ankles, cut into fringes and hung with metal discs and bells. Heavy and cumbersome as it may be, it in no way hinders him dancing hours on end as he prepares himself for his journey. Leaping, dancing, singing and beating his drum, with his eyes closed yet never colliding with the audience packed into the yurt, he summons his guardian spirits. He speaks to them in language they can understand. Birds are called with their specific cries: the cooing of the dove, the hooting of the owl, the cawing of the crow. Animals too are imitated, by his voice and by imitating their movements as they enter into his being. The shaman growls like a bear and steps with its heavy tread, whinnies and stamps his foot like a horse, and if his auxiliary spirit is a snake, as may happen, he twists and writhes on the ground. Finally he collapses, exhausted: his journey has begun.

His route is fraught with dangers and obstacles. First he must ascend and descend a mountain, then find the sacred tree, the Axis of the World, by which he can climb down into the nether regions. There he must cross three rivers. Clouds of darkness gather, in which lurk monstrous beasts; the audience in the yurt strike sparks from fire-stones to light him on his way. For all this time he has been reporting his progress, in song, or sometimes in a high, thin, unnatural-sounding voice which is recognized as that of the evil spirits which have now entered his body. In Corsica, be it noted, the spirits of the dead in the *Squadra d'Arrozza* also speak in high-pitched voices strange to human ears.

The shaman's journey is thus eagerly followed, step by step, by his family and friends. They can make light to encourage him, but they can do nothing to help him cross the ravine spanned by a bridge no more than a hair's-breadth wide and full of the whitened bones of shamans who have failed the test. Evil spirits rain arrows on him; the groans of the dead and the clanking of their chains are heard above the howling of the gale. The horrors of the shamanistic inferno rival those of the medieval Christian hell. The shaman's exploits also call to mind those of Orpheus when he penetrated Hades to rescue Eurydice; Orpheus who, in the words of Mircea Eliade, has 'all the characteristics of a great shaman'. A version of this myth, as has been related, is embodied in a Corsican popular tale, with a woman as the heroic defeated traveller.[11]

The well-initiated, well-prepared shaman triumphs over every difficulty. He dominates the evil spirits because he has learned, during his training, how to capture their energy and turn it against them. He is full of confidence when he approaches the terrible Erlik in his palace standing in the seventh circle of hell, built of black stone and clay. Warding off the fierce dogs that guard it, he addresses the god in a poetic invocation. Translated from the French, one of them runs:

> Dreaded Erlik, I salute you
> Venerated lord of the black face
> Whose body is dark as the night.
> Turn away your long eyes filled with black fire.
> I am come here, to you
> To offer you this cup
> The essence of my heart . . .[12]

Erlik is not implacably hostile to man. After making the formal address the shaman presents him with the spirit of the animal he has sacrificed before leaving home, and demands in return the spirit of the ailing human being he has undertaken to save. Discussions follow, often long and arduous, but the shaman, if sufficiently masterful, ends by getting his way. The god accepts the sacrifice and returns the spirit of the afflicted person. The shaman then travels home by the same perilous route by which he has come. Reaching his yurt, he collapses on to the ground; where he has in fact been lying ever since the start of his journey.

By such means shamans cure many illnesses, save lives. Or are thought to do so. It does in fact seem possible that their dramatic intervention operates as a powerful psychic antidote to certain maladies. To know that such efforts are being made, such hazards faced, such risks run, may well stimulate a strong positive reaction in the patient's system, just as the rites of the *signadori* alleviate certain states of ill-health, if in a lesser degree. The shaman has another duty to perform. If he has failed to cure, or has not been called upon in time, he must act as psychopomp: he who guides the spirits of the dead to the world below. The people of shamanistic societies, like the Corsicans, have an ambivalent attitude to the dead. While ancestors are much respected and often called upon to dispense advice and wisdom, the recently dead are regarded with distrust. It is feared, as in Corsica, that they may linger in their homes and capture the spirits of the living to join them in their journey to the world of the dead. And as in Corsica, a burial is followed by a copious funeral banquet, a farewell gesture to the deceased who, it is thought, will not depart before it has been accomplished. A similar belief must surely underlie the similar Corsican custom.[13]

The shamanistic peoples, at least in the Siberian north, consign all their dead to the underworld. Only the shaman has access to the celestial realm. There he purifies himself of the contamination of the nether regions and intercedes with the gods on behalf of his tribe. To prepare for the ascent he erects a new yurt, and plants in it a birch tree, symbol of the Axis of the World. Nine notches are cut into its trunk representing the nine circles of heaven. An animal is sacrificed, usually a white horse; the shaman and his audience partake of its flesh, which is thought to contain its spirit. The shaman then goes through his repertoire of song and dance and drum-beating until he induces in himself the desired state of ecstasy. He climbs the tree trunk, and as he sets foot on each notch he proclaims that he has reached the corresponding circle of heaven. He speaks loudly to the gods and repeats to the audience their replies, their predictions and their promises to the community. So he continues until he reaches the ninth notch, the ninth circle, before falling to the ground, unconscious. He wakes up only an hour or so later to tell the audience how he has returned from a long and rewarding journey.

Such in broad outline are the practices of the shamans, performed with only minor variations all over the Great North. The differences between them and the *mazzeri* need hardly be underlined. The shamans labour for the welfare of their communities; the *mazzeri* do no more than convey warnings of death. Whereas the shamans act in public, before an audience, employing considerable histrionic skill, the *mazzeri* go about their business discreetly, in the words of Georges Ravis-Giordani, 'clandestinely'.[14] Most significant is the contrast between the authority of the shamans and the subservience of the *mazzeri*: shamans command, *mazzeri* obey. *Mazzeri* are called to go hunting by an unknown unseen power. The shamans decide the time of their journeys and deliberately enter a state of trance by a perfected technique that has earned them the title of 'masters of ecstasy'.[15] They converse with gods and spirits on equal terms, and in so doing may save lives, whereas the *mazzeri* can only transmit decrees of death.

The scope of the shamans' activities is incomparably wider than that of the *mazzeri*. *Mazzeri* hunt in the familiar Corsican maquis, or even in the streets of their villages. The shamans cover vast distances: the Great North of Siberia is three times larger than the surface of Europe. The shamans of certain tribes are said to gallop on eight-hooved horses, others are thought to fly, not like the witches or the *streghe* of European and Corsican tradition, clumsily astride a broomstick or a part of a spinning wheel,[16] but simply by extending their arms, as a bird spreads its wings. In this way they can float over enormous territories as well as explore heaven and hell. The *mazzeri*, on the other hand, are confined to their island. I know of only one *mazzeru* who, as I have told, dreamed of entering a landscape other than that of Corsica. The mountains, he said, were even higher, the land was barren and traversed by great rivers; a scene more resembling the Great North of the shamans, though without the snow.[17] I can offer no explanation for his vision. Had he read books about the Siberian shamans, so that images of their country had lodged in his unconscious? This seems to me most unlikely, for books on exotic subjects were then hard to come by in Corsica, particularly in a remote inland village.

Had he done so, he would have become acquainted with the numerous creatures of shamanistic mythology, which are unknown to the *mazzeri*. While the shamans move at ease in a host of gods and spirits, the *mazzeri* oscillate uneasily between the Christian God and the obscure *Qualcosa* or *Quellu Quassu*. They may indeed appear as poor, cramped, fearful creatures beside the majestic shamans. Yet what they have in common with the shamans is perhaps as significant as what they lack. *Mazzeri*, like the shamans, are intermediaries between their communities and the supernatural powers. Their function, though limited, is not as negative as it might appear to the modern mind. By communicating with the powers that are thought to decree death they can forestall it, explain it, and so diminish some of the terrible violence of its impact. And they may also share with the shamans the role of healers, insofar as they are also *signadori*.[18]

In times past this was perhaps their major activity. The image one can now form of the *mazzeri* may represent no more than a fragment of what they once were. The matter of their dreams, no less than their characteristic style of day-to-day behaviour, suggests that they originated in a pre-agrarian society of hunters and food-gatherers. But while the shamans still inhabit such a world, for the *mazzeri* it is no more than a memory confined to dreams. Long long ago, before the invention of agriculture, the *mazzeri*, one may suppose, formed a privileged caste, operating as healers, seers and controllers of the weather as well as intermediaries between the supernatural dealers of death and the living. Death was perhaps not their overriding preoccupation; if it has become so this is perhaps because it is all that has been left to them after being subjected to various and formidable pressures through the millennia.

Repeated invasions and conquests, the imposition of alien cultures, of law and order that so often led to disorder, combined to marginalize the *mazzeri*. The all-pervading Christian Church assumed the monopoly of contacts with the supernatural. If it never, apparently, persecuted the *mazzeri*, it discredited them by encouraging the population to think of them as ill-baptized. Its one action in connection with the *mazzeri* consisted of rites of exorcism by which they could be divested of their powers. By such subtle means the Church stimulated a psychological conflict which has left few *mazzeri* unscathed. At the same time the Church gained complete control over the practices of *signadori* and so severed them from the *mazzeri*. This view, as I have observed, is shared by Jérôme Pietri and Jean-Victor Angelini, authors of *Le Chamanisme en Corse, ou une religion néolithique*. Following Roccu Multedo in assimilating shamans and *mazzeri*, they regard the practices of both as manifestations of a world-wide Neolithic religion. Although, in *Granite Island*, I ascribed the origins of *mazzerisme* to the Neolithic Age, I now think that pre-Neolithic would be a more suitable term. Shamanism is undoubtedly far older. Mircea Eliade, leading authority on the subject, as I have mentioned, detects representations of shamans in Paleolithic cave engravings.[19]

The Siberian shamans have survived because they have been little affected by Christianity. The evangelization of the Great North was attempted relatively late in history, not before the tenth century, and often with superficial results. Missionaries from various churches and countries, the Orthodox in Russia, the Protestant in Scandinavia, the Catholic in North America, made repeated incursions over the centuries, particularly in the nineteenth; Muslim and Buddhist influences filtered in from Asia; but none of these creeds seriously undermined the indigenous aboriginal animism or the authority of the shamans. A traveller from Alaska recently spoke to me of some Christian missionaries who went there some fifty years ago and left completely frustrated and discouraged. To liken the *mazzeri* to the shamans is to disregard determining factors of religious environment. While it may be said that *mazzeri* belong to the same order of human beings, the resemblance cannot, I think, be pushed further.

Roccu Multedo, however, attributes to the *mazzeri* certain beneficent powers characteristic of shamans. He draws a distinction, as I have explained, between white *mazzeri* and black. The black, designated as *mazzeri acciaccatori*, relish hunting and killing, like some female *mazzeri* described to me by Jean Cesari. The white *mazzeri*, described as *salvatori*, exert themselves to save their prey. This they may achieve by stanching the blood of the inflicted wound, as I have described. Or else they may prevent their victim from crossing a stream, the abode, in Corsica, of evil spirits and the frontier between the worlds of the living and the dead; in traditional Corsican thinking every stream represents the Styx. The *mazzeru salvatore* must also stop his prey from entering a church, which is associated in the popular mind with the office of the dead; to enter a cemetery is just as fatal. Multedo also maintains that the *mazzeri* who are able to travel vast distances, may, like the shamans, act as psychopomps, that is, accompany the doomed to the underworld.[20]

I have, I admit, found no confirmation of these beliefs. But perhaps I arrived too late in Corsica, when the people who could have told me of them had already joined the dead. I can only suggest that the *mazzeri* may once have possessed powers similar to those of the shamans, and that *mazzerisme* and shamanism may once have been analogous, but several thousand years ago.

One may imagine the *mazzeri*, thousands of years ago, at a time before agriculture had tied the Corsicans to particular tracts of soil, a time when men and women roamed freely about the mountains and forests and beaches; hunting wild animals, fishing in streams and in pools and in the sea, scraping shellfish off rocks, gathering nuts and berries. Including chestnuts: the life-giving chestnut tree is indigenous to Corsica, indeed existed there before the island came into being: a recently discovered fossilized imprint of its branches dates from twenty-five million years.[21]

The Scottish writer James Boswell, an enthusiastic disciple of Jean-Jacques Rousseau, felt he was living the life of the earliest Corsicans when he walked across the island with his guides to visit Pasquale Paoli in 1765. 'When we grew hungry,' he recalls, 'we threw stones among the thick branches of the chestnut trees that overshadowed us, and in that way we brought down a shower of chestnuts with which we filled our pockets, and went on eating them with great relish, and when this made us thirsty we lay down by the side of the first brook, and drank sufficiently. It was just being for a little while one of the *prisca gens mortalium*, the primitive race of men . . .'[22]

Thanks to the under-development of Corsica, deplored by some and applauded by others, it is still possible to savour such experiences, even though the Corsicans, who were not really so very primitive when Boswell knew them, now share most of the advantages and disadvantages of the contemporary civilized world. But the crashing technological invasion of the 1960s nonetheless left untouched much of the interior. And though certain traditional types of people, for better or for worse, have disappeared – the human vampires, the storytellers, the bards – the *signadori* are still numerous enough to attract attention. Meanwhile, some thirty *mazzeri* still practise in the extreme south, as though *mazzerisme* were too deeply rooted in the Corsican psyche to be totally eradicated.

The *mazzeri* serve their communities only as messengers of death. They differ from certain shamans and medicine men in that they never act with hostile intent. People called shamans operate both as healers and killers among the Murngin aborigines of Australia, tribes that support themselves essentially by hunting and food-gathering. The killer, known as a 'soul-stealer', performs what is regarded as a duty by killing either enemies of his community or private enemies that have murdered his own kin. He thus commits acts of vengeance such as were carried out by the Corsican bandits. The Corsicans have projected the avenging of the murdered dead into the physical sphere; the Murngin carry out the same obligation by occult means.

The Murngin soul-stealer is initiated by an older shaman with several killings to his credit; he is thought to have obtained his exceptional powers from the spirits of those he has slain. The postulant soul-stealer cannot assume his status in his community until he too has killed at least once and so entered into direct contact with the spirits of the dead. The Murngin are in fact thought to derive their powers from their victims, a belief of which I have found no parallel in Corsica. The technique of the soul-stealers belongs to the mysterious irrational dream-world known to the *mazzeri*. The killer creeps up on his victim when he is asleep, lassoes him round the neck and drags him into the bush. There he thrusts a 'killing stick' into his heart. The man is killed; but being unconscious he knows nothing of what has been done to him until he awakes and the soul-stealer informs him that he has only three days left to live. Though the surgical operation has left no physical trace, the soul-stealer will describe it in sufficient detail to convince the victim that it has really taken place. Utterly demoralized, he invariably dies within the stated number of days. The hostile motivation of the soul-stealers distinguishes them radically from the *mazzeri*, who have no enemies, except their fellows in the neigh-bouring villages when they attack them in the yearly dream battles.[23]

A similar distinction differentiates the *mazzeri* from the sorcerers of the Azande tribes, which are spread over the territories of the southern Sudan, Zaire and the Central African Republic.[24] The sorcerer, it is believed, is born with the 'stuff of witchcraft' in his body. He can send out this substance at will, at night when he is sleeping, to destroy a chosen victim. It floats through the air emitting a bright light until it settles on the doomed person and devours his soul, or spirit, so that he will soon afterwards die. The practice has in common with *mazzerisme* the belief that the spirit can leave the body and travel long distances to remove a spirit from another human being.

The Great North, black Africa, the Australian bush: to such outlandish primitive areas one must look today for activities at all comparable to those of the *mazzeri*. In vain. The *mazzeri* are unique; unique, it seems, in Europe, with a possible extension in northern Sardinia; unique, it seems, in the world. Relic of a primeval way of life, *mazzerisme* is encrusted in Corsica, an island only a little over a hundred miles long by fifty wide, and close to two of the most long-civilized areas of Europe: Tuscany and Provence. Yet there *mazzerisme* has survived, in spite of repeated invasions, occupations, the arrival of hordes of armed, arrogant foreigners. Just because the island has been so often conquered and overrun. All through their history the Corsicans have taken refuge in their mountains, in their natural strongholds enclosed by hardly passable barriers of rock. There they have lived, more or less independent in their social organization, imprisoned by their environment but at liberty to preserve and develop their peculiar inner life. This I hesitate to describe as spiritual because of the moralistic connotations of the word. Rather I should speak of a strong awareness of the unseen powers coming to them by the mediation of the unconscious mind. Poor in material achievements, the Corsicans have been rich in dreams.

CHAPTER 10

Rock

Petrification – ogres – the work of Satan – the
rivers of Paradise – the flying ram – fairies and
giants – *lagramenti* – dreams of death

I recently dreamed that I was commissioned to write a treatise on
Corsica. I was sitting with my pen poised over a blank page. I had no
idea of what to write: no ideas at all. Minutes passed, hours and days,
so it seemed, while I suffered agonies of frustration and shame. Until I
saw my pen tracing four letters: R O C K. That one word was enough.
Enough to contain the physical structure of Corsica, its appearance, its
history, the character of its people and their survival with their specific
culture. Rock can be taken as a symbol of Corsica; the sociologist José
Gil speaks of the 'ultimate rock' which gives all Corsicans, despite
their discords, the sense of belonging to the same community. 'The
ultimate rock': 'a pebble placed in the Mediterranean', to use the
often-quoted expression of the writer and aviator Antoine de Saint-
Exupéry, who took off from Corsica on his last, fatal flight in 1944.[1]

The Corsicans owe to rock their very existence. Subjected to
successive invasions, they retreated inland to their mountain strongholds, enclosed in walls of rock. These natural fortresses were their
dwelling-space through the centuries, determined their means of
living, their social organization, their beliefs and customs and their
dreams. Everywhere in Corsica there is rock: above and below and all
around, underfoot and in the sky. Rock rising in nearly vertical
ranges, or springing up in detached pillars and columns and spires, or
swelling and curling like waves to make caverns and *orii*.[2] Rock of
many colours, running between lilac and grey, between rose and
purple and crimson. To quote José Gil again, the Corsicans live in a
vast sculptured landscape, one created, it seems, by an unbridled

imagination that excelled in conceiving extravagant forms: fantastical architectural shapes that strikingly contrast with the sobriety of the rock-built houses, shapes of men and beasts and monsters, origin of multiple local legends.[3]

Rock has given the Corsicans security; yet the legends connected with it are charged with violence and grief. In Corsican tradition rock has a punitive function; the theme of petrification is prominent. The feminine statue-menhir Santa Maria, near Cambia, was a young girl petrified in punishment for sacrilegious impudence, as has been told. A large statue-menhir found at Luzzipeo, in the Balagne, is said to represent a man punished for a similar fault. During the celebration of Mass he sounded a conch shell, the Corsican bugle that announced the Saracen invasions, the call to arms. But no invasion threatened; the warning was a practical joke. For this frivolous interruption of the sacred office he was turned to stone. The figure, which is intact and large, no less than eight feet high, has been classed by certain observers as female on account of two small hollows on the upper part of the body suggesting breasts, similar to those of the statue-menhir Santa Maria. The interpretation runs counter to the legend. But it better accords with local custom, for during the centuries – perhaps millennia –during which it lay in the maquis, the shepherds rolled the statue over the ground to ensure good pasture: an archaic fertility rite such as are surprisingly rare in Corsica. The statue is now preserved in a dependency of the church at Calenzana which also shelters the sarcophagus of Saint Restituta, martyred by the Romans. Various uncarved menhirs likewise represent people petrified for their misdeeds. A pair of menhirs standing in the valley of the Rizzanese, near Sartene, are named 'a sora e u frate' – the sister (nun) and the monk. They fell in love, it is said, and escaped their respective institutions by night, to meet in this lonely spot. But before they could consummate their guilty passion they were changed to stone.

Dolmens all over Corsica are known as the forges of Satan or the dwellings of ogres. The ogre is a common figure in Corsican popular mythology; perhaps he personifies a pre-Christian evil being analogous to the Devil; in local legend they play similar roles. A dolmen in the Nebbio, near Santo-Pietro-di-Tenda, is said to have been inhabited by an ogre and his mother who terrorized the surrounding region. The shepherds cunningly trapped the ogre in some tar placed outside his home. He tried to save his life by teaching the shepherds how to make *brocciu*, their particular soft cheese, an esteemed Corsican delicacy. The shepherds apparently accepted the recipe, but the ogre and his mother were nevertheless petrified. Only the head of a broken statue-menhir still remains to be seen.[4]

The sinister legends attached to the megalithic monuments echo the long hard struggle of the Christian Church against the earlier faith. It was still alive, as has been told, in the sixth century, to judge by a letter of Pope Gregory the Great, and apparently in the twelfth, when two statue-menhirs were built into the lower courses of the walls of the Pisan cathedral of Sagone, presumably to demonstrate their degradation. Were the ferocious statue-menhirs of Filitosa, found broken laterally and built into a ruined tower, likewise victims of militant Christianity? This is the explanation proposed by archaeologist Joseph Cesari, although no Christian signs or symbols have in fact been found on the site. But the discovery of a statue-menhir incorporated in the structure of a romanesque chapel, now demolished, at a spot known as Murato, less than a mile from Filitosa, lends support to such a hypothesis.[5]

The Devil is much in evidence in Corsican place-legends. He appears in disadvantageous opposition to Saint Martin, friend of the shepherds. Saint Martin laughed at him when he was clumsily ploughing land near his forge in the Niolo, a damaged but imposing dolmen. Enraged, the Devil thereupon broke his plough and flung the ploughshare into the air. It sailed across country to make a hole through a mountain, Capo Tafonato, one of the extraordinary sights of the island. The Devil was considered responsible for the most spectacular features of the landscape. The fabled *Calanche*, a major tourist attraction on the west coast, where a crowd of extraordinary rock formations spring from the face of the red cliffs near Piana, is said to be his work. It was an act of vengeance. Outraged when a shepherdess refused his amorous advances and chased him from her home, he petrified her with her family and their kinsmen and animals; or, according to another version of the tale, he carved the amazing shapes out of the rock in an access of frustration. Saint Martin, attracted by the noise, arrived to bless the spot, whereupon the sea surged up to the foot of the cliffs, making the scene more beautiful but no less horrific. Guy de Maupassant recalled the legend when he visited Corsica in 1880. Standing stupefied, he writes, before those astonishing forms of rose-tinted granite, bleeding in the last evening rays, he detected among their tormented shapes a pair of monks and a bishop of gigantic proportions, a lion crouching by the roadside, a woman suckling her child – the shepherdess who had rejected Satan – and an immense horned head of Satan himself, scowling at the crowd he had imprisoned in bodies of stone.[6]

Are any happy legends attached to the Corsican countryside? Apparently not. Scenes delightful or exalting are not free of sinister connotations. In the neighbourhood of Bocognano a cascade falls some two hundred feet over an escarpment, glittering white in the sunlit mountain air. Known as *Le voile de la mariée* – 'the bride's veil' – it suggests some romantic story of requited love. But no. The heroine of the story is Queen Griselda, wife of the king of Venaco beyond the pass of Vizzavona; royal personages, be it said, unsupported by any historical evidence. Griselda had only one hand; the other had been chopped off in an act of vengeance. She heard that she could recover it by dipping her wrist into a sacred spring on the site of the existing waterfall, which had not yet come into being. Water, in Corsica, is generally associated with evil, as has been told.[7] Does this tale present the opposite view? Not conclusively, for evil water overwhelms the magic spring. The queen came there wearing her bridal veil. But no sooner had she plunged her mutilated arm into the spring, and her hand had begun to take shape, than a frightful ogre who ruled the region removed the rocks that enclosed a dark pool higher up the mountainside where he had his abode. Rocks and water crashed down; the spring was swamped. Griselda and her suite fled in terror, pursued by the ogre who tore off her veil and left it hanging over the precipice as he fell to his death. Or, according to another version of the tale, he was transformed into a statue-menhir that still stands not far away. The tale perhaps reflects a memory of a real landslide and flood, such as are not uncommon in the island. It can be added that a number of medicinal springs exist in Corsica, neglected or unexploited, which are not to my knowledge the subjects of any tales.

Where is the place in Corsica uncontaminated by desperate memories? The Niolo, one might be tempted to imagine. That vast green plateau studded with shining lakes, where the air seems purer and lighter than elsewhere, is the source of four of the principal rivers of the island: the Golo, the Tavignano, the Porto, and the Liamone which derives from its headwaters in the Niolo, the Fiume Grosso. They have been compared to the four rivers of Paradise mentioned in Genesis. Yet the Niolo took no joy in begetting them. According to tradition they are tears: of the place? Of God? Or of some tutelary divinity long since forgotten? No clear answer to the question is forthcoming; but it is generally agreed that the Niolo, sometimes termed 'satanic', was never an earthly paradise. Five peaks rising in procession on the northwestern skyline are named the *Cinque Frati*, 'the five monks'. Holy men who have achieved enlightenment, mounting to heaven? No, one is told: they are fleeing the persecutions of the Giovannali, or else they are Giovannali fleeing the persecutions of their opponents.[8] The tragedy of the Giovannali could not but leave some physical trace on the island. Everywhere pursued by a crusade backed by the Papacy, they were hunted to death and burned, dead and alive. An enormous pyre of their bodies was made on Easter Day, it is said, on the site of the village of Ghisoni. While a horrified crowd looked on, an old priest appeared from the maquis and celebrated the Mass for the Dead over the flames. As he pronounced the words '*Kyrie eleison, Christe eleison*' – 'Lord have mercy, Christ have mercy' – a resounding echo issued from the mountains. The words have given their names to two soaring peaks; but these are less moving, to me, than the rugged little pile of rocks by the village of Carbini, where the sect was inaugurated and, as it is said, the last of its adherents died.

Not all Corsican place-legends are connected with Christianity and the Church. Others reflect the traditional insular code that pervades more elaborate popular tales, as has been shown.[9] Punishment is always meted out to avarice and pride. A girl travelling with a donkey laden with sacks of grain refused charity to a poor wayfarer. For this heartlessness she was turned to stone, along with the donkey and sacks, making a heap of rocks that can still be seen near Luri, in Cap Corse. In another, unnamed spot, a shepherd was surprised to see his ram flying through the air. He summoned his neighbours to witness the feat, then put the ram up for auction and sold it for a high price. The new owner also wanted to show off the talent of the ram. He assembled his friends to watch him throw it over a precipice. The wretched animal bleated despairingly as it fell to die among the sheep grazing below. It was petrified, with the entire flock, to make yet another heap of stones. The shepherd had learned his lesson, one that many Corsicans have had to learn. Bandits to statesmen, including shepherds, Corsicans have an innate appetite for power, or at least a delight in making a grand gesture that will win applause. But such ambitions excite counter-ambitions, envy – *invidia* – and the Evil Eye.[10] Fatally, the Corsicans are tempted to commit the very faults they reprove, and which they know will be their undoing.

A map could be made of legends covering the whole island; I here offer only a selection. They emanate from the physical forces of nature and from reactions to those forces of wonder and fear. Fear predominates. This landscape which globe-trotters rank among the finest in the world, along with New Zealand and the Himalayas, has oppressed rather than stimulated its inhabitants. Yet however overpowering, it is also generous. Everything grows there abundantly, trees and shrubs and flowers: pines and beech and chestnut and olive trees, the ubiquitous holm oak, the exuberant maquis. Fruit trees produce a second blossoming in autumn, roses and oranges decorate gardens nearly all the year round; clusters of mimosa splash golden masses against the snow. Yet the Corsicans have filled the underpopulated spaces with evil and dangerous presences: the Devil, the ogres, the *finzione* which bring warning of death, the spirits of the dead that kill, the *Squadra d'Arrozza* that performs the funerals of the living, while the *mazzeri* go out to kill by night. In the view of the historian of the Corsican Church, S.-B. Casanova, such reactions were a natural response to the sinister aspects of the landscape, he seems unaware of any others. The tormented surface of the island, he writes, 'with its savage gorges, its deep ravines, its inextricable maquis, its dark forests, its bare rocks, its impetuous torrents' combined to strike the imagination and to render Corsicans the most superstitious people in the world.[11]

No doubt these superstitions mask others, relating to a richer and more primitive mythology in part demolished by the Christian Church. Roccu Multedo reports vague memories of giants and fairies. The fairies, who lived by streams, confirmed the Corsican belief in the evil quality of water. They were beautiful; they seduced mortal men. Though Casanova, unexpectedly indulgent, maintains that they were also beneficent, and that a man who managed to capture one ensured his lifelong happiness, popular tales relate that these unnatural unions ended sadly.[12]

As for giants, they are only dimly remembered, usually in connection with the far south. Casanova echoes such a belief when he states that the *mazzeri* sometimes transformed themselves into giants; but I have found no confirmation of this. The well-known Uomo di Cagna, a colossal natural rock formation resembling a human head, is set high up in a mountain range gazing at Bonifacio and Sardinia beyond the sea. It might be that of a petrified giant, although it does not seem to be associated with any legend. Belief in giants may have been based on a reality that has faded from popular memory. Classical scholars who accept the thesis that the ports visited by Odysseus can be identified with real places known to the navigators of antiquity, are of the opinion that the episode of the Laestrygonian giants should be located at Bonifacio, the city perched on a pale limestone promontory overlooking a creek, or fjord, making a deep harbour on the southern tip of the island. Certainly Homer's description fits Bonifacio better than any other port in the western Mediterranean. 'It was an excellent harbour,' one reads, 'closed in on all sides by an unbroken ring of precipitous cliffs . . . No wave, great or small, ever arises there, it was a white calm.' Odysseus dropped anchor and sent a party of men to make contact with the inhabitants living on the cliff above. They found a tribe of cannibal giants, the Laestrygonians, who flung down rocks on the Greek ships, destroying all but one and killing their crews, after which they harpooned their prey 'like fish' and carried them off for supper. It seems not impossible that the dreadful memory of a tribe of very large cannibals in the extreme south lingered on in Corsica through the ages.[13]

Belief in human vampires – *streghe, surpatori* – who entered houses disguised as cats and weasels, was more concrete and lasted, as I have told, into recent times.[14] Trees might also be vampires. According to tradition a chestnut tree in the sumptuous valley of Spelunca snared passing travellers in its branches and sucked away their blood. Another tradition identified mist with hostile spirits known as *lagramenti*. The mists descend on Corsica in autumn and winter; they enfold the mountains, blurring outlines, pouring into valleys like a white foam. They were thought to be full of angry dogs that hounded wayfarers to their deaths over precipices, in lonely spots where their corpses were not found until they had putrefied. The *lagramenti* might also invade villages, and even creep into houses if windows and doors had not been shut in time. If this happened the occupants armed themselves with keys or nails or horseshoes, in the belief that iron repelled evil. By such humble precautions the Corsicans tried to protect themselves against powers of unknown magnitude. The *lagramenti* are perhaps the last of the phantasms with which they have peopled their land, for the name is derived from that of the Saracen chief in Ariosto's *Orlando Furioso*, which must have become known to the Corsicans since the sixteenth century through the education in the Italian classics dispensed by the priests.[15]

All this, one might say, belongs to the past. Rational French state education and materialistic values have discredited the evil spirits and reduced the legends to curiosities of folklore. The ogres have vanished; the Devil no longer roams among the rocks. Nor, indeed, does Saint Martin. The Virgin Mary, author of many Corsican miracles, and Saint Francis, who propagated her cult, alone among the Christian saints have kept an undiminished prestige.[16] It cannot be said that the disappearance of traditional beliefs has been accompanied by any marked revival of Christianity. The churches are too large for present-day congregations; only occasions for family gatherings – christenings, weddings and funerals – and the time-honoured festivals and processions still draw considerable crowds.

Meanwhile, technological progress has reduced the hazards of nature, which may well have accounted for the tenor if not the content of many tragic tales. Roads have replaced mule tracks, motor traffic has superseded mules. If the record of car accidents hardly suggests that travel is less perilous, it is far more rapid and has done much to break the isolation of the mountain villages. Since the end of the last century a railroad tunnels its way through the range dividing the two long-separated areas of Corsica, the *En-Deçà* and the *Au-Delà-des-Monts*;[17] now there is talk of building a fast motorway to link Ajaccio and Bastia. Hydraulic engineering controls and exploits rivers, harnessing them to provide running water, large-scale irrigation, electric current. For whom? Corsican agriculture is still insufficiently rewarding and the villages have lost most of their inhabitants to the towns. Sparsely populated, the interior has become a grandiose spectacle rather than a living space, and this at precisely the period when so many new facilities are available for living there. Though floods and landslides and fires still threaten life and property, the countryside is certainly less menacing than ever before. Will it remain almost empty? Or be overrun by tourists? A recent wave of Alpinists, hikers, pony-trekkers and reckless kayak navigators of the mountain torrents is perhaps indicative. Will non-Corsicans, braving nationalists' indignation, arrive in numbers to settle there? Or will mass unemployment send the Corsicans back to their villages, to wrest a living from their rock-strewn but not unfertile soil?

At all events, the landscape can leave no one indifferent. With its physical and mythical dangers diminished, the Corsican rock retains its mysterious intimidating power. 'It makes one afraid,' my companion said to me. He was no lonely shepherd brought up on tales of *lagramenti* and *finzione*, but a very distinguished Continental-born professor of history at a Parisian university. We were looking at a mountainside that rose abruptly in front of us, a wall of naked granite cut into parallel vertical ravines, as though frowning. In me it induced feelings of helplessness and awe. Corsicans are not insensitive to such influences. They are deeply attached to their environment, but with that love which persists in spite of all that has to be endured from the loved one. Marie Susini, who wrote so often of Corsica but dreaded setting foot there, movingly expresses this tormented relationship when she speaks of the 'sombre anxiety' inspired by the sight of the island, and the 'fear of being unable to meet the demands of that proud land which would transform every story into a destiny.' According to the travel writer Paul Theroux: 'An island of traditional culture cannot be idyllic. It is, instead, completely itself, riddled with magic, superstitions, myths, dangers, rivalries and old routines.' These words were inspired by a journey to the Pacific Isles, but they might just as well have been written about Corsica. Do they apply to islands – small islands at least – the world over?[18]

Or have these negative influences been aggravated by the particularly harsh situation of Corsica: that of a small population struggling to survive in a rugged territory which because of its strategic value attracted a succession of ruthless conquerors? Yet history cannot account for beliefs that took root long before recorded history began: the Megalithic and Neolithic cults of the dead, the dream-hunting of the *mazzeri*, dating, it seems, from pre-Neolithic times. But a tragic history may have nourished primeval beliefs such as would have faded away through the centuries in happier lands. In

Corsica prehistory has soaked into history, and the legacy of the past has endured in an unremitting preoccupation with death.

The drastic changes of the last three decades have altered physical conditions without obliterating underlying beliefs and attitudes. While aircraft zoom through the *lagramenti* or dive low to spray chemical products on forest fires, while helicopters hover over precipices to rescue imprudent wounded Alpinists, there are still *signadori* to dispel the ever-dreaded Evil Eye. There are still those who dream of death and foretell it, ordinary people as well as the *mazzeri* who in the far south practise their prehistoric calling. Many people remember a time when *mazzeri* were active in their villages; others recall personal visions of *finzioni* and the *Squadra d'Arrozza* and spirits of the dead. The peculiar death-haunted dreaming of the Corsicans continues. Outside the island it is hardly known, nor even suspected. Which is why I have written this book.

NOTES

References to sources of which details are provided in the Selected Critical Bibliography (p. 190) are given as SCB, followed by section and subsections.

CHAPTER 1: *Bread of Wood, Wine of Stone*

1 See Lucette Poncin, 'La Mort en Corse', bulletin *A Mimoria*, no. 14 (Ajaccio, 1992), (SCB: VII, B); Florence Aubray et Dominique Rossi, *Evolution de l'espace des morts en Corse* (APERAURC, Sampolo).

2 Statistics supplied by INSEE (Institut national de la statistique et des études économiques, Direction Régionale de la Corse).

3 See Prehistory (SCB: V, B); L. Poncin, op. cit (SCB: VII, B).

4 See S. von Cles-Reden (SCB: V, B). Although the most important groups of Megalithic monuments have been found in southwest Corsica, the thesis of a western origin of the Megalithic faith presented by J. Pietri and J. V. Angelini (SCB: II) is unconvincing. It seems, however, possible that the Megalithic faith reached Corsica in a cultural back-wash from Spain.

5 See J. et L. Jehasse (SCB: V, C).

6 See G. Moracchini-Mazel (SCB: IX).

7 *Voceri*: see Chapter 2 below.

8 See J. Busquet (SCB: VI, B); D. Carrington, *Granite Island* (SCB: XI).

9 See J. Poncin (SCB IX); F. Pomponi (SCB: VII, A).

10 Anti-feudal revolts: see Chapter 7 below. Popular tales: see Chapter 3 below.

11 Constitution of Pasquale Paoli: D. Carrington (SCB: V, E, 1). Boswell's visit (SCB: VIII, B).

12 Charles Bonaparte: Carolus Bonaparte (*sic*), *Exercitationes accademicae in secondam partem. Ethicae de Jur. nat. et Gent* (Corte, 1766).

13 Voltaire (SCB: V, E, 1). *Précis du siècle de Louis XV* (2nd edn. 1769, chap. IX).

14 Napoleon, 'Nouvelle Corse' (SCB: VIII, B).
15 P. Mérimée (SCB: VI, B).
16 J.-B. Marcaggi, *Fleuve de Sang* (SCB: VI, B).
17 X. Versini (SCB: VI, B).
18 J.-B. Marcaggi, *Bandits corses d'hier et d'aujourd'hui*; L. Molinelli Cancellieri (both SCB: VI, B).

CHAPTER 2: *The Dead and the Living*

1 P. Silvani, . . . *Et la Corse fut libérée* (SCB: V, E, 2).
2 See 'Le drapeau . . .' in Pierre Antonetti, *Trois Etudes sur Paoli* (Ajaccio, 1991).
3 See SCB: I.
4 SOMIVAC (Société pour la mise en valeur agricole de la Corse); SETCO (Société d'équipement touristique de la Corse); both instituted in 1957 to stimulate Corsican agriculture and tourism.
5 Statistics supplied by INSEE.
6 Women's emancipation: see Chapter 5 below.
7 Feudal lords: see Chapter 7 below, popular tales: Chapter 3 below.
8 Father Albini (1790–1839) belonged to the Couvent de Saint François founded for the Franciscans at Vico *c.* 1481 and taken over after the French Revolution by the Oblats de Marie. Preaching mission, cross: Louis Delarue, *Prêtre rien que ça* (Nouvelles éditions latines, undated); R. Multedo (1982), (SCB: I).
9 Religious festivals: see C. Tiévant et L. Desideri (SCB: VI, A).
10 *Comparaggiu*: see G. Ravis-Giordani (SCB: VI, A). Bonaparte and Giubega: see D. Carrington, *Napoleon and his Parents* (SCB: V, E, 1).
11 Notably at Corbara: see G. Moracchini avec la collaboration de D. Carrington (SCB: IX).
12 *Catenacciu*: see Francis Leonetti, *Le Pénitent 'Catenacciu'* (Nantes, 1980).
13 See Pierre Lamotte in *Etudes Corses*, no. 10 (Ajaccio, 1954).
14 *Caracolu*: see Pierre Lamotte in *Etudes Corses*, no. 12 (Ajaccio, 1956), (SCB: VII, B); *Granitola*: see Chapter 5 below; see also Lucette Poncin, 'La mort en Corse', bulletin *A Mimoria*, no. 14 (Ajaccio, 1992), (SCB: VII, B); and K. Peraldi (SCB: VIII, A).
15 Bishop's condemnations: see C. F. Giustiniani (SCB: III).
16 *Voceri*: see collections in SCB: VI, C.
17 See F. Pomponi (SCB: VII, A).

18   See S. von Cles-Reden and R. Grosjean (SCB: V, B).

19   'La Corse dans la correspondance de St. Grégoire le Grand', *Bulletin de la Société des Sciences historiques et naturelles de la Corse* (Bastia, 1882).

CHAPTER 3: *Villains, Heroes and Phantoms*

1   Muzarettu, born at Grossa in the southwestern Sartenais; his real name was Marc-Antoine Alfonsi.

2   Popular tales: see SCB: VI, D.

3   Giovanni della Grossa, 1388–c.1464 (SCB: V, D). Local self-government: see Chapter 7 below.

4   Fairies: see F. Ortoli (SCB: VI, D).

5   F. Ortoli (SCB: VI, C).

6   See D. Carrington et P. Lamotte; G. Ravis-Giordani (both SCB: I). Loss of life in First World War: see Chapter 2 above.

7   R. Multedo (1982), (SCB: I), p. 211.

8   Similar beliefs in Brittany: see A. le Braz; in Wales, Sir John Rhys (the Celts appropriated earlier beliefs); in Scotland, J. G. Campbell (all SCB: II).

9   Mother Goddess: see S. von Cles-Reden, G. Camps, J. Cesari (all SCB: V, B), and Chapter 6 below.

10   *Finzione*: see G. Ravis-Giordani, op. cit. (SCB: I).

11   Bandits and shepherds: see J.-B. Marcaggi, *Fleuve de Sang* (SCB: VI, B), and Chapter 1 above.

12   See Chapter 2 above.

13   See SCB: I.

14   R. Multedo (1981), (SCB: I), p. 54.

CHAPTER 4: *The Dream-Hunters*

1   'Wild hunt', 'furious horde': see Chapter 7 below.

2   See the works of R. Multedo (SCB: I); B. Holway (SCB: VII, A); Chapter 5 below.

3   R. Multedo (1975), (SCB: I).

4   High death-rate: see F. Pomponi (SCB: VII, A); and Chapter 2 above.

5   *Streghe, stregoni* flying on *aspa*: R. Multedo (1982), (SCB: I); Sabbath: see Chapter 7 below.

6   Supposed unfaithful wives: see D. Carrington and P. Lamotte, 'Les *mazzeri*' (SCB: I); and B. Holway (SCB: VII, A).

7   R. Multedo (1981), (SCB: I); see Chapter 6 below.

8   Traditional tales: see Chapter 3 above.

9   Sir James Frazer (SCB: XI).

10   M.-M. Rotily-Forcioli (SCB: I).

11   R. Multedo (1975), (SCB: I), p. 80.

12   See R. Multedo (1981), (SCB: I); B. Holway (SCB: VII, A).

13   R. Multedo (1981), (SCB: I), p. 37.

14   R. Multedo (1975), pp. 69–74; (1981), pp. 39–45; D. Carrington and P. Lamotte (all SCB: I).

15   Asphodel: see Lucie Désidéri, in *Arburi, Arbe, Arbigliule* (SCB: X), pp. 272–89; feast of Saint John the Baptist: C. Tiéant et L. Desideri (SCB: VI, A); cypress; *Arburi, Arbe, Arbigliule* (SCB: X), p. 144.

16   All Souls' Day, welcoming of dead; see Chapter 2 above; ambivalent attitude to dead: see Chapter 3 above; 'furious horde': see Chapter 7 below.

17   Book of the Maccabees, I, II, in *La Sainte Bible*, nouvelle édition publiée sous le patronage de la Ligue Catholique de l'Evangile (Paris, 1951). See also M. I. Dimant; M. Wurband et C. Roth (both SCB: XI); Paoli and Boswell: see J. Boswell (SCB: VIII, B).

18   See R. Multedo (1975), (SCB: I), p. 72.

CHAPTER 5: *The Unbaptised*

1   Battlefields: R. Multedo (1975), pp. 73–4; (1981), pp. 43–5; see also D. Carrington et P. Lamotte, 'Les *mazzeri*' and 'A propos des *mazzeri*'. Map R. Multedo (1975), p. 65 (all SCB: I).

2   Evidence from Cap Corse: R. Multedo (1981), (SCB: I), p. 37; *caracolu*: see Chapter 2 above.

3   *Mazzeri* in Sardinia: see B. Holway (SCB: VII, A). Obsidian, trade: see in particular J. Cesari (SCB: V, B). Roger Grosjean postulated that an alien race invaded Corsica, conquered the megalith builders, built towers, and proceeded to Sardinia to build the *nuraghi*, a thesis now rejected: see R. Grosjean, G. Camps, J. Cesari (all SCB: V, B), and Chapter 10 below.

4   See R. Multedo (1975), (SCB: I), p. 46; B. Holway (SCB: VII, A); M. Ceccaldi (SCB: XI).

5   Head in hunt: R. Multedo (1975), p. 64; hunting in Sartenais: R. Multedo (1981), (both SCB: I). Priests forbidden to hunt: see Mgr. Castagnola in S.-B. Casanova (SCB: III), vol. I, pp. 241–3.

6   Asphodel: see Chapter 4 above.

7   Theophrastus, *History of Plants*, vol. 8; Timaeus, quoted by Polybius, XII, 3, 7: Diodorus Siculus, vol. 14; see also O. Jehasse (SCB: V, C).

8   See M. Ehrenberg, *Women in Prehistory* (London, 1989); Joseph Campbell, *The Masks of God* (London, 1968).

9   See G. Camps (SCB: V, B).

10 Healers: see Chapter 7 below. *Voceratrices*: see Chapter 2 above.

11 See Georges Ravis-Giordani, 'La femme corse . . .', in *Pieve e Paesi* (SCB: VII, B).

12 Female statue-menhir of Castaldu: see G. Camps, J. Cesari (both SCB: V, B), *Zicavu* (SCB: VII, B), and Chapter 3 above.

13 Heroines in history: see D. Carrington, *Napoleon and his Parents* (SCB: V, E, 1).

14 See G. Ravis-Giordani (SCB: VII, B).

15 B. Holway (SCB: VII, A).

16 R. Multedo (1981), (SCB: I); shamanism: see SCB: II and Chapter 9 below.

17 See Chapter 6 below.

18 R. Multedo (1981), (SCB: I). Child *mazzeru*: see *La Corse* (Ajaccio), 15 July 1993.

19 Hedgehogs: R. Multedo (1982), (SCB: I), p. 9; see also J. Chevalier, A. Gheerbrant (SCB: XI).

20 See J.-B. Marcaggi (SCB: VIII, B) and Chapter 1 above.

21 Scotland and Wales: see SCB: II.

22 S.-B. Casanova (SCB: III), vol. I, p. xxiv. Sorcerers: see Chapters 6 and 7 below.

23 Trials of the Inquisition: see Chapter 7 below.

24 *Mazzeri* and *Catenacciu*: R. Multedo (1981), (SCB: I).

25 See J. Chevalier, A. Gheerbrant (SCB: XI).

CHAPTER 6: *Written in the Sky*

1   Jean-André Culioli, 1886–1972. A selection of his sung verses is published in M. Giacomo-Marcellesi (SCB: VI, D). Magic rites: see Chapter 8 below.

2   D. Carrington et P. Lamotte, 'Les *mazzeri*' (SCB: I).

3   '*Entre le destin et la science*', *Kyrn*, (SCB: VII, B), no. 371, 13–19 September 1991; *Meridies*, no. 13–14, 1991 (SCB: VII, B).

4 Tommaso Nasica, *Mémoires sur l'enfance et la jeunesse de Napoléon* (Paris, 1858), pp. 15–16, 376; see also D. Carrington, *Napoleon and his Parents* (SCB: V, E, 1).

5 See *Napoléon, Pensées politiques et sociales*, presented by A. Dansette (Paris, 1969), pp. 421-6.

6 See J. Boswell (SCB: VIII, B).

7 F.-D. Guerrazzi, *Pasquale Paoli ossia la rotte de Pontenuovo* (2 vols. Milan, 2nd edn, 1864), quoted by K. Andreani Peraldi (SCB: VIII, A).

8 See E. R. Dodds, *The Greeks and the Irrational* (Berkeley, 1977).

9 Figurine (now in British Museum): see J. Cesari, also R. Grosjean, G. Camps (all SCB: V, B). Statue-menhir of Castaldu: see Chapters 3 and 5 above and S. von Cles-Reden (SCB: V, B), in which the author comments on the absence in Corsica of evidence of the Mother Goddess. Statue-menhir Santa Maria legends: see R. Grosjean (SCB: V, B), R. Multedo (1982), (SCB: I).

10 Seneca, *Consalatio ad. Helviam*, VIII, 8. See J. et L. Jehasse and O. Jehasse (both SCB: V, C).

11 'La croix magique' in F. Ortoli (SCB: VI, D).

12 Bonifacio, *Odyssey*, Laestrygonians: see Louis Moulinier, 'L'épisode des Lestrygons dans l'*Odyssée*', *Etudes Corses*, no. 17, (Ajaccio, 1958), and Chapter 10 below.

13 Funeral banquets: see Lucette Poncin, 'La mort en Corse', *A Mimoria*, no. 14 (Ajaccio, 1991), (SCB: VII, B); Pierre Lamotte, 'Repas et distribution des vivres en l'honneur des morts', in *Etudes Corses*, no. 13, (Ajaccio, 1957); in prehistory: F. de Lanfranchi, 'Une veillée funèbre à l'Age de Fer' in *Rites funéraires . . .* (all SCB: VII, B).

14 See F. Pomponi; X. Versini (both SCB: VII, A).

CHAPTER 7: *Forbidden Ground*

1 S.-B. Casanova (SCB: III), see Chapter 5 above.

2 R. Multedo (1981); (1987), (both SCB: I). See Chapter 9 below.

3 *Benandanti*: C. Ginsburg, *The Night Battles* (SCB: II); G. Ravis-Giordani (SCB: I).

4 See R. Multedo (1975); R. Multedo (1982); G. Ravis-Giordani (all SCB: I).

5 Evil Eye: see Chapter 8 below.

6 R. Multedo, quoted by G. Ravis-Giordani (SCB: I).

7   See F. Pomponi (SCB: VII, A).

8   See X. Versini (SCB: VII, A).

9   F. Lantieri (SCB: III).

10   Albert Memmi, *Portrait du colonisé* (Paris, 1975).

11   N. Lymerich et F. Pena, *Le manuel des inquisiteurs* (Paris, La Haye, 1975) quoted by F. Lantieri (SCB: III).

12   *Voceru*: see Chapter 2 above.

13   See *Arburi, Arbe, Arbigliule* (SCB: X).

14   *Signadori*: see Chapter 8 below.

15   See J. Chevalier, A. Gheerbrant (SCB: XI).

16   Costituzioni di Mgr. Castagnola, 1615, in S.-B. Casanova (SCB: III), vol. I, pp. 240–2. Hunting: ibid.; see Chapter 5 above.

17   C. F. Giustiniani, *Costituzione et Decreti Sinodali* (SCB: III); see Chapter 2 above.

18   Candle of the *Miserere*: see S.-B. Casanova (SCB: III), vol. I, p. xxix.

19   Hedgehogs' teeth: R. Multedo (1982), (SCB: I), and Chapter 5 above. Invulnerability: see R. Multedo, ibid.

20   *Catenacciu*: see Chapter 2 above; Muzarettu: see Chapter 3 above.

21   Popular tales: see Chapter 3 above.

22   Giovannali: see S.-B. Casanova (SCB: III), vol. I, pp. 75-7, who underlines the Franciscan origin of the movement; also D. Carrington, *Granite Island* (SCB: XI), (bibliography), pp. 139–40, offering a summary of events based on research in F. Guerri, 'I Giovannali nella testimonianza di documenti inediti del trecento' in *Corsica Antica e Moderna* (Jan.–April, 1935); Bernard Gui, *Manuel de l'Inquisiteur* (Paris, 1926), and unrevised versions of the Corsican chroniclers Giovanni della Grossa and Pier'Antonio Monteggiani in *Bulletin de la Société des Sciences historiques et naturelles de la Corse* (1910) (SCB: V, D).

23   Sabbath: see Ginsburg, *The Night Battles* and *Ecstasies* . . . (both SCB: II); Margaret Murray, *The Witch-Cult in Western Europe* (London, 1921), *The God of the Witches* (London, 1933); in Corsica: R. Multedo (1975); (1982), (both SCB: I).

24   Feudal lords: deflowering of brides, see Chapter 3 above; foundation of monasteries, gifts to churches: see G. Moracchini avec . . . D. Carrington (SCB: IX); Rinuccio della Rocca, gifts of paintings: see ibid; and D. Carrington in *Etudes Corses*, no. 11 (Ajaccio, 1956).

25   Cult of Diana at Aleria: see J. et L. Jehasse (SCB: V, C); absent in interior: see Chapter 6 above.

26 'Qualcosa', 'quellu quassu': see Chapter 6 above; Squadra d'Arrozza, mubba: see Chapter 3 above.

27 Benandanti as healers: see C. Ginsburg, The Night Battles (SCB: II), pp. 78, 81.

CHAPTER 8: *The Shadow and the Light*

1 Signadori: see R. Multedo (1975); (1982); P. Bertrand-Rousseau (both SCB: I).

2 Medicinal plants: see Chapter 7 above.

3 Evil Eye: see F. T. Elworthy. Incantations: in Scotland, A. Carmichael; in Ethiopia: F. T. Elworthy (all SCB: II).

4 Streghe, surpatori: see Chapter 7 above.

5 Mother Goddess: see Chapter 6 above.

6 Inherited affliction by Evil Eye: R. Multedo (1982), (SCB: I).

7 J. Gil (SCB: VII, A).

8 Popular tales: see Chapter 3 above.

9 Inquisition in Corsica, bishops Castagnola and C. F. Giustiniani: see Chapter 7 above; S.-B. Casanova, vol. I, pp. xxvii–xxviii (all SCB: III).

10 Egg and herb of Ascension: C. Tiévant et L. Desideri (SCB: VI, A); see also Arburi, Arbe, Arbigliule (SCB: X).

11 Shepherds' technique of prophecy: mentioned by bishop Agostino Giustiniani, in Description de la Corse, c. 1531 (SCB: V, D), not to be confused with bishop C. F. Giustiniani, author of Costituzione et Decreti Sinodali (1665), mentioned above and in Chapter 7; bishop Castagnola, ibid. (both SCB: III). Shepherds' predictions: see R. Multedo (1975), (SCB: I); and S.-B. Casanova (SCB: III), vol I, p. xxix.

12 Catenacciu: see Chapter 2 above.

13 Miracula: R. Multedo (1975), p. 81; prayers, see works of R. Multedo and P. Bertrand-Rousseau; magic in sound of words: R. Multedo (1982), p. 45 (all SCB: I).

14 Corsican writers are cited throughout the Bibliography. See in particular VIII.

15 Incantations: in Scotland, A. Carmichael; in Ethiopia, F. T. Elworthy (both SCB: II); Siberian shamans: see Chapter 9 below.

16 Christianity in Roman Corsica: see J. et L. Jehasse; O. Jehasse (both SCB: V, C).

17 Franciscans in Corsica: see Chapter 7 above.

18 Painting of Virgin and Child in monastery at Alesani: see G. Moracchini avec . . . D. Carrington (SCB: IX).

19 Statue of Virgin at Fozzano, commissioned by population from Pompeio Bagnoli of Ajaccio, 1635. See Vyrdaghs Fildelis, *Notices historiques sur la Rocca* (Ajaccio, 1962).

20 Fair at Casamaccioli: see Chapter 6 above.

21 Pisan cathedrals: see Chapter 1 above and G. Morrachini-Mazel (SCB: IX). Virgin revered in Ajaccio: *Corse. Guides Bleus*, 1968 (SCB: IV).

22 *Dio vi salvi Regina*: see Cristiani, Llosa, Thomas (SCB: III), and 'Les origines du *Dio vi salvi Regina*' in Pierre Antonetti, *Trois Etudes sur Paoli* (Ajaccio, 1991).

23 Alternative rites of *signadori*: see R. Multedo (1975), (SCB: I).

24 *Mazzeri*'s guilt: see Chapter 5 above.

25 J. Pietri, J. V. Angelini (1994), (SCB: I); shamans (SCB: II) and see Chapter 9 below. Skull of Sampiero: R. Multedo (1982), (SCB: I).

26 *Parc* . . .: see Chapter 2 above. Eagle sacred to shamans: see Chapter 9 below.

27 Unrequited love: R. Multedo (1982), (SCB: I), p. 142. Love potions: see Chapter 7 above. Traditional social code: see Chapter 5 above and M.–R. Marin-Muracciole (SCB: VI, A). Letizia Bonaparte's wedding: see Monica Stirling, *A Pride of Lions* . . . (London, 1961).

28 Statistics published in *Corse-Matin*, 19 February 1994.

CHAPTER 9: *Magicians of the Chase*

1 See R. Multedo (1981); (1987); G. Ravis-Giordani (all SCB: I).

2 M. Eliade; M. Mercier; M. Bouteiller; M. A. Czaplicka; R. Boyer et E. Lot-Falck (all SCB: II).

3 *Benandanti*: C. Ginsburg, *The Night Battles* (SCB: II); see Chapter 7 above.

4 See M. Bouteiller (SCB: II).

5 *Mazzeri*: expression, predisposition, initiation: see Chapter 5 above.

6 Dream-banquets of the *mazzeri*: see Chapter 6 above.

7 Eagle accursed by Corsican shepherds: see Chapter 8 above.

8 Familiarity with animals; in popular tales: see Chapter 3 above; in daily experience: see Chapter 4 above.

9 *Squadra d'Arrozza*; drum predicting death: see Chapter 3 above.

10 Illness in Corsica; herbal and magical cures: see Chapters 7, 8 above.

11 Shamans' vocabulary: M. Mercier (SCB: II), p. 72; incantations of *signadori*: see Chapter 8 above; address to demons: R. Boyer et E. Lot-Falck (SCB: II), p. 682; voices of *Squadra d'Arrozza*: see Chapter 3 above; Corsican version of Orpheus myth: see Chapter 6 above.

12 Address to Erlik: M. Mercier (SCB: II), p. 104.

13 Corsican funeral banquets: see Chapter 6 above.

14 G. Ravis-Giordani (SCB: I).

15 'Masters of ecstasy': M. Mercier (SCB: II).

16 Eight-hooved horses: R. Boyer et E. Lot-Falck (SCB: II); flying of *streghe*: see Chapter 7 above.

17 *Mazzeru*'s dream landscape: see Chapter 6 above.

18 *Mazzeri* also healers: see *signadori*, Chapter 8 above.

19 Church and *mazzeri*, exorcisms: see Chapter 6 above; Church and *signadori*: see Chapter 8 above. J. Pietri et J.-V. Angelini: see (SCB: I) and Chapter 8 above. *Granite Island* (SCB: XI); Eliade (SCB: II) op. cit.

20 See R. Multedo (1981); (1987) (both SCB: I). *Mazzere* described by J. Cesari: see Chapter 5 above.

21 Chestnut tree in Corsica: M. Conrad (SCB: X), p. 70.

22 J. Boswell (SCB: VIII, B).

23 See W. Lloyd Warner (SCB: II).

24 Azande sorcerers: see E. Evans Pritchard (SCB: II).

CHAPTER 10: *Rock*

1 See J. Gil (SCB: VII, A); Curtis Cate, *Antoine de Saint-Exupéry* (Paris, 1973).

2 *Orii*: see Chapter 6 above.

3 Legends relating to rock: see selections in the works of R. Multedo (SCB: I) and in *A Lettera*, no. 3, 1993, 'La pétrification . . .' (SCB: VII, B).

4 Statue-menhirs and menhirs: see R. Grosjean (SCB: V, B), and Chapters 1 and 6. Saint Restituta: see Chapter 8 above.

5 Pisan cathedral of Sagone: see Moracchini-Mazel (SCB: IX). R. Grosjean postulates an invasion by an alien people, the '*Torréens*', who defeated the megalith builders and erected the tower at Filitosa and others elsewhere in southern Corsica before passing to Sardinia where they constructed the *nuraghi*, a thesis that has been rejected, see G. Camps, J. Cesari (both SCB: V, B). Sardinia: see also Chapter 5 above.

6   See G. de Maupassant; 'La patrie de Colomba' in *Chroniques insulaires*, a collection of his reminiscences of a journey in Corsica. A similar description of the *calanche* appears in his novel *Une vie* (both SCB: VIII, B). Quotations are given in my rendering of the original French.

7   Water associated with evil: see Chapter 4 above.

8   Giovannali: see Chapter 7 above.

9   Popular tales: see Chapter 3 above.

10   Evil Eye: see Chapter 8 above.

11   Warnings of death, *finzione, Squadra d'Arrozza*: see Chapter 3 above; response to landscape: see S.-B. Casanova (SCB: III), vol. I, p. xxii.

12   See R. Multedo (1982) (SCB: I). Fairies: S.-B. Casanova (SCB: III), vol. I, p. xxvi; in popular tales: see Chapter 3 above.

13   Giants: S.-B Casanova (SCB: III), vol. I. Cannibalism: see Chapter 6 above. *The Odyssey*, Bonifacio: see Louis Moulinier, *'L'épisode des Lestrygons dans l'Odyssée'* in *Etudes Corses*, no. 17 (Ajaccio, 1958).

14   *Streghe, surpatori*: see Chapter 7 above.

15   *Lagramenti*: see R. Multedo (1982), (SCB: I), and K. Peraldi (SCB: VIII, A).

16   Virgin Mary, miracles: see Chapter 8 above. Saint Francis: see Chapters 7 and 8 above.

17   Division of Corsica: see Chapters 1 and 5 above.

18   M. Susini (SCB: VIII, C); see Chapter 8 above. Quotation given in my rendering of the original French. Paul Theroux, *The Happy Isles of Oceania* (London, 1992).

SELECTED CRITICAL BIBLIOGRAPHY

X   CORSICAN FLORA

XI   OTHER WORKS CONSULTED

Abbreviations:

BSSHNC   Bulletin de la Société des Sciences historiques et naturelles de la Corse

CRDP   Centre Régional de Documentation Pédagogique

Much has been written about Corsica, in Greek, Latin, Italian, French, English, German and Corsican, from the period of antiquity to the present time, by travellers to the island and by the Corsicans themselves. The following bibliography lists the works that have most contributed to this book. They are indicated in the Notes by the name of the author, sometimes followed by a shortened title, and by the code classification of the bibliography. Other works consulted are mentioned in full.

I   'MAZZERI' AND OCCULT PHENOMENA IN CORSICA

My principal source of information on these subjects is the confidences of the *mazzeri*, the *signadori* and their friends. Most of these people prefer to remain anonymous; I mention in the Acknowledgements those who are willing to be named. Few works have been published on these subjects; surprisingly, because the Corsicans have a natural inclination to write about their island and the number of books produced there every year is high in relation to the size of the population. The following are listed in chronological sequence.

Dorothy Carrington et Pierre Lamotte, '*Les mazzeri*', *Etudes Corses*, nouvelle série, no. 15–16 (Ajaccio, 1957).

Dorothy Carrington et Pierre Lamotte, '*A propos des mazzeri (renseignements de M. Claude Faucheux)*', *Etudes Corses*, nouvelle série, no. 17 (Ajaccio, 1958).

Georges Ravis-Giordani, '*Signes, figures et conduites de l'entre-vie-et-mort: finzione, mazzeri et streie corses*', *La mort en Corse et dans les sociétés méditerranéennes*, *Etudes Corses*, no. 12–13 (Ajaccio, 1979). (See VII, B below). Clear, concise treatment of a wide variety of material.

Roccu Multedo has published four books on Corsican occult phenomena in which he has assembled evidence taken from personal experience (the most valuable element in his work), and popular beliefs and legends culled from various sources, oral and written. Though some of his hypotheses may be contested, and his arguments tend to be distorted by his attempt to assimilate the *mazzeri* with the shamans, this body of work is invaluable to anyone interested in such subjects.

Le 'mazzerisme' et le folklore magique de la Corse (Cervione, 1975).
Le mazzerisme, un chamanisme corse (Nice, 1981; republished 1994).
Le folklore magique de la Corse (Nice, 1982).
Le mazzerisme, est-il un chamanisme corse? (CRET, 1987).

Also consulted:

Pierrette Bertrand Rousseau, *Ile de Corse et magie blanche* (Paris, 1978). A comprehensive study of the *signadori*.

Roccu Multedo, '*Le mazzerisme est-il un chamanisme corse?*' in *Rites funéraires et pratiques magico-religieuses en Corse d'hier et d'aujourd'hui. Actes des 3èmes rencontres culturelles interdisciplinaires de l'Alta Rocca* (Musée de Levie, 1992). (See VII, B below.)

Dorothy Carrington, '*Les mazzeri messagers de la mort: phénomène de la culture corse*' in *Rites funéraires et pratiques magico-religieuses en Corse d'hier et d'aujourd'hui. Actes des 3èmes rencontres culturelles interdisciplinaires de l'Alta Rocca* (Musée de Levie, 1992). (See VII, B below.)

Dorothy Carrington, '*Les mazzeri, chasseurs de rêve*', published with team of hunting experts under the direction of Paul Simonpoli in *La chasse en Corse*, Parc Naturel Régional de Corse (Ajaccio, 1995).

Marie-Madeleine Rotily-Forcioli, *Le mazzere que j'ai connu*, illuminating close-up account of a *mazzere*, the text of which has been most generously communicated to me by the author; to be published shortly.

II   OCCULT PHENOMENA OUTSIDE CORSICA

Out of a vast number of existing works, the following are selected for being particularly relevant to my subject.

Frederick Thomas Elworthy, *The Evil Eye. An Account of this ancient and widespread Superstition* (London, 1895).

Sir John Rhys, *Celtic Folklore, Welsh and Manx* (London, 1901).

J. G. Campbell, *Witchcraft and Second Sight in the Highlands and Islands of Scotland . . .* (Glasgow, 1902)

M. A. Czaplica, *Aboriginal Siberia* (Oxford, 1914).

Anatole le Braz, *Le Légende de la Mort chez les Bretons Armoricains* (Paris, 1922).

Alexander Carmichael, *Carmina Gadelica, Hymns and Incantations collected in the Highlands and Islands of Scotland and translated into English* (5 vols. London, 1928–54).

Marcelle Bouteiller, *Chamanisme et guérison magique* (Paris, 1950).

Mircea Eliade, *Le chamanisme et les techniques archaïques de l'extase* (Paris, 1951; edn. used, English translation, Bollingen Foundation, 1970).

W. Lloyd Warner, *A Black Civilisation, a Social Study of an Australian Tribe* (New York, 1958).

Régis Boyer et Eveline Lot-Falck, *Les Religions de l'Europe du Nord* (Paris, 1974).

E. E. Evans Pritchard, *Witchcraft, Oracles and Magic among the Azande* (Oxford, 1976).

Mario Mercier, *Chamanisme et chamans* (Paris, 1977; edn. used, 1987).

Carlo Ginsburg, *The Night Battles*, translated by John and Anne Tedeschi (London, 1982).

Carlo Ginsburg, *Ecstasies, Deciphering the Witches' Sabbath*, translated by Raymond Rosenthal (London, 1990).

III   CHRISTIANITY IN CORSICA

The ecclesiastical writings here cited, on the whole hostile to Corsican occultism, throw light on the powerful influence in Corsica of the Catholic Church.

'*Costituzione di Mgr. Castagnola*' (Pisa, 1615). Included in S.-B. Casanova (see below) vol. I, pp. 240–3.

Mgr. Carlo Fabrizio Giustiniani, *Costituzione et Decreti Sinodali* (Leghorn, 1661). Record of a synod held in 1657.

Chanoine S.-B. Casanova, *Histoire de l'Eglise Corse* (4 vols. Ajaccio-Bastia, 1931–8). Though misunderstanding the *mazzeri*, the author is a learned and trustworthy guide to his immense subject.

Françoise Lantieri, *Le corps entre la sorcellerie et la folie. Procès de l'Inquisition en Corse 1572–1678*. Thèse du 3ème cycle, Université de Corse, 1978.

Mgrs. Cristiani, Llosa, Thomas, *Dio vi Salvi Regina. Madre universale* (Ajaccio, 1982).

IV   GENERAL INFORMATION

Janine Renucci, *Corse traditionnelle et Corse nouvelle* (Lyon, 1974).

Roland Gant, *Blue Guide. Corsica* (London, 1990).

Janine Renucci, *La Corse. Série: Que-sais-je?* (Presses universitaires de France, 1992).

Guide Gallimard, *Corse-du-Sud. Haute Corse* (Paris, 1993).

Georges Ravis–Giordani, *Le guide de la Corse* (Besançon, 1993).

Guides Bleus Corse (Collection Hachette, last edn. 1994; Also consulted, edn. 1968).

V   PREHISTORY AND HISTORY

A General works including prehistory

Pierre Antonetti, *Histoire de la Corse* (Paris, 1973).

Francis Pomponi, *Histoire de la Corse* (Paris, 1979).

Paul Arrighi et Antoine Olivesi (eds.), *Histoire de la Corse*, with contributions from Eugène Bonifay, René Emmanuelli, François–Xavier Emmanuelli, Fernand Ettori, Roger Grosjean, Jean Jehasse, Laurence Jehasse, Antoine Olivesi, Huguette Taviani (Toulouse, 1986).

B Prehistory

Sibylle von Cles–Reden, *The Realm of the Great Goddess* (London, 1961). Survey of megalithic monuments in the Near East and Europe with perceptive chapter on Corsica.

Roger Grosjean, *La Corse avant l'histoire* (Paris, 1966). Survey by an archaeologist working in the field, discoverer of many prehistoric monuments and author of some contested hypotheses.

Gabriel Camps, *Préhistoire d'une île. Les Origines de la Corse* (Paris, 1988). Reliable professional assessment.

Joseph Cesari avec le concours de Franck Leandri, Paul Nebbia et Jean-Claude Ottaviani, *Corse des origines* (Guides archéologiques de la France, Imprimerie nationale, Paris, 1994). Corsica from its origins to the Roman conquest examined by a team of experts.

C Classical antiquity

Olivier Jehasse, *Corsica Classica* (Ajaccio, 1981).
Jean et Laurence Jehasse, *La Corse antique* (CRDP de la Corse, 1993).

D Corsican chroniclers and historians

The sum of the work of Corsican chroniclers and historians covers the island's history from early times to the late eighteenth century, each one writing of his own and preceding periods.

Histoire de la Corse comprenant la description de cette île d'aprés A. Giustiniani, la chronique de Giovanni della Grossa et de Monteggiani, remaniée par Ceccaldi, la chronique de Ceccaldi et la chronique de Filippini, translated into French from the original Italian by *Abbé Letteron* (BSSHNC, Bastia, 1888–90). *Filippini*, 1529–94, revised and added to the work of his predecessors and published the whole at Tournon, 1594, as *La Historia di Corsica* . . . Unrevised texts of *Della Grossa* and *Monteggiani* are published by *Letteron* in the original Italian (*BSSHNC*, 1910).

Pietro Cirneo, *De rebus Corsicis*, history of Corsica to the author's death in 1506. Translated from Latin by Abbé Letteron (*BSSHNC*, 1884).

Agostino Giustiniani (see above), *Description de la Corse (c. 1531)*. Text re-translated into French and edited by Antoine-Marie Graziani (Ajaccio, 1993).

Ambrogio Rossi, *Osservazioni storiche sopra la Corsica*. Rossi, 1754–1820, was the author of a history of Corsica to 1814 in 17 volumes of which 13 are published, covering the years 1705–1814 (*BSSHNC*, 1895–1906).

Francesco-Ottaviano Renucci, *Storia della Corsica* (2 vols. Bastia, 1833–4). Vivid account of the Bonaparte family by a contemporary and admirer of Napoleon.

E Special periods

1. Seventeenth Century

Antoine-Marie Graziani et José Stromboni, *Les Feux de la Saint Laurent* (Ajaccio, 1992).

2. Eighteenth Century

René Emmanuelli, *Vie de Pascal Paoli* (Lumio, 1970).
Peter Adam Thrasher, *Pasquale Paoli, an Enlightened Hero, 1725–1807* (London, 1970).
Sebastien Costa, *Grand Chancelier du Roi de Corse*, Theodore de Neuhoff,

Mémoires 1732–1736 (2 vols. Aix, 1972). Translated and edited by Renée Luciani. An intimate account of the short reign of a revolutionary monarch.

Voltaire, *De la Corse* (1769; edn. used, Bastia, 1994). *Précis du siècle de Louis XV* (2nd edn. chap. LX).

Dorothy Carrington, 'The Corsican Constitution of Pasquale Paoli', *The English Historical Review* (July, 1973).

Dorothy Carrington, 'Le texte original de la constitution de Pasquale Paoli', *BSSHNC*, no. 619–20 (Bastia, 1976). The original text of the constitution promulgated in 1755, translated into French, with commentary.

Jean Defranceschi, *Le Corse française (30 novembre 1789–15 juin 1794)* (Paris, 1990).

Desmond Gregory, *The Ungovernable Rock* (London and Toronto, Associated University Presses, 1985). Balanced account of the ill-starred British attempt to rule Corsica, 1794–6.

J.-B. Marcaggi, *La Genèse de Napoléon* (Paris, 1902). Well-informed account by a fellow-Corsican.

Xavier Versini, *Monsieur de Buonaparte ou le livre inachevé* (Paris, 1977).

Dorothy Carrington, *Napoleon and his Parents on the Threshold of History* (London, 1990).

3. Modern period

Paul Silvani, *La Corse des années ardentes, 1939–1946* (Paris, 1976).

Paul Silvani, . . . *Et la Corse fut libérée* (Ajaccio, 1993).

VI   TRADITION

A Code and custom

Madeleine-Rose Marin-Muracciole, *L'honneur des femmes en Corse du XIIIe siècle à nos jours* (Paris, 1964).

Georges Ravis-Giordani, 'Saint Jean aux jardins d'Adonis . . .', *Symposium Rito y Mystero* (La Coruna, October, 1971).

Claire Tiévant et Lucie Desideri, *Almanach de la mémoire et des coutumes* (Paris, 1986).

B Vendetta and bandits

Prosper Mérimée, *Colomba* (Paris, 1840). Masterly novel inspired by facts coloured by romantic tendencies of the age.

J.-B. Marcaggi, *Fleuve de Sang* (1898; edn used, Ajaccio, 1993). Story based on harsh fact with no concessions to romanticism by one of the best Corsican writers.

J. Busquet, *Le droit de la Vendetta et les paci corses* (Paris, 1920). Learned analysis of the vendetta as an unwritten popular code of justice.

J.-B. Marcaggi, *Bandits Corses d'Hier et d'Aujourd'hui* (Ajaccio, 1932).

Xavier Versini, *Un siècle de banditisme en Corse, 1814-1914* (Paris, 1964).

Lucia Molinelli Cancellieri, *Spada, Dernier Bandit Corse* (Paris, 1986).

Stephen Wilson, *Feuding, Conflict and Banditry in Nineteenth-Century Corsica* (Cambridge, 1988).

C Poetry and song

Frédéric Ortoli, *Les voceri de l'île de Corse* (Paris, 1887). Collections of funeral laments improvised in verse and song.

J.-B. Marcaggi, *Les chants de la mort et de la vendetta de la Corse* (Paris, 1898). *Voceri* inspired by passion of vengeance.

Fernand Ettori, 'Le vocero comme catharsis des tensions familiales et sociales', *La mort en Corse et dans les sociétés méditerranéennes, Etudes Corses*, no. 12–13 (Ajaccio, 1979). (See VII, B below.)

Ghjuvan-Paolo Poletti, *Cantata Corsica, Poème musical* . . . Poetry set to music, marking an evolution in tradition, by Corsica's foremost singer and musician.

D Popular tales

The following collections are selected from a large number published since the latter part of the last century.

Frédéric Ortoli, *Les Contes populaires de l'île de Corse* (Paris, 1883).

Geneviève Massignon, *Contes Corses* (Paris, 1984).

Mathée Giacomo-Marcellesi, *Contra Salvatica, Légendes et contes de Corse du Sud suivis des chansons de Jean-André Culioli* (Aix-en-Provence, 1989).

VII   CORSICAN SOCIETY PAST AND PRESENT

A Single studies

The following are selected from a large number on account of their relevance to this book.

Bradley Holway, *Adaptation, Class and Politics in Rural Corsica*. Thesis in social anthropology for McGill University, Montreal, 1978. Objective study of a village in the Alta Rocca with interesting observations on the colpadori (*mazzeri*).

Francis Pomponi, '*En amont de la mort, médecine et morbidité en Corse au XIXe siècle*', *La mort en Corse et dans les sociétés méditerranéennes, Etudes Corses*, no. 12–13 (Ajaccio, 1979). (See VII, B below.) Statistical study of a neglected subject.

José Gil, *La Corse. Entre la Liberté et la Terreur* (Ajaccio, 1984). Professional sociological analysis.

Gabriel Xavier Culioli, *Le complexe corse* (Paris, 1990).

Xavier Versini, *Ajaccio. De Pierres et d'Ombres* (Mans, 1991). Glimpses of Ajaccio in the past two centuries.

B Collected studies

Particular articles are cited in the Notes.

Pieve e Paesi (Paris, 1978).

Le Courier du Parc (quarterly 1970–1987); *Corse Nature* (twice yearly from April 1994); both edited by Mme Judais-Bolelli, présidente de *L'Association des Amis du Parc Naturel Régional de Corse*.

La mort en Corse et dans les sociétés méditerranéennes, Etudes Corses, no. 12–13 (1979). Articles from this noteworthy collection are cited in I; VI, C; VII, A, above.

Zicavu, una mimoria per dumani (Edisud, 1985). Analysis of history and conditions of a mountain village by a team of writers, using the French language, with valuable contributions by Jacques and Lucette Poncin.

A Mimoria, bulletin of the association 'A Mimoria', coordinated by Lucette Poncin, author of a number of articles in this collection of close studies of rural life. Appearing about four times yearly since 1989.

Corse, destin d'une île, Meridies, Jan.–Dec. 1991 (Monte Real, Portugal).

A Lettera, a journal appearing about four times yearly devoted to Corsican culture.

Kyrn (Ajaccio, 1970–93) appearing weekly.

Rites funéraires et pratiques magico-religieuses en Corse d'hier et d'aujourd'hui. Actes des 3èmes rencontres culturelles interdisciplinaires de l'Alta Rocca, septembre 1992 (Musée de Levie).

ADECEC, Association pour le développement d'études du centre-est de la Corse (Cervione). A publication appearing at intervals since 1970, directed by the president, M. A. Monti. Includes numerous studies in the Corsican language.

VIII LITERATURE

Since the eighteenth century, Corsica has inspired a rich and varied production of descriptive and fictional works, both by Corsicans and visitors to their island, among whom feature some illustrious names. It is impossible here to do more than pin-point some outstanding works, more especially those that are in harmony with my personal vision of the island. I refer readers looking for a wider selection to the following bibliographical publications.

A Bibliographical works

H. Yvia Croce, *Anthologie des écrivains corses* (2 vols). Vol. I, *XIXe siècle et période contemporaine* (Ajaccio, 1930).

Katty Andreani Peraldi, *La représentation de la mort dans le roman corse du XVIIIe siècle à nos jours* (Ajaccio, 1993). Examines 200 Corsican novels written 1762–1992, in Italian, French and Corsican. A work of literary as well as bibliographical interest.

B Eighteenth- and nineteenth-century writers

James Boswell, *An Account of Corsica, the Journal of a Tour to that Island and Memoirs of Pascal Paoli* (London, 1768). Unique account of Corsica as an independent nation created by Pasquale Paoli.

Napoleon Bonaparte, 'Nouvelle Corse', written *c.* 1789. A lurid tale that offers an early romantic vision of Corsica, published, together with other youthful writings of this author, by Frédéric et Guido Biagi in *Napoléon inconnu* . . . (2 vols. Paris, 1895).

Gustave Flaubert, visited Corsica in 1840. His travel journal is published in *Par les champs et par les grèves* (Paris, 1910).

Prosper Mérimée, *Colomba* (Paris, 1840). (See VI, B above.)

Alexandre Dumas, *Les frères corses* (Paris, 1841).

Edward Lear, *Journal of a Landscape Painter in Corsica* (London, 1870). Reproductions of drawings executed on the spot by an artist who captures the dimension of the Corsican mountains better than any of those who have worked in the island; see Giansily, *Dictionnaire des peintres corses et de la Corse 1800–1950* (Ajaccio, 1993).

Guy de Maupassant, *Une vie* (Paris, 1883). Includes romantic descriptions of the Corsican landscape as the setting of a honeymoon. His notes of travel in the island are collected in *Chroniques insulaires* (Bastia, 1987).

J.-B. Marcaggi, *Fleuve de Sang*; see VI, B above.

C Modern writers

Residing in Paris, the following outstanding Corsican fiction writers set their novels in Corsica.

Angelo Rinaldi, eight novels since 1969 including *La loge du gouverneur* (Paris, 1969), Prix Fénélon 1970, and *La maison des Atlantes* (Paris, 1971), Prix Fémina 1971.

Marie Susini, seven novels since 1953 including *Plein Soleil* (Paris, 1953); *La Fiera* (Paris, 1954) and an essay, *La renfermée. La Corse* (Paris, 1981), a poignant expression of her love-hate relationship with her homeland.

Patrice Franceschi, *Quelque Chose qui prend les hommes* (Paris, 1993). Spellbinding picture of Corsican rural life by one who has lived abroad.

IX ARCHITECTURE AND ART

Geneviève Moracchini avec la collaboration de Dorothy Carrington, *Trésors oubliés des églises de Corse* (Paris, 1959).

Geneviève Moracchini-Mazel, *Les églises romanes de Corse* (2 vols. Paris, 1967).

Joseph Orsolini, *L'Art de la fresque en Corse, 1450–1520* (Parc naturel régional de la Corse, 1990).

Jacques Poncin, *Paysages bâtis en Corse* (Ajaccio, 1992).

Marie-Dominique Roche, *Le Musée Fesch, Ajaccio* (Ajaccio, 1993). Finely illustrated description of remarkable collection of paintings bequeathed to the town by Napoleon's half-uncle, Joseph Fesch.

X CORSICAN FLORA

Plants have played an important part in Corsican traditional life both for utilitarian and medicinal purposes. The following well-illustrated publications indicate their various uses, their medicinal qualities, and the beliefs with which they have been associated.

Arburi, Arbe, Arbigliule, savoirs populaires sur les plantes de la Corse (Parc Naturel Régional de Corse, 1988).

Marcelle Conrad, *Plantes et Fleurs rencontrées. L'île pas à pas* (Parc Naturel Régional de Corse, 1990).

XI OTHER WORKS CONSULTED

Sir James George Frazer, *The Golden Bough* (1922 edn; used, New York, 1942).

Max Wurband et Cecil Roth, *Le peuple Juif, 4000 ans de survivance* (Paris, 1967).

Max I. Dimant, *Les Juifs, Dieu et l'Histoire* (Paris, 1968).

Geoffrey Parrinder, *Witchcraft, European and African* (London, 1968).

Lucy Mair, *Witchcraft* (Toronto, 1969).

Mathieu Ceccaldi, *Dictionnaire Corse–Français* (Paris, 1974).

Jean Chevalier, Alain Gheerbrant, *Dictionnaire des Symboles* (Paris, 1984).

Hilda Ellis Davidson, *The Seer in Celtic and other Traditions* (Edinburgh, 1989).

The following learned journals present original texts and a wide variety of studies invaluable to anyone seeking a close knowledge of Corsica:

Bulletin de la Société de Sciences historiques et naturelles de la Corse, appearing quarterly since 1881, has published the Corsican chroniclers (see V, D above) translated into French; indispensable to an understanding of Corsican history.

Etudes Corses (see VII, B above), appearing quarterly since 1954, offers many studies of importance, some of which are quoted in the above Bibliography and in the Notes.

I owe various items of interest to the two well-informed Corsican daily newspapers: *Corse-Matin* and *La Corse*.

Finally, I mention my *Granite Island, a Portrait of Corsica* (London, 1971) in which I present certain themes more fully developed in this book.

INDEX